STEVE EMANUEL'S
BOOTCAMP FOR THE MBE:
MBE SELF-ASSESSMENT TEST

EMANUEL BAR REVIEW ADVISORS

Steven L. Emanuel
Founder and Editor-in-Chief
Emanuel Bar Review

Joel Wm. Friedman
Jack M. Gordon Professor of Procedural Law and Jurisdiction and
   Director of Tulane ITESM Ph.D. Program
Tulane University Law School

James J. Rigos
Owner and Editor-in-Chief
Rigos Professional Education Programs

STEVE EMANUEL'S
Bootcamp for the MBE

MBE
Self-Assessment Test

Edited by
STEVEN L. EMANUEL

Founder & Editor-in-Chief,
Emanuel Bar Review
Member, NY, CT, MD and VA bars

www.aspenlaw.com

Emanuel Bar Review is a division of Aspen Publishers, a Wolters Kluwer company.

© 2010 Aspen Publishers. All Rights Reserved.
http://lawschool.aspenpublishers.com

Certain publicly disclosed questions and answers from past MBE examinations have been included herein with the permission of the NCBE, the copyright owner. These questions and answers are the only actual MBE questions and answers included in Aspen Publisher's materials. Permission to use the NCBE's questions does not constitute an endorsement by NCBE or otherwise signify that NCBE has reviewed or approved any aspect of these materials or the company or individuals who distribute these materials.

Some questions that have been included herein come from the following NCBE publications:
"Multistate Bar Examination Questions 1992," Copyright © 1992, National Conference of Bar Examiners. All Rights Reserved.
"Sample MBE," Copyright © 1995 by the National Conference of Bar Examiners. All Rights Reserved.
"Sample MBE II," Copyright © 1997 by the National Conference of Bar Examiners. All Rights Reserved.
"Sample MBE III," Copyright © 2002 by the National Conference of Bar Examiners. All Rights Reserved.
"MBE-OPE 1," Copyright © 2006 by the National Conference of Bar Examiners. All Rights Reserved.

No part of this publication may be reproduced or transmitted in any form or by any means, electronic or mechanical, including photocopy, recording, or any information storage and retrieval system, without permission in writing from the publisher. Requests for permission to make copies of any part of this publication should be mailed to:

Aspen Publishers
Attn: Permissions Department
76 Ninth Avenue, 7th Floor
New York, NY 10011-5201

For information about Emanuel Bar Review (including Emanuel Multistate Review), contact:

email: info@emanuelbarprep.com
phone: 1-888-MBE-PREP
fax: 781-207-5815
website: www.emanuelbarprep.com

Printed in the United States of America.

1 2 3 4 5 6 7 8 9 0

ISBN 978-0-7355-9741-9

TABLE OF CONTENTS

Preface vii
Self-Assessment Test
   Subject Matter Breakdown of Questions 1
   Questions — A.M. Exam 3
   Questions — P.M. Exam 47
   Answers — A.M. Exam 91
   Answers — P.M. Exam 145
   Raw-to-Scaled Score Conversion Chart... 199
   Answer Sheet — A.M. Exam 203
   Answer Sheet — P.M. Exam 205

PREFACE

Dear Bootcamp enrollee:

First, welcome to Steve Emanuel's Bootcamp for the MBE. We promise to do everything we can to help you succeed on the MBE.

Now, a few words about this book. The book consists of a single 200-question simulated MBE, which we call the "Self-Assessment Test," together with detailed explanatory answers, specifically written and tailored to maximize your performance on your upcoming bar exam. These explanatory answers — together with our other course materials — will help you master the fine-line distinctions, subtleties, and black-letter rules that are most frequently tested on the MBE.

Use this Self-Assessment Test to familiarize yourself with what the MBE is like, *before you take the online lecture portion(s) of our course*. We've tried hard to make the Self-Assessment Test as much like a real MBE as we can. And we've tried to make it reflect the legal sub-issues and judicial trends that the examiners are most frequently testing these days. This means that:

- This Test has the *same distribution of subjects* as a "real" MBE: 34 questions in each of Contracts and Torts, and 33 questions in each of the other four subjects (Constitutional Law, Criminal Law and Procedure, Evidence, and Real Property)

- It has approximately the *same distribution of topics* within each subject as a real MBE. For instance, it has the same 2-to-1 mix between substantive and procedural Criminal Law questions, and the same mix between sales (i.e., UCC) and non-sales questions within the Contracts questions. The examiners can only test you on these topics, and on the sub-issues within them, in so many ways — and we've carefully highlighted the most-tested areas in this Sample Test and in our other materials.

- Many of the questions are based on *actual questions* that have appeared on past MBEs. However, we have converted these actual questions to the current MBE format, which features somewhat shorter fact patterns, almost no multiple-question fact patterns, and almost no use of proper names.

- We've extensively researched and written these explanatory *answers* to ensure accuracy. I have personally, over the space of many months, researched original sources like Restatements and multi-volume treatises to give you not only "the right answer" but also a detailed chain of reasoning that will help you with other questions you may encounter in the same subject areas. You can see a partial listing of our sources if you look at the abbreviations note at the start of the answers, on p. 92.

If possible, you should take the Self-Assessment Test under actual, timed, testing conditions. That is, you should:

- take three uninterrupted hours to complete the first 100 questions (we recommend 9 a.m.-noon);
- take a one-hour lunch break (we recommend noon to 1 p.m.); and then
- take another three uninterrupted hours to complete the second set of 100 questions in the afternoon (we recommend 1-4 p.m.).

We want to give you the best possible pre-course preparation. Therefore, we recommend that when you take the Self-Assessment Test, you observe these real-MBE constraints:

- No notes or books
- Realistic time constraints. Since the A.M. and P.M. sessions of the MBE are 100 questions each in exactly 3 hours, this means that you should allow yourself only *1 minute 48 seconds per question.*
- Entering your answers on the real-life "bubble" answer sheets provided at the very end of this book.

Don't worry if the questions seem hard — they *are* hard, because they're designed so that the median candidate (the 50th percentile performer) nationally will get only a raw score of about 135, or 68% of the questions correct. And these are folks who have already completed their bar-exam preparation, whereas you're just beginning that preparation.

You'll want to consult the raw-to-scaled score conversion chart at the end of the book (p. 199) — this will help you figure out what scaled score you would have received for any given "raw" score (i.e., for any given number of correct answers out of the 200 questions).

By way of illustration, to just pass the California Bar Exam — usually considered the toughest in America — if you had the same relative performance on the MBE as on the essays and performance test, you would need a scaled MBE score of 144. To achieve a 144 on the Self-Assessment Test, you would need to answer about 133 questions, or slightly less than 67%, correctly.

If you want to work on just a single one of the six subjects at a time, the table on p. 1 will let you see which questions focus on that subject.

The entire Emanuel Bar Review team joins me in saying that we're glad you chose Steve Emanuel's Bootcamp for the MBE. GOOD LUCK.

Steve Emanuel

Larchmont, NY

April, 2010

SUBJECT MATTER BREAKDOWN OF QUESTIONS

This listing tells you which questions involve which subject, for the Self-Assessment Test.

CONSTITUTIONAL LAW

12, 28, 32, 35, 38, 39, 40, 42, 43, 53, 57, 62, 69, 89, 94, 95, 96, 107, 120, 131, 139, 141, 145, 148, 152, 153, 162, 165, 168, 172, 174, 185, 197

CONTRACTS

1, 2, 6, 22, 24, 25, 29, 31, 44, 55, 58, 63, 71, 74, 90, 93, 101, 102, 118, 123, 125, 143, 144, 163, 164, 167, 169, 173, 180, 188, 193, 195, 198, 199

CRIMINAL LAW

5, 11, 18, 20, 30, 45, 54, 56, 60, 64, 65, 70, 75, 79, 82, 83, 87, 97, 104, 114, 122, 128, 132, 150, 155, 157, 170, 171, 176, 181, 189, 194, 200

Of the above, the following involve Criminal Procedure: 5, 18, 30, 60, 75, 82, 83, 122, 128, 176, 194

EVIDENCE

3, 9, 10, 19, 34, 36, 49, 59, 67, 68, 72, 76, 80, 91, 100, 111, 115, 117, 124, 129, 130, 136, 137, 138, 140, 147, 151, 154, 175, 178, 182, 184, 187

REAL PROPERTY

13, 14, 15, 21, 23, 26, 37, 41, 47, 48, 51, 61, 66, 78, 84, 92, 98, 106, 108, 109, 113, 116, 126, 127, 133, 134, 135, 142, 149, 159, 160, 161, 177

TORTS

4, 7, 8, 16, 17, 27, 33, 46, 50, 52, 73, 77, 81, 85, 86, 88, 99, 103, 105, 110, 112, 119, 121, 146, 156, 158, 166, 179, 183, 186, 190, 191, 192, 196

QUESTIONS
SELF-ASSESSMENT TEST
A.M. EXAM
TIME: 3 HOURS

Directions: Each of the questions or incomplete statements below is followed by four suggested answers or completions. You are to choose the best of the stated alternatives. Answer all questions according to the generally accepted view, except where otherwise noted.

For the purposes of this test, you are to assume that Articles 1 and 2 of the Uniform Commercial Code have been adopted. You are to assume that the 2001 proposed amendments to Article 1 and the 2003 proposed amendments to Article 2 have not been adopted. You are also to assume relevant application of Article 9 of the UCC concerning fixtures. The Federal Rules of Evidence are deemed to control. The terms "Constitution," "constitutional," and "unconstitutional" refer to the federal Constitution unless indicated to the contrary. You are to assume that there is no applicable statute unless otherwise specified; however, survival actions and claims for wrongful death should be assumed to be available where applicable. You should assume that joint and several liability, with pure comparative negligence, is the relevant rule unless otherwise indicated.

1. In a single writing, a painter contracted with a farmer to paint three identical barns on the farmer's rural estate for $2,000 each. The contract provided for the farmer's payment of $6,000 upon the painter's completion of the work on all three barns. The painter did not ask for any payment when the first barn was completely painted, but she demanded $4,000 after painting the second barn. The farmer rightfully refused the painter's demand for payment. The painter then immediately terminated the contract without painting the third barn. What is the painter entitled to recover from the farmer?

   (A) Nothing, because payment was expressly conditioned on completion of all three barns.

   (B) The painter's expenditures plus anticipated "profit" in painting the first two barns, up to a maximum recovery of $4,000.

   (C) The reasonable value of the painter's services in painting the two barns, less the farmer's damages, if any, for the painter's failure to paint the third barn.

   (D) The amount that the combined value of the two painted barns has been increased by the painter's work.

   [Q3020]

2. On November 15, a carpenter in a signed writing contracted with a homeowner for an agreed price to personally remodel the homeowner's kitchen according to specifications provided by the homeowner, and to start work on December 1. The carpenter agreed to provide all materials for the job in addition to all of the labor required.

   On November 26 the carpenter without legal excuse repudiated the contract, and the homeowner, after a reasonable and prolonged effort, could not find anyone to remodel his kitchen for a price approximating the price agreed to by the carpenter. If one year later the homeowner brings an action for specific performance against the carpenter, which of the following will provide the carpenter with the best defense?

   (A) An action for equitable relief not brought within a reasonable time is barred by laches.

   (B) Specific performance is generally not available as a remedy to enforce a contractual duty to perform personal services.

   (C) Specific performance is generally not available as a remedy in the ease of an anticipatory repudiation.

   (D) Specific performance is not available as a remedy where even nominal damages could have been recovered as a remedy at law.

   [Q2141]

3. The defendant, a man, has been charged with murdering the victim. The defendant defends on the grounds that the murder was really committed by a particular woman, who has since died. The defendant offers a properly authenticated photocopy of a transcript of a deposition in a civil suit brought against the woman by the victim's family for the victim's death, in which the woman said, "Yes, I killed him because I hated him." The civil suit was brought because the woman was known to have quarreled with and disliked the victim. Upon proper objection by the prosecution, the statement should be

   (A) admitted as a declaration against interest

   (B) admitted as former testimony by a person now unavailable;

   (C) inadmissible as hearsay not within any

exception

(D) inadmissible, because the original rather than a photocopy must be offered

[Q6001]

4. A corporation designed and built a processing plant for the manufacture of an explosive chemical. An engineer was retained by the corporation to design a filter system for the processing plant. She prepared an application for a permit to build the plant's filter system and submitted it to the state's Department of Environmental Protection (DEP). As required by DEP regulations, the engineer submitted a blueprint to the DEP with the application for permit. The blueprint showed the entire facility and was signed and sealed by her as a licensed professional engineer.

After the project was completed, a portion of the processing plant exploded, injuring the plaintiff. During discovery in an action by the plaintiff against the engineer, it was established that the explosion was caused by a design defect in the processing plant that was unrelated to the filter system designed by the engineer.

In that action, will the plaintiff prevail?

(A) Yes, if the engineer signed, sealed, and submitted a blueprint that showed the design defect.

(B) Yes, because all of the plant's designers are jointly and severally liable for the defect.

(C) No, because the engineer owed no duty to the plaintiff to prevent the particular risk of harm.

(D) No, if the engineer was an independent contractor of the corporation.

[Q3032]

5. The defendant sold heroin to a football player. The football player was later stopped by police for speeding. The police searched the football player's car and found the heroin concealed under the rear seat. The defendant is charged with illegally selling heroin.

The defendant's motion to prevent introduction of the heroin into evidence will most probably be

(A) granted, because the heroin was not in plain view.

(B) granted, because the scope of the search was excessive.

(C) denied, because the defendant has no standing to object to the search.

(D) denied, because the search was proper as incident to a valid full custodial arrest.

[Q4049]

6. On December 15, a lawyer received from a stationer an offer consisting of its catalog and a signed letter stating, "We will supply you with as many of the items in the enclosed catalog as you order during the next calendar year. We assure you that this offer and the prices in the catalog will remain firm throughout the coming year." On January 15, having at that time received no reply from the lawyer, the stationer notified the lawyer that, effective February 1, it was increasing the prices of certain specified items in its catalog.

Is the price increase effective with respect to catalog orders the stationer receives from the lawyer during the month of February?

(A) No, because the stationer's original offer, including the price term, became irrevocable under the doctrine of promissory estoppel.

(B) No, because the stationer is a

merchant with respect to office supplies; and its original offer, including the price term, was irrevocable throughout the month of February.

(C) Yes, because the stationer received no consideration to support its assurance that it would not increase prices.

(D) Yes, because the period for which the stationer gave assurance that it would not raise prices was longer than three months.

[Q3028]

7. A driver, returning from a long shift at a factory, fell asleep at the wheel and lost control of his car. As a result, his car collided with a police car driven by an officer who was returning to the station after having responded to an emergency. The police officer was injured in the accident. The police officer sued the driver in negligence for her injuries. The driver moved for summary judgment, arguing that the common-law firefighters' rule barred the suit.

Should the court grant the motion?

(A) No, because the firefighters' rule does not apply to police officers.

(B) No, because the police officer's injuries were not related to any special dangers of her job.

(C) Yes, because the accident would not have occurred but for the emergency.

(D) Yes, because the police officer was injured on the job.

[Q7006]

8. A neighbor, who lived next door to a homeowner, went into the homeowner's garage without permission and borrowed the homeowner's chain saw. The neighbor used the saw to clear broken branches from the trees on the neighbor's own property. After he had finished, the neighbor noticed several broken branches on the homeowner's trees that were in danger of falling on the homeowner's roof. While the neighbor was cutting the homeowner's branches, the saw broke.

In a suit for conversion by the homeowner against the neighbor, will the homeowner recover?

(A) Yes, for the actual damage to the saw.

(B) Yes, for the value of the saw before the neighbor borrowed it.

(C) No, because when the saw broke, the neighbor was using it to benefit the homeowner.

(D) No, because the neighbor did not intend to keep the saw.

[Q3003]

9. In an accident case, the defendant testified in his own behalf that he was going 30 m.p.h. On cross-examination, the plaintiff's counsel did not question the defendant with regard to his speed. Subsequently, the plaintiff's counsel calls a police officer to testify that, in his investigation following the accident, the defendant told him he was driving 40 m.p.h. The officer's testimony is

(A) admissible as a prior inconsistent statement.

(B) admissible as an admission.

(C) inadmissible, because it lacks a foundation.

(D) inadmissible, because it is hearsay not within any exception.

[Q4015]

10. In a civil action for breach of an oral contract, the defendant admits that there had been discussions, but denies that he ever entered into an agreement with the plaintiff.

Which of the following standards of admissibility should be applied by the court to evidence proffered as relevant to prove whether a contract was formed?

(A) Whether a reasonable juror would find the evidence determinative of whether the contract was or was not formed.

(B) Whether the evidence has any tendency to make the fact of contract formation more or less probable than without the evidence.

(C) Whether the evidence is sufficient to prove, absent contrary evidence, that the contract was or was not formed.

(D) Whether the evidence makes it more likely than not that a contract was or was not formed.

[Q7078]

11. The defendant decided to kill his boss, the CEO of the company, after she told the defendant that he would be fired if his work did not improve. The defendant knew the CEO was scheduled to go on a business trip on Monday morning. On Sunday morning, the defendant went to the company parking garage and put a bomb in the company car that the CEO usually drove. The bomb was wired to go off when the car engine started. The defendant then left town. At 5 a.m. Monday, the defendant, after driving all night, was overcome with remorse and had a change of heart. He called the security officer on duty at the company and told him about the bomb. The security officer said he would take care of the matter. An hour later, the officer put a note on the CEO's desk telling her of the message. He then looked at the car but could not see any signs of a bomb. He printed a sign saying "DO NOT USE THIS CAR," put it on the windshield, and went to call the police. Before the police arrived, a vice president of the same company got into the car and started the engine. The bomb went off, killing her.

The jurisdiction defines murder in the first degree as any homicide committed with premeditation and deliberation or any murder in the commission of a common-law felony. Second-degree murder is defined as all other murder at common law. Manslaughter is defined by the common law.

The defendant is guilty of

(A) murder in the first degree, because, with premeditation and deliberation, he killed whoever would start the car.

(B) murder in the second degree, because he had no intention of killing the vice president.

(C) manslaughter, because at the time of the explosion, he had no intent to kill, and the death of the vice president was in part the fault of the security officer.

(D) only attempted murder of the CEO, because the death of the vice president was the result of the security officer's negligence.

[Q3133]

12. A man bought an antique car from a car dealer in State A. Under State A law, a person who buys from such a dealer acquires good title, even if the property was stolen from a previous owner. The man showed the car at an antique car show in State B. A woman recognized the car as having been stolen from her. Under State B law, a person whose property is stolen may reclaim it, even if the current possessor is an innocent purchaser. The woman sued the man in a State B court to reclaim the car. The man defended, claiming that he had good title under the law of State A. Nevertheless, the State B court applied

State B law, and the woman prevailed. The man did not appeal. The sheriff gave the woman possession of the car. Several months later, the woman drove the car to State A. The man brought a new suit against the woman, claiming that the State B court in the prior suit should have applied the State A law, which protected innocent purchasers. The woman appeared and moved to dismiss the suit.

What should the State A court do?

(A) Apply the federal law of sale of goods, because the car has moved in interstate commerce.

(B) Apply the State A law, because the car is currently located in State A.

(C) Dismiss the suit, because the State A court must give full faith and credit to the State B judgment.

(D) Remove the case to federal court, because the car has moved in interstate commerce, and therefore the case raises a federal question.

[Q7051]

13. A grantor, who owned a farm in fee simple, conveyed the farm to a grantee by warranty deed. A neighbor, who owned the adjoining property, asserted title to the farm and brought an appropriate action against the grantee to quiet title to the farm. The grantee demanded that the grantor defend the grantee's title under the deed's covenant of warranty, but the grantor refused. The grantee then successfully defended at her own expense.

The grantee brought an appropriate action against the grantor to recover the grantee's expenses incurred in defending against the neighbor's action to quiet title to the farm.

In this action, the court should decide for

(A) the grantee, because in effect it was the grantor's title that was challenged.

(B) the grantee, because the grantor's deed to her included the covenant of warranty.

(C) the grantor, because the title he conveyed was not defective.

(D) the grantor, because the neighbor may elect which of the grantor or the grantee to sue.

[Q3159]

14. A mother owned a two-family apartment house on a small city lot not suitable for partition-in-kind. Upon the mother's death, her will devised the property to "my son and my daughter."

A week ago, a creditor of the son obtained a money judgment against the son, and properly filed the judgment in the county where the property is located. A statute in the jurisdiction provides: any judgment properly filed shall, for ten years from filing, be a lien on the real property then owned or subsequently acquired by any person against whom the judgment is rendered.

The son needed cash, but the daughter did not wish to sell the property. The son commenced a partition action against the daughter and the creditor.

Assume that the court properly ordered a partition by judicial sale.

After the sale, the creditor's judgment will be a lien on

(A) all of the property.

(B) only a one-half interest in the property.

(C) all of the proceeds of sale of the property.

(D) only the portion of the proceeds of sale due the son.

[Q1066]

15. A landowner mortgaged the land to a bank to secure his preexisting obligation to the bank. The mortgage was promptly and properly recorded. The landowner and a buyer then entered into a valid written contract for the purchase and sale of the land, which provided for the transfer of "a marketable title, free of encumbrances." The contract did not expressly refer to the mortgage.

    Shortly after entering into the contract, the buyer found another property that much better suited her needs and decided to try to avoid her contract with the landowner. When the buyer discovered the existence of the mortgage, she asserted that the title was encumbered and that she would not close. The landowner responded by offering to provide for payment and discharge of the mortgage at the closing from the proceeds of the closing. The buyer refused to go forward, and the landowner brought an appropriate action against her for specific performance.

    If the court holds for the landowner in this action, it will most likely be because

    (A) the mortgage is not entitled to priority because it was granted for preexisting obligations.

    (B) the doctrine of equitable conversion supports the result.

    (C) The landowner's arrangements for the payment of the mortgage fully satisfied the landowner's obligation to deliver marketable title.

    (D) the existence of the mortgage was not the buyer's real reason for refusing to close.

    [Q2081]

16. For ten years, a vacationer and his neighbor have owned summer vacation homes on adjoining lots. A stream flows through both lots. As a result of a childhood swimming accident, the vacationer is afraid of water and has never gone close to the stream.

    The neighbor built a dam on her property that has completely stopped the flow of the stream to the vacationer's property.

    In a suit by the vacationer against the neighbor, will the vacationer prevail?

    (A) Yes, if the damming unreasonably interferes with the use and enjoyment of the vacationer's property.

    (B) Yes, if the neighbor intended to affect the vacationer's property.

    (C) No, because the vacationer made no use of the stream.

    (D) No, if the dam was built in conformity with all applicable laws.

    [Q3041]

17. A driver was driving his car near an owner's house when the owner's child darted into the street in front of the driver's car. As the driver swerved and braked his car to avoid hitting the child, the car skidded up into the owner's driveway and stopped just short of the owner, who was standing in the driveway and had witnessed the entire incident. The owner suffered serious emotional distress from witnessing the danger to his child and to himself. Neither the owner nor his property was physically harmed.

    If the owner asserts a claim for damages against the driver, will the owner prevail?

    (A) Yes, because the driver's entry onto the owner's land was unauthorized.

    (B) Yes, because the owner suffered serious emotional distress by witnessing the danger to his child and to himself.

    (C) No, unless the driver was negligent.

    (D) No, unless the owner's child was

exercising reasonable care.

[Q3149]

18. A landlord was the owner of a three-dwelling-unit residential building. She lived in an apartment on the third floor, her son lived with his wife in an apartment on the second floor, and the ground floor apartment was rented to a police officer and his family. One day, while the son and his wife were out of town, the landlord and the officer were having coffee together in the landlord's apartment. During the course of their conversation, the landlord said that she was worried about her son because once, while visiting him, she saw a substance in his apartment which she believed to be cocaine. Since she really did not know what cocaine looked like, however, she was not sure. The officer said, "If you'd like, I'll have a look and let you know whether or not there is anything for you to worry about."

Using her key to open the door to the son's apartment, the landlord brought the officer inside. The officer did not see any coke, but he noticed a television in the living room which looked like one stolen from an appliance store in the neighborhood. Without saying anything about the television to the landlord, the officer obtained a search warrant by submitting an affidavit indicating that he had seen certain items in the son's apartment which he had probable cause to believe were stolen. Later, he returned, entered, and thoroughly searched the apartment pursuant to the warrant. The television which he had seen on his first visit was not stolen, but during the course of his search, he found several items which were stolen. The son was charged with burglary.

If the son makes an appropriate motion to suppress the use of stolen items found in his apartment, his motion should be

(A) denied, since the stolen items were obtained as the result of a lawful search.

(B) denied, since it would not serve the interests of justice to require a police officer to ignore a discovery which he has probable cause to believe is contraband.

(C) granted, if the search warrant was issued as the result of information obtained in an unlawful search.

(D) granted, since his possession of stolen items is not necessarily proof that he stole those items.

[Q5080]

19. The plaintiff was injured when the ladder on which she was standing collapsed without warning. Immediately following the accident, the plaintiff was taken to a hospital where she remained for approximately six hours. At the trial of the plaintiff's action against the manufacturer of the ladder, the plaintiff's attorney offered a properly authenticated record from the hospital. After examining the record, the defendant's attorney, outside the presence of the jury, moved to exclude a portion of the record which read: "History: Ladder collapsed. Patient fell." The motion to exclude that portion of the record should be

(A) granted, if, but only if, it can be excluded without causing any physical damage to the record.

(B) granted, because it has no bearing on the plaintiff's medical condition.

(C) denied, if the history was taken for the purpose of diagnosis or treatment.

(D) granted, since hospital personnel are not experts in determining the causes of accidents.

[Q5081]

20. A woman wanted to make some money, so she decided to sell cocaine. She asked a man, who was reputed to have access to illegal drugs, to supply her with cocaine so she could resell it. The man agreed and sold the woman a bag of white powder. The woman then repackaged the white powder into smaller containers and sold one to an undercover police officer, who promptly arrested the woman. The woman immediately confessed and said that the man was her supplier. Upon examination, the white powder was found not to be cocaine or any type of illegal substance.

    If the man knew the white powder was not cocaine but the woman believed it was, which of the following is correct?

    (A) Both the man and the woman are guilty of attempting to sell cocaine.

    (B) Neither the man nor the woman is guilty of attempting to sell cocaine.

    (C) The man is guilty of attempting to sell cocaine, but the woman is not.

    (D) The man is not guilty of attempting to sell cocaine, but the woman is.

    [Q3002]

21. A businessman owned in fee simple Lot 1 in a properly approved subdivision, designed and zoned for industrial use. An investor owned the adjoining Lot 2 in the same subdivision. The plat of the subdivision was recorded as authorized by statute.

    Twelve years ago, the businessman erected an industrial building wholly situated on Lot 1 but with one wall along the boundary common with Lot 2. The construction was done as authorized by a building permit, validly obtained under applicable statutes, ordinances, and regulations. Further, the construction was regularly inspected and passed as being in compliance with all building code requirements.

    Lot 2 remained vacant until six months ago, when the investor began excavation pursuant to a building permit authorizing the erection of an industrial building situated on Lot 2 but with one wall along the boundary common with Lot 1. The excavation caused subsidence of a portion of Lot 1 that resulted in injury to the business owner's building. The excavation was not done negligently or with any malicious intent to injure. In the jurisdiction, the time to acquire title by adverse possession or rights by prescription is 10 years.

    The businessman brought an appropriate action against the investor to recover damages resulting from the injuries to the building on Lot 1.

    In such lawsuit, judgment should be for

    (A) the businessman if, but only if, the subsidence would have occurred without the weight of the building on Lot 1.

    (B) the businessman, because a right for support, appurtenant to Lot 1, had been acquired by adverse possession or prescription.

    (C) the investor, because Lots 1 and 2 are urban land, as distinguished from rural land and, therefore, under the circumstances the businessman had the duty to protect any improvements on Lot 1.

    (D) the investor, because the construction and the use to be made of the building were both authorized by the applicable law.

    [Q3087]

22. A retailer of lighting fixtures, in a signed writing, contracted with an apartment developer for the sale to the developer of 50 identical sets of specified bathroom fixtures, 25 sets to be delivered on March

1, and the remaining 25 sets on April 1. The agreement did not specify the place of delivery, or the time or place of payment.

Which of the following statements is correct?

(A) The retailer must tender 25 sets to the developer at the developer's place of business on March 1, but does not have to turn them over to the developer until the developer pays the contract price for the 25 sets.

(B) The retailer has no duty to deliver the 25 sets on March 1 at the developer's place of business unless the developer tenders the contract price for the 25 sets on that date.

(C) The retailer must deliver 25 sets on March 1, and the developer must pay the contract price for the 25 sets within a reasonable time after their delivery.

(D) The retailer must deliver 25 sets on March 1, but the developer's payment is due only upon the delivery of all 50 sets.

[Q3103]

23. A landowner executed and delivered a promissory note and a mortgage securing the note to a mortgage company, which was named as payee in the note and as mortgagee in the mortgage. The note included a statement that the indebtedness evidenced by the note was "subject to the terms of a contract between the maker and the payee of the note executed on the same day" and that the note was "secured by a mortgage of even date." The mortgage was promptly and properly recorded. Subsequently, the mortgage company sold the landowner's note and mortgage to a bank and delivered to the bank a written assignment of the note and mortgage. The assignment was promptly and properly recorded. The mortgage company retained possession of both the note and the mortgage in order to act as collecting agent. Later, being short of funds, the mortgage company sold the note and mortgage to an investor at a substantial discount. The mortgage company executed a written assignment of the note and mortgage to the investor and delivered to him the note, the mortgage, and the assignment. The investor paid value for the assignment without actual knowledge of the prior assignment to the bank and promptly and properly recorded his assignment. The principal of the note was not then due, and there had been no default in payment of either interest or principal.

If the issue of ownership of the landowner's note and mortgage is subsequently raised in an appropriate action by the bank to foreclose, the court should hold that

(A) the investor owns both the note and the mortgage.

(B) the bank owns both the note and the mortgage.

(C) the investor owns the note and the bank owns the mortgage.

(D) the bank owns the note and the investor owns the mortgage.

[Q1123]

24. A contractor contracted with a warehouse owner to construct for $500,000 a warehouse and an access driveway at highway level on the owner's property. Shortly after commencing work on the driveway, which required for the specified level some excavation and removal of surface material, the contractor unexpectedly encountered a large mass of solid rock. The contractor informed the owner (accurately) that because of the rock the driveway as specified would cost at

least $20,000 more than figured, and demanded for that reason a total contract price of $520,000. Since the owner was expecting warehousing customers immediately after the agreed completion date, he signed a writing promising to pay the additional $20,000. Following timely completion of the warehouse and driveway, which conformed to the contract in all respects, the owner refused to pay the contractor more than $500,000.

What is the maximum amount to which the contractor is entitled?

(A) $500,000, because there was no consideration for the owner's promise to pay the additional $20,000.

(B) $500,000, because the owner's promise to pay the additional $20,000 was exacted under duress.

(C) $520,000, because the modification was fair and was made in the light of circumstances not anticipated by the parties when the original contract was made.

(D) $520,000, provided that the reasonable value of the contractor's total performance was that much or more.

[Q2004]

25. A famous chef entered into a written agreement with his friend, a well-known interior decorator respected for his unique designs, in which the decorator agreed, for a fixed fee, to design the interior of the chef's new restaurant, and, upon the chef's approval of the design plan, to decorate and furnish the restaurant accordingly. The agreement was silent as to assignment or delegation by either party. Before beginning the work, the decorator sold his decorating business to a buyer under an agreement in which the decorator assigned to the buyer, and the buyer agreed to complete, the chef-decorator contract. The buyer, also an experienced decorator of excellent repute, advised the chef of the assignment, and supplied him with information confirming both the buyer's financial responsibility and past commercial success.

Is the chef obligated to permit the buyer to perform the chef-decorator agreement?

(A) Yes, because the agreement contained no prohibition against assignment or delegation.

(B) Yes, because the chef received adequate assurances of the buyer's ability to complete the job.

(C) No, because the decorator's duties were of a personal nature, involving his reputation, taste, and skill.

(D) No, because the decorator's purported delegation to the buyer of his obligations to the chef effected a novation.

[Q3072]

26. A testator owned in fee simple a farm of 300 acres. He died and by will duly admitted to probate devised the farm to his surviving widow, for life with remainder in fee simple to his three children, two daughters and a son. All three children survived the testator.

At the time of the testator's death, there existed a mortgage on the farm that the testator had given ten years before to secure a loan for the purchase of the farm. At his death, there remained unpaid $40,000 in principal, payable in installments of $4,000 per year for the next ten years. In addition, there was due interest at the rate of 10% per annum, payable annually with the installment of principal. The widow took possession and out of a gross income of $50,000 per year realized $25,000 net after paying all expenses and charges except the installment of principal and interest due on the mortgage.

The daughters wanted the three children, including the son, to each contribute one-third of the amounts needed to pay the mortgage installments. The son objected, contending that the widow should pay all of these amounts out of the profits she had made in operation of the farm. When foreclosure of the mortgage seemed imminent, the son sought legal advice.

If the son obtained sound advice relating to his rights, he was told that

(A) his only protection would lie in instituting an action for partition to compel the sale of the life estate of the widow and to obtain the value of the son's one-third interest in remainder.

(B) he could obtain appropriate relief to compel the widow personally to pay the sums due because the income is more than adequate to cover these amounts.

(C) he could be compelled personally to pay his share of the amounts due because discharge of the mortgage enhances the principal.

(D) he could not be held personally liable for any amount but that his share in remainder could be lost if the mortgage installments are not paid.

[Q1107]

27. A customer fell and injured himself when he slipped on a banana peel while shopping at a grocer's store. The banana peel was fresh and clean except for a mark made by the heel of the customer's shoe. In an action brought by the customer against the grocer, these are the only facts in evidence.

Should the trial judge permit the case to go to the jury?

(A) No, because the customer had an obligation to watch where he stepped.

(B) No, because there is not a reasonable basis for inferring that the grocer knew or should have known of the banana peel.

(C) Yes, because it is more likely than not that the peel came from a banana offered for sale by the grocer.

(D) Yes, because the grocer could foresee that a customer might slip on a banana peel.

[Q7083]

28. Insurance is provided in a particular state only by private companies. Although the state insurance commissioner inspects insurance companies for solvency, the state does not regulate their rates or policies. A particular insurance company charges higher rates for burglary insurance to residents of one part of a county in the state than to residents of another section of the same county because of the different crime rates in those areas.

A resident of that county was charged the higher rate by the insurance company because of the location of her residence. The resident sues the insurance company, alleging that the differential in insurance rates unconstitutionally denies her the equal protection of the laws.

Will the resident's suit succeed?

(A) Yes, because the higher crime rate in the resident's neighborhood demonstrates that the county police are not giving persons who reside there the equal protection of the laws.

(B) Yes, because the insurance rate differential is inherently discriminatory.

(C) No, because the constitutional

29. For an agreed price of $20 million, a builder contracted with a developer to design and build on the developer's commercial plot a 15-story office building. In excavating for the foundation and underground utilities, the contractor encountered a massive layer of granite at a depth of 15 feet. By reasonable safety criteria, the building's foundation required a minimum excavation of 25 feet. When the contract was made, neither the developer nor the contractor was aware of the subsurface granite, for the presence of which neither party had hired a qualified expert to test.

    Claiming accurately that removal of enough granite to permit the construction as planned would cost him an additional $3 million and a probable net loss on the contract of $2 million, the contractor refused to proceed with the work unless the developer would promise to pay an additional $2.5 million for the completed building.

    If the developer refuses and sues the contractor for breach of contract, which of the following will the court probably decide?

    (A) The contractor is excused under the modern doctrine of supervening impossibility, which includes severe impracticability.

    (B) The contractor is excused, because the contract is voidable on account of the parties' mutual mistake concerning an essential underlying fact.

    (C) The developer prevails, because the contractor assumed the risk of encountering subsurface granite that was unknown to the developer.

    (D) The developer prevails, unless subsurface granite was previously unknown anywhere in the vicinity of the developer's construction site.

    [Q1172]

30. State troopers lawfully stopped a driver on the turnpike for exceeding the speed limit by four miles per hour. One trooper approached the car to warn the driver to drive within the speed limit. The other trooper remained in the patrol car and ran a computer check of the license number of the driver's car. The computer check indicated that there was an outstanding warrant for the driver's arrest for unpaid traffic tickets. The troopers then arrested the driver. After handcuffing her, the troopers searched her and the car, and discovered 10 glassine bags of heroin in a paper bag on the back seat of the car. Later it was learned that the driver had paid the outstanding traffic tickets 10 days earlier and the warrant had been quashed, but the clerk of the court had failed to update the computer, which continued to list the warrant as outstanding. The driver was charged with unlawful possession of heroin. Her attorney filed a motion to suppress the use as evidence of the heroin found in the car.

    Should the motion be granted?

    (A) No, because the troopers could reasonably rely on the computer report and the search was incident to arrest.

    (B) No, because troopers may lawfully search the passenger compartment of a car incident to a valid traffic stop.

    (C) Yes, because there was no arrest for the traffic violation and no lawful arrest could be made on the basis of

(D) Yes, because there was no probable cause or reasonable suspicion to believe drugs were in the car.

[Q7042]

31. A developer, needing a water well on one of his projects, met several times about the matter with a well driller. Subsequently, the driller sent the developer an unsigned typewritten form captioned "WELL DRILLING PROPOSAL" and stating various terms the two had discussed but not agreed upon, including a "proposed price of $5,000." The form concluded, "This proposal will not become a contract until signed by you [the developer] and then returned to and signed by me [the driller]."

The developer signed the form and returned it to the driller, who neglected to sign it but promptly began drilling the well at the proposed site on the developer's project. After drilling for two days, the driller told the developer during one of the developer's daily visits that he would not finish unless the developer would agree to pay twice the price recited in the written proposal. The developer refused, the driller quit, and the developer hired a substitute driller to drill the well to completion for a price of $7,500.

In an action by the developer against the driller for damages, which of the following is the probable decision?

(A) The developer wins, because his signing of the driller's form constituted an acceptance of an offer by the driller.

(B) The developer wins, because the driller's commencement of performance constituted an acceptance by the driller of an offer by the developer and an implied promise by the driller to complete the well.

(C) The driller wins, because he never signed the proposal as required by its terms.

(D) The driller wins, because his commencement of performance merely prevented the developer from revoking his offer, made on a form supplied by the driller, and did not obligate the driller to complete the well.

[Q1041]

32. Small retailers located in the state of Yellow are concerned about the loss of business to certain large retailers located nearby in bordering states. In an effort to deal with this concern, the legislature of Yellow enacted a statute requiring all manufacturers and wholesalers who sell goods to retailers in Yellow to do so at prices that are no higher than the lowest prices at which they sell them to retailers in any of the states that border Yellow. Several manufacturers and wholesalers who are located in states bordering Yellow and who sell their goods to retailers in those states and in Yellow bring an action in federal court to challenge the constitutionality of this statute.

Which of the following arguments offered by these plaintiffs is likely to be most persuasive in light of applicable precedent?

The state statute

(A) deprives them of their property or liberty without due process of law.

(B) imposes an unreasonable burden on interstate commerce.

(C) deprives them of a privilege or immunity of national citizenship.

(D) denies them the equal protection of the laws.

33. The plaintiff suffered a serious injury while participating in an impromptu basketball game at a public park. The injury occurred when the plaintiff and the defendant, on opposing teams, each tried to obtain possession of the ball when it rebounded from the backboard after a missed shot at the basket. During that encounter, the plaintiff was struck and injured by the defendant's elbow. The plaintiff now seeks compensation from the defendant.

   At the trial, evidence was introduced tending to prove that the game had been rough from the beginning, that elbows and knees had frequently been used to discourage interference by opposing players, and that the plaintiff had been one of those making liberal use of such tactics.

   In this action, will the plaintiff prevail?

   (A) Yes, if the defendant intended to strike the plaintiff with his elbow.

   (B) Yes, if the defendant intended to cause a harmful or offensive contact with the plaintiff.

   (C) No, because the plaintiff impliedly consented to rough play.

   (D) No, unless the defendant intentionally used force that exceeded the players' consent.

34. Charged with forcible rape, the defendant relied on a defense of alibi. At the trial, the alleged victim testified that the defendant was the man who accosted her on the street, dragged her into the basement of an apartment building, and forced her to submit to sexual intercourse. During the case, the defendant's attorney offered the testimony of a woman who stated that she was familiar with the victim's reputation in the community and that the victim was thought of as a prostitute. The defendant's attorney also offered into evidence a certified court record indicating that the victim had been convicted of prostitution, a misdemeanor, two months prior to the alleged rape.

   Upon proper objection by the prosecution to both the woman's testimony and the court record, which of the following should the court admit?

   (A) The woman's testimony only.

   (B) The court record only.

   (C) The woman's testimony and the court record.

   (D) Neither the woman's testimony nor the court record.

35. A city has an ordinance that prohibits the location of "adult theaters and bookstores" (theaters and bookstores presenting sexually explicit performances or materials) in residential or commercial zones within the city. The ordinance was intended to protect surrounding property from the likely adverse secondary effects of such establishments. "Adult theaters and bookstores" are freely permitted in the areas of the city zoned industrial, where those adverse secondary effects are not as likely. A storekeeper is denied a zoning permit to open an adult theater and bookstore in a building owned by him in an area zoned commercial. As a result, the storekeeper brings suit in an appropriate court challenging the constitutionality of the zoning ordinance.

   Which of the following statements regarding the constitutionality of this city ordinance is most accurate?

   (A) The ordinance is valid, because a city may enforce zoning restrictions on speech-related businesses to ensure that the messages they disseminate are acceptable to the residents of adjacent property.

(B) The ordinance is valid, because a city may enforce this type of time, place, and manner regulation on speech-related businesses, so long as this type of regulation is designed to serve a substantial governmental interest and does not unreasonably limit alternative avenues of communication.

(C) The ordinance is invalid, because a city may not enforce zoning regulations that deprive potential operators of adult theaters and bookstores of their freedom to choose the location of their businesses.

(D) The ordinance is invalid, because a city may not zone property in a manner calculated to protect property from the likely adverse secondary effects of adult theaters and bookstores.

[Q2193]

36. A drug enforcement agent had been informed that a person arriving from Europe on a particular airline flight, and answering to a particular description, would be carrying cocaine in his baggage. When the agent saw a man answering that description (the defendant), the agent stopped him and searched his bag. In it, he found a small brass statue with a false bottom. Upon removing the false bottom, the agent found one ounce of cocaine. At the defendant's drug trial, he claimed that he had purchased the statue as a souvenir and was unaware that there was cocaine hidden it its base.

At trial the prosecution now offers to prove that the defendant was convicted fifteen years earlier of illegally importing cocaine by hiding it in the base of a brass statue. If the defendant's attorney objects, the court should rule that proof of the defendant's prior conviction is

(A) admissible, as evidence of habit.

(B) admissible, because it is evidence of a distinctive method of operation.

(C) inadmissible, because evidence of previous conduct by a defendant may not be used against him.

(D) inadmissible, because the prior conviction occurred more than ten years before the trial.

[Q5136]

37. A landowner executed an instrument in the proper form of a deed, purporting to convey his land to a friend. The landowner handed the instrument to the friend, saying, "This is yours, but please do not record it until after I am dead. Otherwise, it will cause me no end of trouble with my relatives." Two days later, the landowner asked the friend to return the deed to him because he had decided that he should devise the land to the friend by will rather than by deed. The friend said that he would destroy the deed and a day or so later falsely told the landowner that the deed had been destroyed. Six months ago, the landowner, who had never executed a will, died intestate, survived by a daughter as his sole heir at law. The day after the landowner's death, the friend recorded the deed from him. As soon as the daughter discovered this recording and the friend's claim to the land, she brought an appropriate action against the friend to quiet title to the land.

For whom should the court hold?

(A) The daughter, because the death of the landowner deprived the subsequent recordation of any effect.

(B) The daughter, because the friend was

dishonest in reporting that he had destroyed the deed.

(C) The friend, because the deed was delivered to him.

(D) The friend, because the deed was recorded by him.

[Q7009]

38. A city has had a severe traffic problem on its streets. As a result, it enacted an ordinance prohibiting all sales to the public of food or other items by persons selling directly from trucks, cars, or other vehicles located on city streets. The ordinance included an inseverable grandfather provision exempting from its prohibition vendors who, for 20 years or more, have continuously sold food or other items from such vehicles located on the streets of the city.

A retail ice cream vendor qualifies for this exemption and is the only food vendor that does. A yogurt company is a business similar to the ice cream company, but the yogurt company has been selling to the public directly from trucks located on the streets of the city only for the past ten years. The yogurt company filed suit in an appropriate federal district court to enjoin enforcement of this ordinance on the ground that it denies the yogurt company the equal protection of the laws.

In this case, the court will probably rule that the ordinance is

(A) constitutional, because it is narrowly tailored to implement the city's compelling interest in reducing traffic congestion and, therefore, satisfies the strict scrutiny test applicable to such cases.

(B) constitutional, because its validity is governed by the rational basis test, and the courts consistently defer to economic choices embodied in such legislation if they are even plausibly justifiable.

(C) unconstitutional, because the nexus between the legitimate purpose of the ordinance and the conduct it prohibits is so tenuous and its provisions are so underinclusive that the ordinance fails to satisfy the substantial relationship test applicable to such cases.

(D) unconstitutional, because economic benefits or burdens imposed by legislatures on the basis of grandfather provisions have consistently been declared invalid by courts as per se violations of the equal protection clause of the Fourteenth Amendment.

[Q1021]

39. A federal statute prohibits the sale or resale, in any place in this country, of any product intended for human consumption or ingestion into the human body that contains designated chemicals known to cause cancer, unless the product is clearly labeled as dangerous.

The constitutionality of this federal statute may most easily be justified on the basis of the power of Congress to

(A) regulate commerce among the states.

(B) enforce the Fourteenth Amendment.

(C) provide for the general welfare.

(D) promote science and the useful arts.

[Q1026]

40. A man intensely disliked his neighbors, who were of a different race. One night, intending to frighten his neighbors, he spray-painted their house with racial epithets and threats that they would be lynched. The man was arrested and prosecuted under a state law providing that "any person who threatens violence against another person with the intent to cause that person to fear for his or her life

or safety may be imprisoned for up to five years." In defense, the man claimed that he did not intend to lynch his neighbors, but only to scare them so that they would move away.

Can the man constitutionally be convicted under this law?

(A) No, because he was only communicating his views and had not commenced any overt action against the neighbors.

(B) Yes, because he was engaged in trespass when he painted the words on his neighbors' house.

(C) Yes, because his communication was a threat by which he intended to intimidate his neighbors.

(D) Yes, because his communication was racially motivated and thus violated the protections of the Thirteenth Amendment.

[Q7095]

41. A landowner owned land in fee simple. A small house on the land was occupied, with the landowner's oral permission, rent-free, by the landowner's son and the son's college classmate. The son was then 21 years old.

The landowner, by properly executed instrument, conveyed the land to "my beloved son, his heirs and assigns, upon the condition precedent that he earn a college degree by the time he reaches the age of 30. If, for any reason, he does not meet this condition, then the land shall become the sole property of my beloved daughter, her heirs and assigns." At the time of the conveyance, the son and the classmate attended a college located several blocks from the land. Neither had earned a college degree.

One week after the delivery of the deed to the son, the son recorded the deed and immediately told the classmate that he, the son, was going to begin charging the classmate rent since "I am now your landlord." There is no applicable statute.

The son and the classmate did not reach agreement, and the son served the appropriate notice to terminate whatever tenancy the classmate had. The son then sought, in an appropriate action, to oust the classmate.

Who should prevail?

(A) The son, because the conveyance created a fee simple subject to divestment in the son.

(B) The son, because the landowner's conveyance terminated the classmate's tenancy.

(C) The classmate, because the landowner's permission to occupy preceded the landowner's conveyance to the son.

(D) The classmate, because he is a tenant of the landowner, not of the son.

[Q1173]

42. A newly enacted federal statute appropriates $100 million in federal funds to support basic research by universities located in the United States. The statute provides that "the ten best universities in the United States" will each receive $10 million. It also provides that "the ten best universities" shall be "determined by a poll of the presidents of all the universities in the nation, to be conducted by the United States Department of Education." In responding to that poll, each university president is required to apply the well-recognized and generally accepted standards of academic quality that are specified in the statute. The provisions of the statute are inseverable.

Which of the following statements about this statute is correct?

(A) The statute is unconstitutional, because the reliance by Congress on a poll of individuals who are not federal officials to determine the recipients of its appropriated funds is an unconstitutional delegation of legislative power.

(B) The statute is unconstitutional, because the limitation on recipients to the ten best universities is arbitrary and capricious and denies other high-quality universities the equal protection of the laws.

(C) The statute is constitutional, because Congress has plenary authority to determine the objects of its spending and the methods used to achieve them, so long as they may reasonably be deemed to serve the general welfare and do not violate any prohibitory language in the Constitution.

(D) The validity of the statute is nonjusticiable, because the use by Congress of its spending power necessarily involves political considerations that must be resolved finally by those branches of the government that are closest to the political process.

[Q2145]

43. A company wanted to expand the size of the building it owned that housed the company's supermarket by adding space for a coffeehouse. The company's building was located in the center of five acres of land owned by the company and devoted wholly to parking for its supermarket customers.

City officials refused to grant a required building permit for the coffeehouse addition unless the company established in its store a child care center that would take up space at least equal to the size of the proposed coffeehouse addition, which was to be 20% of the existing building. This action of city officials was authorized by provisions of the applicable zoning ordinance.

In a suit filed in state court against appropriate officials of the city, the company challenged this child care center requirement solely on constitutional grounds. The lower court upheld the requirement even though city officials presented no evidence and made no findings to justify it other than a general assertion that there was a shortage of child care facilities in the city. The company appealed.

The court hearing the appeal should hold that the requirement imposed by the city on the issuance of this building permit is

(A) constitutional, because the burden was on the company to demonstrate that there was no rational relationship between this requirement and a legitimate governmental interest, and the company could not do so because the requirement is reasonably related to improving the lives of families and children residing in the city.

(B) constitutional, because the burden was on the company to demonstrate that this requirement was not necessary to vindicate a compelling governmental interest, and the company could not do so on these facts.

(C) unconstitutional, because the burden was on the city to demonstrate that this requirement was necessary to vindicate a compelling governmental interest, and the city failed to meet its burden under that standard.

(D) unconstitutional, because the burden

was on the city to demonstrate a rough proportionality between this requirement and the impact of the company's proposed action on the community, and the city failed to do so.

[Q3162]

44. A worker, aged 60, who had no plans for early retirement, had worked for a company for 20 years as a managerial employee-at-will when he had a conversation with the company's president about the worker's post-retirement goal of extensive travel around the United States. A month later, the president handed the worker a written, signed resolution of the company's Board of Directors stating that when and if the worker should decide to retire, at his option, the company, in recognition of his past service, would pay him a $2,000-per-month lifetime pension. (The company had no regularized retirement plan for at-will employees.) Shortly thereafter, the worker retired and immediately bought a $30,000 recreational vehicle for his planned travels. After receiving the promised $2,000 monthly pension from the company, for six months, the worker, now unemployable elsewhere, received a letter from the company, advising him that the pension would cease immediately because of recessionary budget constraints affecting in varying degrees all managerial salaries and retirement pensions.

In a suit against the company, for breach of contract, the worker will probably

(A) win, because he retired from the company as bargained-for consideration for the Board's promise to him of a lifetime pension.

(B) win, because he timed his decision to retire and to buy the recreational vehicle in reasonable reliance on the Board's promise to him of a lifetime pension.

(C) lose, because the Board's promise to him of a lifetime pension was an unenforceable gift promise.

(D) lose, because he had been an employee-at-will throughout his active service with the company.

[Q3169]

45. A young man and two of his friends were members of a teenage street gang. While they were returning from a dance late one evening, their car collided with a car driven by an elderly woman. After an argument, the young man attacked the elderly woman with his fists and beat her to death. The two friends watched, and when they saw the woman fall to the ground they urged the young man to flee. The young man was eventually apprehended and tried for manslaughter, but the jury could not decide on a verdict.

If the friends are subsequently tried as accomplices to manslaughter, they should be

(A) acquitted, because the young man was not convicted of the offense.

(B) acquitted, because they did not assist or encourage the young man to commit the crime.

(C) convicted, because they urged the young man to flee.

(D) convicted, because they made no effort to intervene.

[Q3070]

46. An electrical engineer designed an electronic game. The engineer entered into a licensing agreement with a toy company under which the company agreed to manufacture the game according to the engineer's specifications and to market it and pay a royalty to the engineer.

A child, whose parents had purchased the game for her, was injured while playing the game. The child recovered a judgment against the toy company on the basis of a finding that the game was defective because of the engineer's improper design.

In a claim for indemnity against the engineer, will the toy company prevail?

(A) Yes, because as between the engineer and the toy company, the engineer was responsible for the design of the game.

(B) Yes, because the toy company and the engineer were joint tortfeasors.

(C) No, because the toy company, as the manufacturer, was strictly liable to the child.

(D) No, if the toy company, by a reasonable inspection, could have discovered the defect in the design of the game.

[Q4052]

47. A grantor owned a tract of land in fee simple. By warranty deed, she conveyed the land in fee simple to her lawyer for a recited consideration of "$10 and other valuable consideration." The deed was promptly and properly recorded. One week later, the grantor and the lawyer executed a written document that stated that the conveyance of the property was for the purpose of establishing a trust for the benefit of the grantor's child. The lawyer expressly accepted the trust and signed the document with the grantor. This written agreement was not authenticated to be eligible for recordation and there never was an attempt to record it.

The lawyer entered into possession of the land and distributed the net income from it to the child at appropriate intervals.

Five years later, the lawyer conveyed the property in fee simple to a buyer by warranty deed. The buyer paid the fair market value of the property, had no knowledge of the written agreement between the grantor and the lawyer, and entered into possession of the property.

The grantor's child made demand upon the buyer for distribution of income at the next usual time the lawyer would have distributed. The buyer refused. The child brought an appropriate action against the buyer for a decree requiring her to perform the trust the lawyer had theretofore recognized.

In such action, judgment should be for

(A) the child, because a successor in title to the trustee takes title subject to the grantor's trust.

(B) the child, because equitable interests are not subject to the recording act.

(C) the buyer, because, as a bona fide purchaser, she took free of the trust encumbering the lawyer's title.

(D) the buyer, because no trust was ever created since the grantor had no title at the time of the purported creation.

[Q3005]

48. A seller owned a piece of land in fee simple, as the land records showed, when he contracted to sell the land to a buyer. Two weeks later, the buyer paid the agreed price and received a warranty deed. A week thereafter, when neither the contract nor the deed had been recorded and while the seller remained in possession of the property, a creditor of the seller properly filed a money judgment against the seller. The creditor knew nothing of the buyer's interest.

A statute in the jurisdiction provides: "Any judgment properly filed shall, for ten years from filing, be a lien on the real property then owned or subsequently acquired by any person against whom the judgment is rendered."

The recording act of the jurisdiction provides: "No conveyance or mortgage of real property shall be good against subsequent purchasers for value and without notice unless the same be recorded according to law."

The creditor brought an appropriate action to enforce her lien against the property in the buyer's hands.

If the court decides for the buyer, it will most probably be because

(A) the doctrine of equitable conversion applies.

(B) the jurisdiction's recording act does not protect creditors.

(C) the seller's possession gave the creditor constructive notice of the buyer's interest.

(D) the buyer was a purchaser without notice.

[Q3123]

49. A passenger is suing a defendant for injuries suffered in the crash of a small airplane, alleging that the defendant had owned the plane and negligently failed to have it properly maintained. The defendant has asserted in defense that he never owned the plane or had any responsibility to maintain it. At trial, the passenger calls a witness to testify that the witness had sold to the defendant a liability insurance policy on the plane. The testimony of the witness is

(A) inadmissible, because the policy itself is required under the original document rule.

(B) inadmissible, because of the rule against proof of insurance where insurance is not itself at issue.

(C) admissible to show that the defendant had little motivation to invest money in maintenance of the airplane.

(D) admissible as some evidence of the defendant's ownership of or responsibility for the airplane.

[Q3136]

50. A car owner washed her car while it was parked on a public street, in violation of a statute that prohibits the washing of vehicles on public streets during rush hours. The statute was enacted only to expedite the flow of automobile traffic. Due to a sudden and unexpected cold snap, the car owner's waste water formed a puddle that froze. A pedestrian slipped on the frozen puddle and broke her leg. The pedestrian sued the car owner to recover for her injury. At trial, the only evidence the pedestrian offered as to negligence was the car owner's admission that she had violated the statute. At the conclusion of the proofs, both parties moved for a directed verdict.

How should the trial judge proceed?

(A) Deny both motions and submit the case to the jury, because, on the facts, the jury may infer that the car owner was negligent.

(B) Deny both motions and submit the case to the jury, because the jury may consider the statutory violation as evidence that the car owner was negligent.

(C) Grant the car owner's motion, because the pedestrian has failed to offer adequate evidence that the car owner was negligent.

(D) Grant the pedestrian's motion, because of the car owner's admitted statutory violation.

[Q7020]

51. A large tract of land was owned by a religious order. On the land, the order erected a large residential building where its members reside. The land is surrounded by rural residential properties and its only access to a public way is afforded by an easement over a strip of land 30 feet wide. The easement was granted to the order by deed from a neighbor, who owned one of the adjacent residential properties. The order built a driveway on the strip, and the easement was used for 20 years without incident or objection.

    Last year, as permitted by the applicable zoning ordinance, the order constructed a 200-bed nursing home and a parking lot on their land, using all of the land that was available for such development. The nursing home was very successful, and on Sundays visitors to the nursing home overflowed the parking facilities on the land and parked all along the driveway from early in the morning through the evening hours. After two Sundays of the resulting congestion and inconvenience, the neighbor erected a barrier across the driveway on Sundays preventing any use of the driveway by anyone seeking access to the order's land. The order objected.

    The neighbor brought an appropriate action to terminate the easement.

    The most likely result in this action is that the court will hold for

    (A) the neighbor, because the order excessively expanded the use of the dominant tenement.

    (B) the neighbor, because the parking on the driveway exceeded the scope of the easement.

    (C) the order, because expanded use of the easement does not terminate the easement.

    (D) the order, because the neighbor's use of self help denies her the right to equitable relief.

    [Q2021]

52. A thirteen-year-old girl was a member of a national young people's scouting organization. As part of a scouting project, she planned to spend an entire weekend camping alone in the woods. The defendant, who knew about the project, phoned the scout's mother the day after the scout left home. The defendant said, "We have your daughter. We've already beaten her up once, just to hear her scream. Next time, we might kill her." The defendant instructed the mother to deliver a cash ransom to a specified location within one hour. Since there was no way to locate the scout's campsite in the woods, the mother could not find out whether the defendant was telling the truth. Horrified that her daughter might be beaten and injured or killed, she delivered the ransom as instructed. She remained in a hysterical state until the scout returned from her camping trip, and the mother realized that the ransom demand had been a hoax. The mother, who already suffered from a heart ailment, had a heart attack the day after the scout's return.

    If the mother asserts a claim against the defendant for assault, the court should find for

    (A) the mother, because the defendant was aware that his conduct would frighten her.

    (B) the mother, because the court will transfer the defendant's intent.

    (C) the defendant, because the mother did not perceive injury being inflicted upon the scout.

    (D) the defendant, because the mother had no reason to expect to be touched by the defendant.

[Q5018]

53. The United States Congress enacted a federal statute providing that any state may "require labeling to show the state or other geographic origin of citrus fruit that is imported into the receiving state." Pursuant to the federal statute, a state that produced large quantities of citrus fruit enacted a law requiring all citrus fruit imported into the state to be stamped with a two-letter postal abbreviation signifying the state of the fruit's origin. The law did not impose any such requirement for citrus fruit grown within the state. When it adopted the law, the state legislature declared that its purpose was to reduce the risks of infection of local citrus crops by itinerant diseases that have been found to attack citrus fruit. A national association of citrus growers sued to have the state law declared unconstitutional. The association claims that the law is prohibited by the negative implications of the commerce clause of the Constitution.

Which of the following is the best argument in favor of the state's effort to have this lawsuit dismissed?

(A) Any burden on interstate commerce imposed by the state law is outweighed by a legitimate state interest.

(B) Congress has the authority to authorize specified state regulations that would otherwise be prohibited by the negative implications of the commerce clause, and it has done so in this situation.

(C) The state law does not discriminate against out-of-state citrus growers or producers.

(D) The state law furthers a legitimate state interest, the burden it imposes on interstate commerce is only incidental, and the state's interest cannot be satisfied by other means that are less burdensome to interstate commerce.

[Q7084]

54. The defendant suffered a severe head injury in an accident which occurred three years ago. As a result, she experienced eight incidents of sudden unconsciousness, each lasting approximately two minutes. All the incidents occurred within a three-month period immediately following the accident, and all occurred while the defendant was at home. Last week she was driving her automobile in a lawful manner when she suddenly lost consciousness as a result of the head injury which occurred three years ago. Her car swerved out of control onto the sidewalk, striking and permanently injuring a pedestrian. Drake was charged with violating a state statute which defines the crime of "reckless maiming" as "causing permanent injury to another person by acting in knowing disregard of the plain and strong likelihood that death or serious personal injury will result."

Which of the following is the defendant's most effective argument in defense against the charge of reckless maiming?

(A) The pedestrian head injury was not the result of any culpable conduct by the defendant.

(B) After losing consciousness while driving, the defendant was no longer capable of exercising control over the operation of her vehicle.

(C) The defendant reasonably believed that she would not have any further incidents of unconsciousness.

(D) The defendant did not know that her driving would lead to death or serious injury.

[Q5050]

55. On June 1, a wholesaler received a purchase-order form from a retailer and new customer, in which the latter ordered 1,000 anti-recoil widgets for delivery no later than August 30 at a delivered total price of $10,000, as quoted in the wholesaler's current catalog. Both parties are merchants with respect to widgets of all types. On June 2, the wholesaler mailed to the retailer its own form, across the top of which the wholesaler's president had written, "We are pleased to accept your order." This form contained the same terms as the retailer's form except for an additional printed clause in the wholesaler's form that provided for a maximum liability of $100 for any breach of contract by the retailer.

As of June 5, when the retailer received the wholesaler's acceptance form, which of the following is an accurate statement concerning the legal relationship between the wholesaler and the retailer?

(A) There is no contract, because the liability-limitation clause in the wholesaler's form is a material alteration of the retailer's offer.

(B) There is no contract, because the retailer did not consent to the liability-limitation clause in the wholesaler's form.

(C) There is an enforceable contract whose terms include the liability-limitation clause in the wholesaler's form, because liquidation of damages is expressly authorized by the Uniform Commercial Code.

(D) There is an enforceable contract whose terms do not include the liability-limitation clause in the wholesaler's form.

[Q2034]

56. Angry because her co-worker had insulted her, the defendant decided to get revenge. Because she worked for an exterminator, the defendant had access to cans of a poison gas called Terminate which was often used to kill termites and other insects. The defendant did not want to kill the co-worker, so she carefully read the use manual supplied by the manufacturer. The manual said that Terminate was not fatal to human beings, but that exposure to it could cause serious ailments including blindness and permanent respiratory irritation. When she was sure that no one would see her, the defendant brought a can of Terminate to the parking lot and released the poison gas into the co-worker's car, hoping to blind her but not kill her. At lunchtime, the co-worker and her friend sat together in the co-worker's car. As a result of their exposure to the Terminate in the car, the friend died and the co-worker became so ill that she was hospitalized for over a month.

If the defendant is charged with the murder of the friend, she should be found

(A) guilty, because the friend's death resulted from an act which the defendant performed with the intent to cause great bodily harm to a human being.

(B) guilty, because the use of poison gas is an inherently dangerous activity.

(C) not guilty, because she did not know that the friend would be exposed to the poison gas.

(D) not guilty, because she did not intend to cause the death of any person.

[Q5017]

57. Which of the following acts by the United States Senate would be constitutionally IMPROPER?

(A) The Senate decides, with the House of

Representatives, that a disputed state ratification of a proposed constitutional amendment is valid.

(B) The Senate determines the eligibility of a person to serve as a senator.

(C) The Senate appoints a commission to adjudicate finally a boundary dispute between two states.

(D) The Senate passes a resolution calling on the President to pursue a certain foreign policy.

[Q1087]

58. A carpenter contracted with a homeowner to remodel the homeowner's home for $10,000, to be paid on completion of the work. On May 29, relying on his expectation that he would finish the work and have the homeowner's payment on June 1, the carpenter contracted to buy a car for "$10,000 in cash, if payment is made on June 1; if payment is made thereafter, the price is $12,000." The carpenter completed the work according to specifications on June 1 and demanded payment from the homeowner on that date. The homeowner, without any excuse, refused to pay. Thereupon, the carpenter became very excited, suffered a minor heart attack, and, as a result, incurred medical expenses of $1,000. The reasonable value of the carpenter's services in remodeling the homeowner's home was $13,000.

In an action by the carpenter against the homeowner, which of the following should be the carpenter's measure of recovery?

(A) $10,000, the contract price.

(B) $11,000, the contract price plus $1,000 for the medical expenses incurred because the homeowner refused to pay.

(C) $12,000, the contract price plus $2,000, the bargain that was lost because the carpenter could not pay cash for the car on June 1.

(D) $13,000, the amount the homeowner was enriched by the carpenter's services.

[Q7099]

59. The plaintiff sued the defendant for illegal discrimination, claiming that the defendant fired him because of his race. At trial, the plaintiff called a witness, expecting him to testify that the defendant had admitted the racial motivation. Instead, the witness testified that the defendant said that he had fired the plaintiff because of his frequent absenteeism. While the witness is still on the stand, the plaintiff offers a properly authenticated secret tape recording he had made at a meeting with the witness in which the witness related the defendant's admissions of racial motivation.

The tape recording is

(A) admissible as evidence of the defendant's racial motivation and to impeach the witness's testimony.

(B) admissible only to impeach the witness's testimony.

(C) inadmissible, because it is hearsay not within any exception.

(D) inadmissible, because a secret recording is an invasion of the witness's right of privacy under the U.S. Constitution.

[Q3026]

60. Acting with a warrant and with probable cause, police arrested the defendant on charges of marijuana cultivation. They advised him of his *Miranda* rights. The defendant asked to have his attorney present and was permitted to telephone her office. He left a message that he had been arrested. When the attorney received the

message, she telephoned the county sheriff, asking where the defendant was being held. The sheriff said that he did not know. As a result, it took the attorney several hours to find the defendant. While waiting for the attorney, one of the officers said to the defendant, "Why don't you tell us about it?" whereupon the defendant admitted growing the marijuana. The defendant was subsequently charged with violating a state law which prohibits growing marijuana.

The defendant's attorney made an appropriate motion to prevent the use of the defendant's statement as evidence against him. The motion should be

(A) granted, because the defendant asserted his right to have an attorney present.

(B) granted, only if the sheriff actually knew the defendant's whereabouts when he said that he did not.

(C) denied, if the sheriff actually did not know the defendant's whereabouts when he said that he did not.

(D) denied, because the defendant waived his right to remain silent when he admitted growing the marijuana.

[Q5136]

61. A brother and sister owned a parcel as joint tenants, upon which was situated a two-family house. The brother lived in one of the two apartments and rented the other apartment to a tenant. The brother got in a fight with the tenant and injured him. The tenant obtained and properly filed a judgment for $10,000 against the brother.

The statute in the jurisdiction reads: Any judgment properly filed shall, for ten years from filing, be a lien on the real property then owned or subsequently acquired by any person against whom the judgment is rendered.

The sister, who lived in a distant city, knew nothing of the tenant's judgment. Before the tenant took any further action, the brother died. The common-law joint tenancy is unmodified by statute.

The sister then learned the facts and brought an appropriate action against the tenant to quiet title to the land.

The court should hold that the tenant has

(A) a lien against the whole of the property, because he was a tenant of both the brother and the sister at the time of the judgment.

(B) a lien against the brother's undivided one-half interest in the land, because his judgment was filed prior to the brother's death.

(C) no lien, because the sister had no actual notice of the tenant's judgment until after the brother's death.

(D) no lien, because the brother's death terminated the interest to which the tenant's lien attached.

[Q1090]

62. The vaccination of children against childhood contagious diseases (such as measles, diphtheria, and whooping cough) has traditionally been a function of private doctors and local and state health departments. Because vaccination rates have declined in recent years, especially in urban areas, the President proposes to appoint a Presidential Advisory Commission on Vaccination which would be charged with conducting a national publicity campaign to encourage vaccination as a public health measure. No federal statute authorizes or prohibits this action by the President. The activities of the Presidential Advisory Commission on Vaccination would be financed entirely from funds appropriated by Congress to the Office of the President for "such other

purposes as the President may think appropriate."

May the President constitutionally create such a commission for this purpose?

(A) Yes, because the President has plenary authority to provide for the health, safety, and welfare of the people of the United States.

(B) Yes, because this action is within the scope of executive authority vested in the President by the Constitution, and no federal statute prohibits it.

(C) No, because the protection of children against common diseases by vaccination is a traditional state function and, therefore, is reserved to the states by the Tenth Amendment.

(D) No, because Congress has not specifically authorized the creation and support of such a new federal agency.

[Q3109]

63. A client consulted a lawyer about handling the sale of the client's building, and asked the lawyer what her legal fee would be. The lawyer replied that her usual charge was $100 per hour, and estimated that the legal work on behalf of the client would cost about $5,000 at that rate. The client said, "Okay; let's proceed with it," and the lawyer timely and successfully completed the work. Because of unexpected title problems, the lawyer reasonably spent 75 hours on the matter and shortly thereafter mailed the client a bill for $7,500, with a letter itemizing the work performed and time spent. The client responded by a letter expressing his good-faith belief that the lawyer had agreed to a total fee of no more than $5,000. The client enclosed a check in the amount of $5,000 payable to the lawyer and conspicuously marked, "Payment in full for legal services in connection with the sale of [the client's] building." Despite reading the "Payment in full..." language, the lawyer, without any notation of protest or reservation of rights, endorsed and deposited the check to her bank account. The check was duly paid by the client's bank. A few days later, the lawyer unsuccessfully demanded payment from the client of the $2,500 difference between the amount of her bill and the check, and now sues the client for that difference.

What, if anything, can the lawyer recover from the client?

(A) Nothing, because the risk of unexpected title problems in a real-property transaction is properly allocable to the seller's attorney and thus to the lawyer in this case.

(B) Nothing, because the amount of the lawyer's fee was disputed in good faith by the client, and the lawyer impliedly agreed to an accord and satisfaction.

(C) $2,500, because the client agreed to an hourly rate for as many hours as the work reasonably required, and the sum of $5,000 was merely an estimate.

(D) The reasonable value of the lawyer's services in excess of $5,000, if any, because there was no specific agreement on the total amount of the lawyer's fee.

[Q2123]

64. A young man and an older man planned to break into a federal government office to steal food stamps. The young man telephoned a woman one night and asked whether the woman wanted to buy some "hot" food stamps. The woman, who understood that "hot" meant stolen, said, "Sure, bring them right over." The young man and the older man then successfully

executed their scheme. That same night they delivered the food stamps to the woman, who bought them for $500. The woman did not ask when or by whom the stamps were stolen. All three were arrested. The woman was brought to trial on a charge of conspiracy to steal food stamps.

On the evidence stated, the woman should be found

(A) guilty, because when a new confederate enters a conspiracy already in progress, she becomes a party to it.

(B) guilty, because she knowingly and willingly aided and abetted the conspiracy and is chargeable as a principal.

(C) not guilty, because although the woman knew the stamps were stolen, she neither helped to plan nor participated or assisted in the theft.

(D) not guilty, because the young man and the older man had not been convicted of or charged with conspiracy, and the woman cannot be guilty of conspiracy by herself.

[Q4002]

65. A student broke into a professor's office in order to look at examination questions. The questions were locked in a drawer, and the student could not find them. The student believed that looking at examination questions was a crime, but in this belief he was mistaken.

Charged with burglary, the student should be

(A) acquitted, because he did not complete the crime and he has not been charged with attempt.

(B) acquitted, because what he intended to do when he broke in was not a crime.

(C) convicted, because he had the necessary mental state and committed the act of breaking and entering.

(D) convicted, because factual impossibility is not a defense.

[Q4037]

66. A landlord leased an apartment to a tenant by written lease for two years ending on the last day of a recent month. The lease provided for $700 monthly rental. The tenant occupied the apartment and paid the rent for the first 15 months of the lease term, until he moved to a new job in another city. Without consulting the landlord, the tenant moved a friend into the apartment and signed an informal writing transferring to the friend his "lease rights" for the remaining nine months of the lease. The friend made the next four monthly $700 rental payments to the landlord. For the final five months of the lease term, no rent was paid by anyone, and the friend moved out with three months left on the lease term. The landlord was on an extended trip abroad, and did not learn of the default and the vacancy until last week. The landlord sued the tenant and the friend, jointly and severally, for $3,500 for the last five months' rent.

What is the likely outcome of the lawsuit?

(A) Both the tenant and the friend are liable for the full $3,500, because the tenant is liable on privity of contract and the friend is liable on privity of estate as assignee.

(B) The friend is liable for $1,400 on privity of estate, which lasted only until he vacated, and the tenant is liable for $2,100 on privity of contract and estate for the period after the friend vacated.

(C) The friend is liable for $3,500 on privity of estate and the tenant is not liable, because the landlord's failure to object to the friend's payment of rent relieved the tenant of liability.

(D) The tenant is liable for $3,500 on privity of contract and the friend is not liable, because a sublessee does not have personal liability to the original landlord.

[Q7004]

67. A state statute provides that the owner of any motor vehicle operated on the public roads of the state is liable for damage resulting from the negligence of any person driving the vehicle with the owner's permission. A woman was injured when a vehicle operated by a priest struck her while she was walking across the street. At the scene of the accident, the priest apologized to the woman, saying, "I'm sorry. It isn't my car. I didn't know that the brakes were bad." The woman subsequently instituted an action against an accountant for her damages, asserting that the accountant owned the vehicle. She alleged that the accountant was negligent in permitting the vehicle to be driven by the priest while he (the accountant) knew that the brakes were in need of repair, and that he was also vicariously liable under the statute for the negligence of the priest. The accountant denied ownership of the vehicle. At the trial, the plaintiff offered testimony by a car mechanic that on the day after the accident the accountant hired him to completely overhaul the brakes. Upon objection by the accountant, the evidence is

(A) admissible, to show that the accountant was the owner of the vehicle.

(B) admissible, to show that the brakes were in need of repair on the day of the accident.

(C) inadmissible, because the condition of the vehicle on any day other than that of the accident is irrelevant to show its condition at the time the accident occurred.

(D) inadmissible, under a policy which encourages safety precautions.

[Q5072]

68. The plaintiff sued the defendant for breach of a commercial contract in which the defendant had agreed to sell the plaintiff all of the plaintiff's requirements for widgets. The plaintiff called an expert witness to testify as to damages. The defendant seeks to show that the expert had provided false testimony as a witness in his own divorce proceedings.

This evidence should be

(A) admitted only if elicited from the expert on cross-examination.

(B) admitted only if the false testimony is established by clear and convincing extrinsic evidence.

(C) excluded, because it is impeachment on a collateral issue.

(D) excluded, because it is improper character evidence.

[Q3013]

69. Plaintiff challenged the constitutionality of a state tax law, alleging that it violated the equal protection clauses of both the United States Constitution and the state constitution. The state supreme court agreed and held the tax law to be invalid. It said: "We hold that this state tax law violates the equal protection clause of the United States Constitution and also the equal protection clause of the state constitution because we interpret that provision of the state constitution to contain exactly the same prohibition against discriminatory legislation as is contained in the equal protection clause of

the Fourteenth Amendment to the United States Constitution."

The state sought review of this decision in the United States Supreme Court, alleging that the state supreme court's determination of the federal constitutional issue was incorrect.

How should the United States Supreme Court dispose of the case if it believes that this interpretation of the federal Constitution by the state supreme court raises an important federal question and is incorrect on the merits?

(A) Reverse the state supreme court decision, because the equal protection clause of a state constitution must be construed by the state supreme court in a manner that is congruent with the meaning of the equal protection clause of the federal Constitution.

(B) Reverse the state supreme court decision with respect to the equal protection clause of the federal Constitution and remand the case to the state supreme court for further proceedings, because the state and federal constitutional issues are so intertwined that the federal issue must be decided so that this case may be disposed of properly.

(C) Refuse to review the decision of the state supreme court, because it is based on an adequate and independent ground of state law.

(D) Refuse to review the decision of the state supreme court, because a state government may not seek review of decisions of its own courts in the United States Supreme Court.

[Q1010]

70. The defendant, while intoxicated, drove his car through a playground crowded with children just to watch the children run to get out of his way. His car struck one of the children, killing her instantly.

Which of the following is the best theory for finding the defendant guilty of murder?

(A) Transferred intent.

(B) Felony murder, with assault with a deadly weapon as the underlying felony.

(C) Intentional killing, since he knew that the children were there and he deliberately drove his car at them.

(D) Commission of an act highly dangerous to life, without an intent to kill but with disregard of the consequences.

[Q4035]

71. Under a written agreement a manufacturer of pastries promised to sell its entire output of baked buns at a specified unit price to a bakery, for one year. The bakery promised not to sell any other supplier's baked buns. Shortly after making the contract, and before the manufacturer had tendered any buns, the bakery decided that the contract had become undesirable because of a sudden, sharp decline in its customers' demand for baked buns. It renounced the agreement, and the manufacturer sues for breach of contract.

Which of the following will the court probably decide?

(A) The bakery wins, because mutuality of obligation was lacking in that the bakery made no express promise to buy any of the manufacturer's baked buns.

(B) The bakery wins, because the agreement was void for indefiniteness of quantity and total price for the year involved.

(C) The manufacturer wins, because the bakery's promise to sell at retail the manufacturer's baked buns exclusively, if it sold any such buns at all, implied a promise to use its best efforts to sell bakery's one-year output of baked buns.

(D) The manufacturer wins, because under the applicable law both parties to a sale-of-goods contract impliedly assume the risk of price and demand fluctuations.

[Q1017]

72. A defendant was charged with aggravated assault. At trial, the victim testified that the defendant beat her savagely, but she was not asked about anything said during the incident. The prosecutor then called a witness to testify that when the beating stopped, the victim screamed: "I'm dying-don't let [the defendant] get away with it!"

Is the testimony of the witness concerning the victim's statement admissible?

(A) No, because it is hearsay not within any exception.

(B) No, because the victim was not asked about the statement.

(C) Yes, as a statement under belief of impending death, even though the victim did not die.

(D) Yes, as an excited utterance.

[Q7037]

73. The Rapido is a sports car manufactured by the defendant, a car maker. The Rapido has an excellent reputation for mechanical reliability with one exception, which is that the motor may stall if the engine has not had an extended warm-up. The plaintiff had just begun to drive her Rapido in city traffic without a warm-up when the engine suddenly stalled. Behind the plaintiff, a car driven by an elderly man tried to stop, but rear-ended the plaintiff's car. The plaintiff suffered no external physical injuries as a result of the collision. However, the shock of the crash caused her to suffer a severe heart attack.

The plaintiff brought an action against the defendant based on strict liability in tort. During the trial, the plaintiff presented evidence of an alternative engine design of equal cost that would eliminate the stalling problem without impairing the functions of the engine in any way. The defendant moves for a directed verdict at the close of the evidence.

This motion should be

(A) denied, because the jury could find that an unreasonably dangerous defect in the engine was a proximate cause of the collision.

(B) denied, if the jury could find that the Rapido was not crashworthy.

(C) granted, because the elderly man's failure to stop within an assured clear distance was a superseding cause of the collision.

(D) granted, if a person of normal sensitivity would not have suffered a heart attack under these circumstances.

[Q3146]

74. In a signed writing, a buyer contracted to purchase a 25-foot travel trailer from an RV dealer for $15,000, cash on delivery no later than June 1. The buyer arrived at the dealer's sales lot on Sunday, May 31, to pay for and take delivery of the trailer, but refused to do so when he discovered that the spare tire was missing.

The dealer offered to install a spare tire on Monday when its service department would open, but the buyer replied that he did not want the trailer and would purchase another one elsewhere.

Which of the following is accurate?

(A) The buyer had a right to reject the trailer, but the dealer was entitled to a reasonable opportunity to cure the defect.

(B) The buyer had a right to reject the trailer and terminate the contract under the perfect tender rule.

(C) The buyer was required to accept the trailer, because the defect could be readily cured.

(D) The buyer was required to accept the trailer, because the defect did not substantially impair its value.

[Q2106]

75. "The Heights" was a poor neighborhood in a city. Because many of the residents of The Heights had been complaining about the exploitation of tenants by absentee landlords, and about the lack of law enforcement in their neighborhood, the City Attorney instituted a campaign of neighborhood reform in The Heights. The City Attorney obtained a series of warrants for inspection of buildings in The Heights. He accomplished this by presenting an affidavit which stated that many health and safety violations had been observed in buildings located in The Heights by police and building inspectors traveling through the neighborhood. Pursuant to the warrants, police officers and building inspectors were ordered to inspect certain buildings. As a result, an apartment building owned by a landlord was found to have more than twenty violations of the city's building code. The landlord was prosecuted under a state law which made it a felony for any landlord to willfully fail to correct health and safety violations in a building which he or she owned.

If the landlord moves to suppress the evidence against him which was obtained as a result of the inspection of his building, his motion should be

(A) granted, unless the affidavit which was submitted in support of the request for a warrant specifically stated that violations had been observed in the landlord's building.

(B) granted, because the inspections were part of a general scheme to enforce the law in a particular neighborhood only.

(C) denied, because no warrant is needed to inspect buildings for health or safety violations.

(D) denied, because the inspection was part of a reasonable administrative scheme to enforce generally-applicable health and safety codes in The Heights.

[Q5022]

76. At a defendant's trial for burglary, his friend supported the defendant's alibi that they were fishing together at the time of the crime. On cross-examination, the friend was asked whether his statement on a credit card application that he had worked for his present employer for the last five years was false. The friend denied that the statement was false.

The prosecutor then calls the manager of the company for which the friend works, to testify that although the friend had been first employed five years earlier and is now employed by the company, there had been a three-year period during which he had not been so employed. The testimony of the manager is

(A) admissible, in the judge's discretion, because the friend's credibility is a fact of major consequence to the case.

(B) admissible, as a matter of right,

because the friend "opened the door" by his denial on cross-examination.

(C) inadmissible, because whether the friend lied in his application is a matter that cannot be proved by extrinsic evidence.

(D) inadmissible, because the misstatement by the friend could have been caused by a misunderstanding of the application form.

[Q3122]

77. As an encyclopedia salesman approached the grounds on which a reclusive homeowner's house was situated, he saw a sign that said, "No salesmen. Trespassers will be prosecuted. Proceed at your own risk." Although the salesman had not been invited to enter, he ignored the sign and drove up the driveway toward the house. As he rounded a curve, a powerful explosive charge buried in the driveway exploded, and the salesman was injured.

Can the salesman recover damages from the homeowner for his injuries?

(A) Yes, if the homeowner was responsible for the explosive charge under the driveway.

(B) Yes, unless the homeowner, when he planted the charge, intended only to deter, not to harm, a possible intruder.

(C) No, because the salesman ignored the sign, which warned him against proceeding further.

(D) No, if the homeowner reasonably feared that intruders would come and harm him or his family.

[Q3195]

78. A grantor owned in fee simple two adjoining lots, Lots 1 and 2. He conveyed in fee simple Lot 1 to an investor. The deed was in usual form of a warranty deed with the following provision inserted in the appropriate place:

"Grantor, for himself, his heirs and assigns, does covenant and agree that any reasonable expense incurred by grantee, his heirs and assigns, as the result of having to repair the retaining wall presently situated on Lot 1 at the common boundary with Lot 2, shall be reimbursed one-half the costs of repairs; and by this provision the parties intend a covenant running with the land."

The investor conveyed Lot 1 in fee simple to a housewife by warranty deed in usual and regular form. The deed omitted any reference to the retaining wall or any covenant. Fifty years after the grantor's conveyance to the investor, the housewife conveyed Lot 1 in fee simple to a student by warranty deed in usual form; this deed omitted any reference to the retaining wall or the covenant.

There is no statute that applies to any aspect of the problems presented except a recording act and a statute providing for acquisition of title after ten years of adverse possession.

All conveyances by deeds were for a consideration equal to fair market value.

The deed from the grantor to the investor was never recorded. All other deeds were promptly and properly recorded.

Lot 2 is now owned by the grantor's son, who took by intestate succession from the grantor, now dead.

The student expended $3,500 on the retaining wall. Then he obtained all of the original deeds in the chain from the grantor to him. Shortly thereafter, the student discovered the covenant in the grantor's deed to the investor. He demanded that the grantor's son pay $1,750, and when the son refused, the student instituted an appropriate action to recover that sum from the son. In such action, the son asserted all defenses available to him.

If judgment is for the grantor's son, it will be because

(A) the student is barred by adverse possession.

(B) the investor's deed from the grantor was never recorded.

(C) the student did not know about the covenant until after he had incurred the expenses and, hence, could not have relied on it.

(D) the student's expenditures were not proved to be reasonable and customary.

[Q2107]

79. The defendant, while eating in a restaurant, noticed that a departing customer at the next table had left a five-dollar bill as a tip for the waitress. The defendant reached over, picked up the five-dollar bill, and put it in his pocket. As he stood up to leave, another customer who had seen him take the money ran over to him and hit him in the face with her umbrella. Enraged, the defendant choked the customer to death.

The defendant is charged with murder. He requests the court to charge the jury that they can find him guilty of voluntary manslaughter rather than murder. The defendant's request should be

(A) granted, because the jury could find that the defendant acted recklessly and not with the intent to cause death or serious bodily harm.

(B) granted, because the jury could find that being hit in the face with an umbrella constitutes adequate provocation.

(C) denied, because the evidence shows that the defendant intended to kill or to cause serious bodily harm.

(D) denied, because the evidence shows that the defendant provoked the assault on himself by his criminal misconduct.

[Q4038]

80. In a civil trial for fraud arising from a real estate transaction, the defendant claimed not to have been involved in the transaction. The plaintiff called a witness to testify concerning the defendant's involvement in the fraudulent scheme, but to the plaintiff's surprise the witness testified that the defendant was not involved, and denied making any statement to the contrary. The plaintiff now calls a second witness to testify that the first witness had stated, while the two were having a dinner conversation, that the defendant was involved in the fraudulent transaction.

Is the testimony of the second witness admissible?

(A) No, because a party cannot impeach the party's own witness.

(B) No, because it is hearsay not within any exception.

(C) Yes, but only to impeach the first witness.

(D) Yes, to impeach the first witness and to prove the defendant's involvement.

[Q7019]

81. A law student rented a furnished apartment. His landlord began to solicit his advice about her legal affairs, but he refused to provide it. The landlord then demanded that he vacate the apartment immediately. The landlord also engaged in

a pattern of harassment, calling the student at home every evening and entering his apartment without his consent during times when he was at school. During these unauthorized visits she removed the handles from the bathroom and kitchen sinks, but did not touch anything belonging to the student. The lease has a year to run, and the student is still living in the apartment. The student has sued the landlord for trespass to land.

Is he likely to prevail?

(A) No, because he has no standing to sue for trespass.

(B) No, because the landlord caused no damage to his property.

(C) Yes, for compensatory damages only.

(D) Yes, for injunctive relief, compensatory damages, and punitive damages.

[Q7088]

82. The police had, over time, accumulated reliable information that a rock singer operated a large cocaine-distribution network, that he and his accomplices often resorted to violence, and that they kept a small arsenal of weapons in his home.

One day, the police received reliable information that a large brown suitcase with leather straps containing a supply of cocaine had been delivered to the singer's home and that it would be moved to a distribution point the next morning. The police obtained a valid search warrant to search for and seize the brown suitcase and the cocaine and went to the singer's house.

The police knocked on the singer's door and called out, "Police. Open up. We have a search warrant." After a few seconds with no response, the police forced the door open and entered. Hearing noises in the basement, the police ran down there and found the singer with a large brown suitcase with leather straps. They seized the suitcase and put handcuffs on the singer. A search of his person revealed a switchblade knife and a .45-caliber pistol.

The police then fanned out through the house, looking in every room and closet. They found no one else, but one officer found an Uzi automatic weapon in a box on a closet shelf in the singer's bedroom.

In addition to charges relating to the cocaine in the suitcase, the singer is charged with unlawful possession of weapons.

The singer moves pretrial to suppress the use as evidence of the Uzi automatic weapon. The singer's motion to suppress should be

(A) granted, because the search exceeded the scope needed to find out if other persons were present.

(B) granted, because once the object of the warrant—the brown suitcase—had been found and seized, no further search of the house is permitted.

(C) denied, because the police were lawfully in the bedroom and the weapon was immediately identifiable as being subject to seizure.

(D) denied, because the police were lawfully in the house and had probable cause to believe that weapons were in the house.

[Q3068]

83. Police officers received a tip that drug dealing was occurring at a certain ground-floor duplex apartment. They decided to stake out the apartment. The stakeout revealed that a significant number of people visited the apartment for short periods of time and then left. A man exited the apartment and started to walk briskly

away. The officers grabbed the man and, when he struggled, wrestled him to the ground. They searched him and found a bag of heroin in one of his pockets. After discovering the heroin on the man, the police decided to enter the apartment. They knocked on the door, which was opened by the woman who lived there. The police asked if they could come inside, and the woman gave them permission to do so. Once inside, the officers observed several bags of heroin on the living room table. The woman is charged with possession of the heroin found on the living room table. She moves pretrial to suppress the heroin on the ground that it was obtained by virtue of an illegal search and seizure.

Should the woman's motion be granted?

(A) No, because the tip together with the heroin found in the man's pocket provided probable cause for the search.

(B) No, because the woman consented to the officers' entry.

(C) Yes, because the officers' decision to enter the house was the fruit of an illegal search of the man.

(D) Yes, because the officers did not inform the woman that she could refuse consent.

[Q7022]

84. A grantor owned a tract of land in fee simple. By warranty deed he conveyed the land to his nephew for life "and from and after the death of my nephew to my niece, her heirs and assigns."

Subsequently the niece died, devising all of her estate to the niece's boyfriend. The niece was survived by a cousin, her sole heir-at-law.

Shortly thereafter the nephew died, survived by the grantor, the niece's boyfriend, and the niece's cousin.

Title to the land now is in

(A) the grantor, because the contingent remainder never vested and the grantor's reversion was entitled to possession immediately upon the nephew's death.

(B) the boyfriend, because the vested remainder in the niece was transmitted by her will.

(C) the cousin, because she is the niece's heir.

(D) either the grantor or the cousin, depending upon whether the destructibility of contingent remainders is recognized in the applicable jurisdiction.

[Q1151]

85. A well-known movie actor was drinking Vineyard wine at a nightclub. A bottle of the Vineyard wine, with its label plainly showing, was on the table in front of the actor. An amateur photographer asked the actor if he could take his picture and the actor said, "Yes." Subsequently, the photographer sold the photo to the bottler of Vineyard wine. The bottler, without the actor's consent, used the photo in a wine advertisement in a nationally circulated magazine. The caption below the photo stated, "[The actor] enjoys his Vineyard wine."

If the actor sues the bottler to recover damages as a result of the bottler's use of the photograph, will the actor prevail?

(A) No, because the actor consented to being photographed.

(B) No, because the actor is a public figure.

(C) Yes, because the bottler made commercial use of the photograph.

(D) Yes, unless the actor did, in fact, enjoy his Vineyard wine.

[Q3192]

86. A four-year-old child sustained serious injuries when a playmate pushed him from between two parked cars into the street, where he was struck by a car. The child, by his representative, sued the driver of the car, the playmate's parents, and his own parents. At trial, the child's total injuries were determined to be $100,000. The playmate's parents were determined to be 20% at fault because they had failed to adequately supervise her. The driver was found to be 50% at fault. The child's own parents were determined to be 30% at fault for failure to adequately supervise him. The court has adopted the pure comparative negligence doctrine, with joint and several liability, in place of the common-law rules relating to plaintiff's fault. In addition, the common-law doctrines relating to intra-family liability have been abrogated.

How much, if anything, is the child's representative entitled to recover from the driver?

(A) $30,000.

(B) $50,000.

(C) $100,000.

(D) Nothing.

[Q7072]

87. During an altercation between two men at a company picnic, the victim suffered a knife wound in his abdomen and the defendant was charged with assault and attempted murder. At his trial, the defendant seeks to offer evidence that he had been drinking at the picnic and was highly intoxicated at the time of the altercation.

In a jurisdiction that follows the common- law rules concerning admissibility of evidence of intoxication, the evidence of the defendant's intoxication should be

(A) admitted without limitation.

(B) admitted subject to an instruction that it pertains only to the attempted murder charge.

(C) admitted subject to an instruction that it pertains only to the assault charge.

(D) excluded altogether.

[Q4007]

88. A bus passenger was seated next to a woman whom he did not know. The woman stood to exit the bus, leaving a package on the seat. The passenger lightly tapped the woman on the back to get her attention and to inform her that she had forgotten the package. Because the woman had recently had back surgery, the tap was painful and caused her to twist and seriously injure her back.

If the woman sues the passenger to recover for the back injury, will she prevail?

(A) No, because she is presumed to have consented to the ordinary contacts of daily life.

(B) No, because she was not put in apprehension because of the touching.

(C) Yes, because the passenger intentionally touched her.

(D) Yes, because the passenger's intentional touching seriously injured her.

[Q7063]

89. A public high school has had a very high rate of pregnancy among its students. In order to assist students who keep their babies to complete high school, the high school has established an infant day-care center for children of its students, and also offers classes in child care. Because the

child-care classes are always overcrowded, the school limits admission to those classes solely to students at the high school who are the mothers of babies in the infant day-care center.

A male student at the high school has legal custody of his infant son. The school provides care for his son in the infant day-care center, but will not allow the male student to enroll in the child-care classes. He brings suit against the school challenging, on constitutional grounds, his exclusion from the child-care classes.

Which of the following best states the burden of persuasion in this case?

(A) The student must demonstrate that the admission requirement is not rationally related to a legitimate governmental interest.

(B) The student must demonstrate that the admission requirement is not as narrowly drawn as possible to achieve a substantial governmental interest.

(C) The school must demonstrate that the admission policy is the least restrictive means by which to achieve a compelling governmental interest.

(D) The school must demonstrate that the admission policy is substantially related to an important governmental interest.

[Q2155]

90. A lawyer entered into a contract with a painter by the terms of which the painter was to paint the lawyer's office for $1,000 and was required to do all of the work over the following weekend so as to avoid disruption of the lawyer's business. The painter commenced work on Saturday morning, and had finished half the painting by the time he quit work for the day. That night, without the fault of either party, the office building was destroyed by fire.

Which of the following is an accurate statement?

(A) Both parties' contractual duties are discharged, and the painter can recover nothing from the lawyer.

(B) Both parties' contractual duties are discharged, but the painter can recover in quasi-contract from the lawyer.

(C) Only the painter's contractual duty is discharged, because the lawyer's performance (payment of the agreed price) is not impossible.

(D) Only the painter's contractual duty is discharged, and the painter can recover his reliance damages from the lawyer.

[Q1121]

91. In a civil trial arising from a car accident at an intersection, the plaintiff testified on direct that he came to a full stop at the intersection. On cross-examination, the defendant's lawyer asked whether the plaintiff claimed that he was exercising due care at the time, and the plaintiff replied that he was driving carefully. At a sidebar conference, the defendant's lawyer sought permission to ask the plaintiff about two prior intersection accidents in the last 12 months where he received traffic citations for failing to stop at stop signs. The plaintiff's lawyer objected.

Should the court allow defense counsel to ask the plaintiff about the two prior incidents?

(A) No, because improperly failing to stop on the recent occasions does not bear on the plaintiff's veracity and does not contradict his testimony in this case.

(B) No, because there is no indication that failing to stop on the recent occasions led to convictions.

(C) Yes, because improperly failing to

stop on the recent occasions bears on the plaintiff's credibility, since he claims to have stopped in this case.

(D) Yes, because improperly failing to stop on the recent occasions tends to contradict the plaintiff's claim that he was driving carefully at the time he collided with the defendant.

[Q7012]

92. A man owns a small lot in fee simple, and a woman owns the adjoining large lot in fee simple. The man has kept the lawns and trees on the small lot trimmed and neat. The woman "lets nature take its course" at the large lot. The result on the large lot is a tangle of underbrush, fallen trees, and standing trees that are in danger of losing limbs. Many of the trees on the large lot are near the small lot. In the past, debris and large limbs have been blown from the large lot onto the small lot. By local standards the large lot is an eyesore that depresses market values of real property in the vicinity, but the condition of the large lot violates no applicable laws or ordinances.

The man demanded that the woman keep the trees near the small lot trimmed. The woman refused.

The man brought an appropriate action against the woman to require her to abate what the man alleges to be a nuisance. In the lawsuit, the only issue is whether the condition of the large lot constitutes a nuisance.

The strongest argument that the man can present is that the condition of the large lot

(A) has an adverse impact on real estate values.

(B) poses a danger to the occupants of the small lot.

(C) violates community aesthetic standards.

(D) cannot otherwise be challenged under any law or ordinance.

[Q3175]

93. A buyer entered into a written contract to purchase from a seller 1,000 sets of specially manufactured ball bearings of a nonstandard dimension for a price of $10 per set. The seller correctly calculated that it would cost $8 to manufacture each set. Delivery was scheduled for 60 days later. Fifty-five days later, after the seller had completed production of the 1,000 sets, the buyer abandoned the project requiring use of the specially manufactured ball bearings and repudiated the contract with the seller. After notifying the buyer of his intention to resell, the seller sold the 1,000 sets of ball bearings to a salvage company for $2 per set. The seller sued the buyer for damages.

What damages should the court award to the seller?

(A) $2 per set, representing the difference between the cost of production and the price the buyer agreed to pay.

(B) $6 per set, representing the difference between the cost of manufacture and the salvage price.

(C) $8 per set, representing the lost profits plus the unrecovered cost of production.

(D) Nominal damages, as the seller failed to resell the goods by public auction.

[Q7031]

94. The governor of a state proposes to place a Christmas nativity scene, the components of which would be permanently donated to the state by private citizens, in the state Capitol Building rotunda where the state legislature meets annually. The governor further proposes to display this state-owned nativity scene annually from

December 1 to December 31, next to permanent displays that depict the various products manufactured in the state. The governor's proposal is supported by all members of both houses of the legislature.

If challenged in a lawsuit on establishment clause grounds, the proposed nativity scene display would be held

(A) unconstitutional, because the components of the nativity scene would be owned by the state rather than by private persons.

(B) unconstitutional, because the nativity scene would not be displayed in a context that appeared to depict and commemorate the Christmas season as a primarily secular holiday.

(C) constitutional, because the components of the nativity scene would be donated to the state by private citizens rather than purchased with state funds.

(D) constitutional, because the nativity scene would be displayed alongside an exhibit of various products manufactured in the state.

[Q3165]

95. A state statute prohibits the use of state-owned or state-operated facilities for the performance of abortions that are not "necessary to save the life of the mother." That statute also prohibits state employees from performing any such abortions during the hours they are employed by the state.

A woman was in her second month of pregnancy. She sought an abortion at a state-owned and state-operated hospital. The woman did not claim that the requested abortion was necessary to save her life. The officials in charge of the hospital refused to perform the requested abortion solely on the basis of the state statute. The woman immediately filed suit against those officials in an appropriate federal district court. She challenged the constitutionality of the state statute and requested the court to order the hospital to perform the abortion she sought. In this case, the court will probably hold that the state statute is

(A) unconstitutional, because a limit on the availability of abortions performed by state employees or in state-owned or state-operated facilities to situations in which it is necessary to save the life of the mother impermissibly interferes with the fundamental right of the woman to decide whether to have a child.

(B) unconstitutional, because it impermissibly discriminates against poor persons who cannot afford to pay for abortions in privately owned and operated facilities and against persons who live far away from privately owned and operated abortion clinics.

(C) constitutional, because it does not prohibit a woman from having an abortion or penalize her for doing so, it is rationally related to the legitimate governmental goal of encouraging childbirth, and it does not unduly burden the voluntary performance of abortions by private physicians in private facilities.

(D) constitutional, because the use of state-owned or state-operated facilities and access to the services of state employees are privileges and not rights and, therefore, a state may condition them on any basis it chooses.

[Q2162]

96. The National Ecological Balance Act prohibits the destruction or removal of any wild animals located on lands owned by the United States without express

permission from the Federal Bureau of Land Management. Violators are subject to fines of up to $1,000 per offense.

After substantial property damage was inflicted on residents of a state by hungry coyotes, the state legislature passed the Coyote Bounty Bill, which offers $25 for each coyote killed or captured within the state. A National Forest, owned by the federal government, is located entirely within that state. Many coyotes live in the National Forest.

Without seeking permission from the Bureau of Land Management, a hunter shot several coyotes in the National Forest and collected the bounty from the state. As a result, he was subsequently tried in federal district court, convicted, and fined $1,000 for violating the National Ecological Balance Act. The hunter appealed his conviction to the United States Court of Appeals.

On appeal, the Court of Appeals should hold the National Ecological Balance Act, as applied to the hunter, to be

(A) constitutional, because the property clause of Article IV, Section 3, of the Constitution authorizes such federal statutory controls and sanctions.

(B) constitutional, because Article I, Section 8, of the Constitution authorizes Congress to enact all laws necessary and proper to advance the general welfare.

(C) unconstitutional, because Congress may not use its delegated powers to override the Tenth Amendment right of the state to legislate in areas of traditional state governmental functions, such as the protection of the property of its residents.

(D) unconstitutional, because Congress violates the full faith and credit clause of Article IV when it punishes conduct that has been authorized by state action.

[Q2079]

97. A professional basketball player was scheduled to play in an important basketball game on Sunday. On Friday, after wagering heavily on the game, a gambler attacked the player with a baseball bat. The gambler's intent was to inflict injuries severe enough to require hospitalization and thus keep the player from playing as planned. As a result of the beating, the player was taken to a hospital, where he was treated by a doctor. The following day, the doctor injected the player with a medicine to relieve his pain. Because of an allergic reaction to the drug, the player died within minutes.

If the gambler is charged with the murder of the player, he should be found

(A) not guilty, because the player's allergic reaction to the drug was an intervening cause of death.

(B) not guilty, if the player's death was proximately caused by the doctor's negligence.

(C) guilty, only if the player's death was proximately caused by the gambler's attack.

(D) guilty, unless the doctor's conduct is found to be reckless or grossly negligent.

[Q5099]

98. A developer owned five adjoining rectangular lots, numbered 1 through 5 inclusive, all fronting on Main Street. All of the lots are in a zone limited to one- and two-family residences under the zoning ordinance. Two years ago, the developer

conveyed Lots 1, 3, and 5. None of the three deeds contained any restrictions. Each of the new owners built a one-family residence.

One year ago, the developer conveyed Lot 2 to a doctor. The deed provided that each of the doctor and the developer, their respective heirs and assigns, would use Lots 2 and 4 respectively only for one-family residential purposes. The deed was promptly and properly recorded. The doctor built a one-family residence on Lot 2.

Last month, the developer conveyed Lot 4 to a woman who operated a pharmacy. The deed contained no restrictions. The deed from the developer to the doctor was in the title report examined by the pharmacist's lawyer. The pharmacist obtained a building permit and commenced construction of a two-family residence on Lot 4.

The doctor, joined by the owners of Lots 1, 3, and 5, brought an appropriate action against the pharmacist to enjoin the proposed use of Lot 4, or, alternatively, damages caused by the pharmacist's breach of covenant.

Which is the most appropriate comment concerning the outcome of this action?

(A) All plaintiffs should be awarded their requested judgment for injunction because there was a common development scheme, but award of damages should be denied to all.

(B) The doctor should be awarded appropriate remedy, but recovery by the other plaintiffs is doubtful.

(C) Injunction should be denied, but damages should be awarded to all plaintiffs, measured by diminution of market value, if any, suffered as a result of the proximity of the pharmacist's two-family residence.

(D) All plaintiffs should be denied any recovery or relief because the zoning preempts any private scheme of covenants.

[Q3055]

99. A traveler was a passenger on a commercial aircraft owned and operated by an airline. The aircraft crashed into a mountain, killing everyone on board. The flying weather was good.

The traveler's legal representative brought a wrongful death action against the airline. At trial, the legal representative offered no expert or other testimony as to the cause of the crash.

On the airline's motion to dismiss at the conclusion of the legal representative's case, the court should

(A) grant the motion, because the legal representative has offered no evidence as to the cause of the crash.

(B) grant the motion, because the legal representative has failed to offer evidence negating the possibility that the crash may have been caused by mechanical failure that the airline could not have prevented.

(C) deny the motion, because the jury may infer that the aircraft crashed due to the airline's negligence.

(D) deny the motion, because in the circumstances common carriers are strictly liable.

[Q3161]

100. A large daily newspaper printed an article by a reporter who worked for it, accusing a well-known local businessman of misusing corporate funds. The businessman commenced a defamation action against the newspaper. As a defense, the newspaper asserted the businessman's

non-compliance with a state law that limited damages for defamation unless a demand for retraction is made.

The newspaper attorney offered the testimony of an editor employed by the paper. The editor testified that it was his job to note retraction demands in an office file, and that as a matter of company policy and practice all such demands were promptly reported to him for that purpose and promptly noted by him. He said that on the morning of trial, he had searched the file for notes of any retraction demand made by the businessman, and found none. If the newspaper's attorney offers the file in evidence, the businessman's objection should be

(A) sustained, since the absence of a notation cannot be used as evidence that an event did not occur.

(B) sustained, since the file is self-serving.

(C) overruled, if the file itself is admissible as a business record.

(D) overruled, since the editor used the file to refresh his recollection.

[Q5025]

QUESTIONS
SELF-ASSESSMENT TEST
P.M. EXAM
TIME: 3 HOURS

Directions: Each of the questions or incomplete statements below is followed by four suggested answers or completions. You are to choose the best of the stated alternatives. Answer all questions according to the generally accepted view, except where otherwise noted.

For the purposes of this test, you are to assume that Articles 1 and 2 of the Uniform Commercial Code have been adopted. You are to assume that the 2001 proposed amendments to Article 1 and the 2003 proposed amendments to Article 2 have not been adopted. You are also to assume relevant application of Article 9 of the UCC concerning fixtures. The Federal Rules of Evidence are deemed to control. The terms "Constitution," "constitutional," and "unconstitutional" refer to the federal Constitution unless indicated to the contrary. You are to assume that there is no applicable statute unless otherwise specified; however, survival actions and claims for wrongful death should be assumed to be available where applicable. You should assume that joint and several liability, with pure comparative negligence, is the relevant rule unless otherwise indicated.

101. An heir, who knew nothing about horses, inherited a thoroughbred colt whose disagreeable behavior made him a pest around the barn. The heir sold the colt for $1,500 to an experienced racehorse-trainer who knew of the heir's ignorance about horses. At the time of sale, the heir said to the trainer, "I hate to say it, but this horse is bad-tempered and nothing special." Soon after the sale, the horse won three races and earned $400,000 for the trainer.

    Which of the following additional facts, if established by the heir, would best support his chance of obtaining rescission of the sale to the trainer?

    (A) The heir did not know until after the sale that the trainer was an experienced racehorse-trainer.

    (B) At a pre-sale exercise session of which the trainer knew that the heir was not aware, the trainer clocked the horse in record-setting time, far surpassing any previous performance.

    (C) The horse was the only thoroughbred that the heir owned, and the heir did not know how to evaluate young and untested racehorses.

    (D) At the time of the sale, the heir was angry and upset over an incident in which the horse had reared and thrown a rider.

    [Q2062]

102. In exchange for a valid and sufficient consideration, an uncle orally promised his nephew, who had no car and wanted a minivan, "to pay to anyone from whom you buy a minivan within the next six months the full purchase price thereof." Two months later, the nephew bought a used minivan on credit from a Ford dealer, for $8,000. At the time, the dealer was unaware of the uncle's earlier promise to the nephew, but learned of it shortly after the sale.

    Can the dealer enforce the uncle's promise to the nephew?

    (A) Yes, under the doctrine of promissory estoppel.

    (B) Yes, because the dealer is an intended beneficiary of the uncle-nephew contract.

    (C) No, because the uncle's promise to the nephew is unenforceable under the suretyship clause of the statute of frauds.

    (D) No, because the dealer was neither identified when the uncle's promise was made nor aware of it when the minivan sale was made.

    [Q3172]

103. A married couple purchased a new mobile home from a retailer of such homes. The mobile home was assembled by a manufacturer and had an "HVAC" (heating, ventilating, and air conditioning) system designed by that manufacturer. The HVAC system contained both a furnace and an air conditioner, neither of which was made by the manufacturer — the furnace was made by a heating company and the air conditioner was made by a cooling company. The manufacturer selected and installed the furnace and the air conditioner into the overall HVAC unit. The furnace and the air conditioner were each controlled by an independent thermostat installed by the manufacturer. Because of the manner in which the manufacturer designed the HVAC system, the first time the system was operated by the couple, cold air was vented into the couple's bedroom to keep the temperature at 68°F. The cold air then activated the heater thermostat, and hot air was pumped

into the bedroom of the couple's six-month-old child. The temperature in the child's room reached more than 170°F before the child's mother became aware of the condition and shut the system off manually. As a result, the child suffered permanent physical injury.

The child, through a duly appointed guardian, has asserted claims against the manufacturer, the heating company, and the cooling company (but not the retailer), all of which claims are based on strict liability in tort. The child will probably recover against

(A) the manufacturer only, because the ventilating system was defectively designed by it.

(B) the heating company only, because it was the excessive heat from the furnace that caused the child's injuries.

(C) the manufacturer and the heating company only, because the combination of the manufacturer's design and the heating company's furnace caused the child's injuries.

(D) the manufacturer, the heating company, and the cooling company, because the combination of the manufacturer's design, the heating company's furnace, and the cooling company's air conditioning unit caused the child's injuries.

[Q4044]

104. While browsing in a clothing store, the defendant decided to take a purse without paying for it. She placed the purse under her coat and took a couple of steps toward the exit. She then realized that a sensor tag on the purse would set off an alarm. She placed the purse near the counter from which she had removed it.

The defendant has committed

(A) no crime, because the purse was never removed from the store.

(B) no crime, because she withdrew from her criminal enterprise.

(C) only attempted larceny, because she intended to take the purse out of the store.

(D) larceny, because she took the purse from its original location and concealed it with the intent to steal.

[Q3098]

105. A construction company was digging a trench for a new sewer line in a street in a high-crime neighborhood. During the course of the construction, there had been many thefts of tools and equipment from the construction area. One night, the construction company's employees neglected to place warning lights around the trench. A delivery truck drove into the trench and broke an axle. While the delivery driver was looking for a telephone to summon a tow truck, thieves broke into the delivery truck and stole $350,000 worth of goods. The delivery company sued the construction company to recover for the $350,000 loss and for $1,500 worth of damage to its truck. The construction company stipulated that it was negligent in failing to place warning lights around the trench, and admits liability for damage to the truck, but denies liability for the loss of the goods.

On cross-motions for summary judgment, how should the court rule?

(A) Deny both motions, because there is evidence to support a finding that the construction company should have realized that its negligence could create an opportunity for a third party to commit a crime.

(B) Grant the construction company's motion, because no one could have foreseen that the failure to place warning lights could result in the loss of a cargo of valuable goods.

(C) Grant the construction company's motion, because the criminal acts of third persons were a superseding cause of the loss.

(D) Grant the delivery company's motion, because but for the construction company's actions, the goods would not have been stolen.

[Q7032]

106. Twenty-five years ago a seller conveyed Lot 1 to a buyer by a warranty deed. The seller at that time also executed and delivered an instrument in the proper form of a deed, purporting to convey Lot 2 to the buyer. The seller thought she had title to Lot 2 but did not; therefore, no title passed by virtue of the Lot 2 deed. Lot 2 consisted of three acres of brushland adjoining the west boundary of Lot 1. The buyer has occasionally hunted rabbits on Lot 2, but less often than annually. No one else came onto Lot 2 except occasional rabbit hunters.

Twenty years ago, the buyer planted a row of evergreens in the vicinity of the opposite (east) boundary of Lot 1 and erected a fence just beyond the evergreens to the east. In fact both the trees and the fence were placed on Lot 3, owned by a neighbor, which bordered the east boundary of Lot 1. The buyer was unsure of the exact boundary, and placed the trees and the fence in order to establish his rights up to the fence. The fence is located ten feet within Lot 3.

Now, the buyer has had his property surveyed and the title checked and has learned the facts.

The period of time to acquire title by adverse possession in the jurisdiction is 15 years.

The buyer consulted his lawyer, who properly advised that, in an appropriate action, the buyer would probably obtain title to

(A) Lot 2 but not to the ten-foot strip of Lot 3.

(B) the ten-foot strip of Lot 3 but not to Lot 2.

(C) both Lot 2 and the ten-foot strip of Lot 3.

(D) neither Lot 2 nor the ten-foot strip of Lot 3.

[Q1063]

107. A federal statute enacted pursuant to the power of Congress to enforce the Fourteenth Amendment prohibits any state from requiring any of its employees to retire from state employment solely because of their age. The statute expressly authorizes employees required by a state to retire from state employment solely because of their age to sue the state government in federal district court for any damages resulting from that state action. On the basis of this federal statute, a retiree who had worked for State X sues the state in federal district court. State X moves to dismiss the suit on the ground that Congress lacks authority to authorize such suits against a state.

Which of the following is the strongest argument that the retiree can offer in opposition to the state's motion to dismiss this suit?

(A) When Congress exercises power vested in it by the Fourteenth Amendment, Congress may enact appropriate remedial legislation expressly subjecting the states to private suits for damages in federal court.

(B) When Congress exercises power vested in it by any provision of the Constitution, Congress has unlimited authority to authorize private actions for damages against a state.

(C) While the Eleventh Amendment restrains the federal judiciary, that amendment does not limit the power of Congress to modify the sovereign immunity of the states.

(D) While the Eleventh Amendment applies to suits in federal court by citizens of one state against another state, it does not apply to such suits by citizens against their own states.

[Q1027]

108. A brother and sister owned a large tract of land in fee simple as joint tenants with rights of survivorship. While the sister was on an extended safari in Kenya, the brother learned that there were very valuable coal deposits within the land, but he made no attempt to inform his sister. Thereupon, the brother conveyed his interest in the land to his wife, who immediately reconveyed that interest to the brother. The common-law joint tenancy is unmodified by statute.

Shortly thereafter, the brother was killed in an automobile accident. His will, which was duly probated, specifically devised his one-half interest in the property to his wife.

The sister then returned from Kenya and learned what had happened. The sister brought an appropriate action against the brother's wife, who claimed a one-half interest in the property, seeking a declaratory judgment that she, the sister, was the sole owner of the land.

In this action, who should prevail?

(A) The brother's wife, because the brother and sister were tenants in common at the time of the brother's death.

(B) The brother's wife, because the brother's will severed the joint tenancy.

(C) The sister, because the joint tenancy was reestablished by the brother's wife's reconveyance to the brother.

(D) The sister, because the brother breached his fiduciary duty as her joint tenant.

[Q1047]

109. A brother and sister owned a property in fee simple as tenants in common, each owning an undivided one-half interest. The two joined in mortgaging the property to an investor by a properly recorded mortgage that contained a general warranty clause. The brother became disenchanted with land-owning and notified his sister that he would no longer contribute to the payment of installments due to the investor. After the mortgage was in default and the investor made demand for payment of the entire amount of principal and interest due, the sister tendered to the investor, and the investor deposited, a check for one-half of the amount due the investor. The sister then demanded a release of her undivided one-half interest. The investor refused to release any interest in the property. The sister promptly brought an action against the investor to quiet title to an undivided one-half interest in the property.

In such action, the sister should

(A) lose, because the investor's title had been warranted by an express provision of the mortgage.

(B) lose, because there was no redemption from the mortgage.

(C) win, because the sister is entitled to marshalling.

(D) win, because the cotenancy of the

mortgagors was in common and not joint.

[Q3065]

110. A mother rushed her eight-year-old daughter to the emergency room at a hospital after the daughter fell off her bicycle and hit her head on a sharp rock. The wound caused by the fall was extensive and bloody.

The mother was permitted to remain in the treatment room, and held the daughter's hand while the emergency room physician cleaned and sutured the wound. During the procedure, the mother said that she was feeling faint and stood up to leave the room. While leaving the room, the mother fainted and, in falling, struck her head on a metal fixture that protruded from the emergency room wall. She sustained a serious injury as a consequence.

If the mother sues the hospital to recover damages for her injury, will she prevail?

(A) Yes, because the mother was a public invitee of the hospital.

(B) Yes, unless the fixture was an obvious, commonly used, and essential part of the hospital's equipment.

(C) No, unless the hospital's personnel failed to take reasonable steps to anticipate and prevent the mother's injury.

(D) No, because the hospital's personnel owed the mother no affirmative duty of care.

[Q3036]

111. A pastor was a well-known clergyman. A large daily newspaper printed an article by a journalist in its employ. The article accused the pastor of misusing church funds. The pastor commenced a defamation action against the newspaper. An issue in the case was whether the journalist, at the time he wrote the article, acted without malice in charging that the pastor had misused church funds. (For this purpose, it was relevant whether the journalist genuinely believed that the misuse had occurred.)

The newspaper's attorney called a bartender, who worked in a bar near the newspaper's office. The bartender stated that on the day after the journalist's article appeared in the newspaper, the journalist told him, "When I wrote that piece on the pastor, I believed every word of it." On objection by the pastor's attorney, the bartender's testimony should be

(A) admitted as evidence that the article was published without malice.

(B) admitted as a declaration of the journalist's state of mind.

(C) admitted as a self-serving declaration.

(D) excluded as hearsay not falling within any exception.

[Q5024]

112. The plaintiff, who was an asbestos insulation installer from 1955 to 1965, contracted asbestosis, a serious lung disorder, as a result of inhaling airborne asbestos particles on the job. The asbestos was manufactured and sold to the plaintiff's employer by an asbestos manufacturer. Because neither the asbestos manufacturer nor anyone else discovered the risk to asbestos installers until 1966, the manufacturer did not provide any warnings of the risks to installers until after that date.

The plaintiff brought an action against the asbestos manufacturer based on strict liability in tort for failure to warn. The case is to be tried before a jury. The jurisdiction has not adopted a comparative fault rule in strict liability cases.

In this action, an issue that is relevant to the case and is a question for the court to decide as a matter of law, rather than for the jury to decide as a question of fact, is whether

(A) a satisfactory, safer, alternative insulation material exists under today's technology.

(B) the defendant should be held to the standard of a prudent manufacturer who knew of the risks, regardless of whether the risks were reasonably discoverable before 1966.

(C) the defendant should reasonably have known of the risks of asbestos insulation materials before 1966, even though no one else had discovered the risks.

(D) the asbestos insulation materials to which the plaintiff was exposed were inherently dangerous.

[Q3023]

113. Several years ago, a man purchased property, financing a large part of the purchase price by a loan from a bank that was secured by a mortgage. The man made the installment payments on the mortgage regularly until last year. Then the man persuaded a woman to buy the property from him, subject to the mortgage to the bank. They expressly agreed that the woman would not assume and agree to pay the man's debt to the bank. The man's mortgage to the bank contained a due-on-sale clause stating, "If Mortgagor transfers his/her interest without the written consent of Mortgagee first obtained, then at Mortgagee's option the entire principal balance of the debt secured by this Mortgage shall become immediately due and payable." However, without seeking the bank's consent, the man conveyed the property to the woman, the deed stating in pertinent part ". . . subject to a mortgage to [the bank] [giving details and recording data]."

The woman took possession of the property and made several mortgage payments, which the bank accepted. Now, however, neither the woman nor the man has made the last three mortgage payments. The bank has brought an appropriate action against the woman for the amount of the delinquent payments.

In this action, judgment should be for

(A) the woman, because she did not assume and agree to pay the man's mortgage debt.

(B) the woman, because she is not in privity of estate with the bank.

(C) the bank, because the man's deed to the woman violated the due-on-sale clause.

(D) the bank, because the woman is in privity of estate with the bank.

[Q1033]

114. A defendant was charged with assault and battery in a jurisdiction that followed the "retreat" doctrine, and he pleaded self-defense. At his trial, the evidence established the following: A man and his wife were enjoying a drink at a tavern when the defendant entered and stood near the door. The wife whispered to her husband that the defendant was the man who had insulted her on the street the day before. The husband approached the defendant and said, "Get out of here, or I'll break your nose." The defendant said, "Don't come any closer, or I'll hurt you." When the husband raised his fists menacingly, the defendant pulled a can of pepper spray from his pocket, aimed it at the husband's face, and sprayed. The husband fell to the floor, writhing in pain.

Should the defendant be convicted?

- (A) No, because he had no obligation to retreat before resorting to nondeadly force.
- (B) No, because there is no obligation to retreat when one is in an occupied structure.
- (C) Yes, because he failed to retreat even though there was an opportunity available.
- (D) Yes, because the husband did not threaten to use deadly force against him.

[Q7096]

115. In a federal civil trial, the plaintiff wishes to establish that, in a state court, the defendant had been convicted of fraud, a fact that the defendant denies.

Which mode of proof of the conviction is LEAST likely to be permitted?

- (A) A certified copy of the judgment of conviction, offered as a self-authenticating document.
- (B) Testimony of the plaintiff, who was present at the time of the sentence.
- (C) Testimony by a witness to whom the defendant made an oral admission that he had been convicted.
- (D) Judicial notice of the conviction, based on the court's telephone call to the clerk of the state court, whom the judge knows personally.

[Q3167]

116. An uncle was the record title holder of a vacant tract of land. He often told friends that he would leave the land to his nephew in his will. The nephew knew of these conversations. Prior to the uncle's death, the nephew conveyed the land by warranty deed to a woman for $10,000. She did not conduct a title search of the land before she accepted the deed from the nephew. She promptly and properly recorded her deed. Last month, the uncle died, leaving the land to the nephew in his duly probated will. Both the nephew and the woman now claim ownership of the land. The nephew has offered to return the $10,000 to the woman.

Who has title to the land?

- (A) The nephew, because at the time of the deed to the woman, the uncle was the owner of record.
- (B) The nephew, because the woman did not conduct a title search.
- (C) The woman, because of the doctrine of estoppel by deed.
- (D) The woman, because she recorded her deed prior to the uncle's death.

[Q7082]

117. In a personal injury action by the plaintiff against the defendant, the plaintiff claimed that the accident occurred because the defendant, who was operating a blue Ford sedan, was driving at an excessive rate of speed. At the trial, the plaintiff's attorney called a witness on the plaintiff's direct case. The witness testified that after hearing a broadcast on a police radio on the day of the accident, she looked out of her window and saw the defendant's blue Ford sedan strike the plaintiff's red convertible on Main Street. The witness said that she did not have a present recollection of what she had heard on the police radio, but that she made a written note of it immediately following the broadcast. The plaintiff's attorney showed her a piece of paper which had been marked for identification, and the witness said that she now remembered that she had heard a police dispatcher saying that officers were in pursuit of a blue Ford sedan which was traveling down Main

Street at an excessive rate of speed.

If the defendant's attorney objects to the testimony of the witness regarding what she heard on the police radio, the court should hold that her testimony is

(A) inadmissible as hearsay, not within any exception.

(B) admissible as a sense impression.

(C) admissible as a past recollection recorded.

(D) admissible as present recollection refreshed.

[Q5068]

118. An accountant entered into a contract with a painter by the terms of which the painter was to paint the accountant's office for $1,000 and was required to do all of the work over the following weekend so as to avoid disruption of the accountant's business.

If the painter had started to paint on the following Saturday morning, he could have finished before Sunday evening. However, he stayed home that Saturday morning to watch the final game of the World Series on TV, and did not start to paint until Saturday afternoon. By late Saturday afternoon, the painter realized that he had underestimated the time it would take to finish the job if he continued to work alone. The painter phoned the accountant at her home and accurately informed her that it was impossible to finish the work over the weekend unless he hired a helper. He also stated that to do so would require an additional charge of $200 for the work. The accountant told the painter that she apparently had no choice but to pay "whatever it takes" to get the work done as scheduled.

The painter hired a helper to help finish the painting and paid the helper $200. The accountant has offered to pay the painter $1,000. The painter is demanding $1,200.

How much is the painter likely to recover?

(A) $1,000 only, because the accountant received no consideration for her promise to pay the additional sum.

(B) $1,000 only, because the accountant's promise to pay "whatever it takes" is too uncertain to be enforceable.

(C) $1,200, in order to prevent the accountant's unjust enrichment.

(D) $1,200, because the impossibility of the painter's completing the work alone discharged the original contract and a new contract was formed.

[Q1120]

119. A secretary worked in an office in a building occupied partly by her employer and partly by a retail glass store. The two areas were separated by walls and were in no way connected, except that the air conditioning unit served both areas and there was a common return-air duct.

The glass store began remodeling, and its employees did the work, which included affixing a plastic surfacing material to counters. To fasten the plastic to the counters, the employees purchased glue, with the brand name Stick, that was manufactured by a glue manufacturer, packaged in a sealed container by that glue manufacturer, and retailed to the glass store by a paint company.

In the course of the remodeling job, one of the glass store's employees turned on the air conditioning and caused fumes from the glue to travel from the glass store through the air conditioning unit and into the secretary's office. The glass store employees did not know that there was common ductwork for the air conditioners. The secretary was permanently blinded by the fumes from the glue.

The label on the container of glue read, "DANGER. Do not smoke near this product. Extremely flammable. Contains Butanone, Tuluol, and Hexane. Use with adequate ventilation. Keep out of the reach of children."

The three chemicals listed on the label are very toxic and harmful to human eyes. The glue manufacturer had received no reports of eye injuries during the ten years that the product had been manufactured and sold.

If the secretary asserts a claim against the paint company, the most likely result is that she will

(A) recover, if she can recover against the glue manufacturer.

(B) recover, because the secretary was an invitee of a tenant in the building.

(C) not recover unless the paint company was negligent.

(D) not recover, because the glue came in a sealed package.

[Q4049]

120. A state statute declares that after five years of continuous service in their positions all state employees, including faculty members at the state university, are entitled to retain their positions during "good behavior." The statute also contains a number of procedural provisions. Any state employee who is dismissed after that five-year period must be given reasons for the dismissal before it takes effect. In addition, such an employee must, upon request, be granted a post-dismissal hearing before an administrative board to seek reinstatement and back pay. The statute precludes any other hearing or opportunity to respond to the charges. That post-dismissal hearing must occur within six months after the dismissal takes effect. The burden of proof at such a hearing is on the state, and the board may uphold the dismissal only if it is supported by a preponderance of the evidence. An employee who is dissatisfied with a decision of the board after a hearing may appeal its decision to the state courts. The provisions of this statute are inseverable.

A teacher who had been employed continuously for seven years as a faculty member at the state university was dismissed. A week before the dismissal took effect, she was informed that she was being dismissed because of a charge that she accepted a bribe from a student in return for raising the student's final grade in her course. At that time she requested an immediate hearing to contest the propriety of her dismissal.

Three months after her dismissal, she was granted a hearing before the state administrative board. The board upheld her dismissal, finding that the charge against her was supported by a preponderance of the evidence presented at the hearing.

The faculty member did not appeal the decision of the state administrative board to the state courts. Instead, she sought a declaratory judgment in federal district court to the effect that the state statute prescribing the procedures for her dismissal is unconstitutional.

In this case, the federal district court should

(A) dismiss the suit, because a claim that a state statute is unconstitutional is not ripe for adjudication by a federal court until all judicial remedies in state courts provided for by state law have been exhausted.

(B) hold the statute unconstitutional,

because the due process clause of the Fourteenth Amendment requires a state to demonstrate beyond a reasonable doubt the facts constituting good cause for termination of a state employee.

(C) hold the statute unconstitutional, because a state may not ordinarily deprive an employee of a property interest in a job without giving the employee an opportunity for some kind of predismissal hearing to respond to the charges against that employee.

(D) hold the statute constitutional, because the due process clause of the Fourteenth Amendment entitles state employees who have a right to their jobs during good behavior only to a statement of reasons for their dismissal and an opportunity for a post-dismissal hearing.

[Q1152]

121. A customer ordered some merchandise from a store. When the merchandise was delivered, the customer decided that it was not what he had ordered, and he returned it for credit. The store refused to credit the customer's account, continued to bill him, and, after 90 days, turned the account over to a bill collector for collection. The bill collector called at the customer's house at 7 p.m. on a summer evening while many of the customer's neighbors were seated on their porches. When the customer opened the door, the bill collector, who was standing just outside the door, raised an electrically amplified bullhorn to his mouth. In a voice that could be heard a block away, the bill collector called the customer a "deadbeat" and asked him when he intended to pay his bill to the store. The customer, greatly angered, slammed the door shut.

If the customer asserts a claim based on defamation against the bill collector, will the customer prevail?

(A) Yes, if the bill collector's remarks were heard by any of the customer's neighbors.

(B) Yes, because the bill collector's conduct was extreme and outrageous.

(C) No, unless the bill collector knew that the customer owed no money to the store.

(D) No, unless the customer suffered some special damage.

[Q4065]

122. A state legislature passed a statute providing that juries in criminal trials were to consist of 6 rather than 12 jurors, and providing that jury verdicts did not have to be unanimous but could be based on 5 votes out of 6 jurors. A defendant was tried for murder. Over his objection, he was tried by a jury composed of 6 jurors. The jurors found him guilty by a vote of 5 to 1 and, over the defendant's objection, the court entered a judgment of conviction, which was affirmed on appeal by the state supreme court. The defendant seeks to overturn his conviction in a habeas corpus action in federal court, claiming his constitutional rights were violated by allowing a jury verdict that was not unanimous and by allowing a jury composed of fewer than 12 members.

How is the federal court likely to rule in this action?

(A) It will set aside the conviction, because the jury was composed of fewer than 12 members.

(B) It will set aside the conviction, because the 6-person jury verdict was not unanimous.

(C) It will set aside the conviction for both

reasons.

(D) It will uphold the conviction.

[Q7017]

123. On June 1, a seller and a buyer contracted in writing for the sale and purchase of the seller's cattle ranch (a large single tract), and to close the transaction on December 1. On October 1, the buyer told the seller, "I'm increasingly unhappy about our June 1 contract because of the current cattle market, and do not intend to buy your ranch unless I'm legally obligated to do so."

If the seller sues the buyer on October 15 for breach of contract, the seller will probably

(A) win, because the buyer committed a total breach by anticipatory repudiation on October 1.

(B) win, because the buyer's October 1 statement created reasonable grounds for the seller's insecurity with respect to the buyer's performance.

(C) lose, because the parties contracted for the sale and conveyance of a single tract, and the seller cannot bring suit for breach of such a contract prior to the agreed closing date.

(D) lose, because the buyer's October 1 statement to the seller was neither a repudiation nor a present breach of the June 1 contract.

[Q3142]

124. At the trial of the case of *Smith v. Jones,* which of the following is LEAST likely to be admitted into evidence for the purpose of determining whether a certain letter was written by Jones?

(A) A sample of Jones's signature, together with the testimony of a handwriting expert that the letter was signed by the same person who created the sample.

(B) A sample of Jones's signature submitted to the jury together with the letter in question.

(C) The testimony of a layperson who stated that he saw Jones sign the letter in question.

(D) Testimony that the letterhead on the letter in question was Jones's.

[Q5048]

125. A sea captain owns an exceptionally seaworthy boat that she charters for sport fishing at a $500 daily rate. The fee includes the use of the boat with the sea captain as the captain, and one other crew member, as well as fishing tackle and bait. On May 1, a customer agreed with the captain that the customer would have the full-day use of the boat on May 15 for himself and his family for $500. The customer paid an advance deposit of $200 and signed an agreement that the deposit could be retained by the captain as liquidated damages in the event the customer canceled or failed to appear.

At the time of contracting, the captain told the customer to be at the dock at 5 a.m. on May 15. The customer and his family, however, did not show up on May 15 until noon. Meantime, the captain agreed at 10 a.m. to take a replacement customer and her family out fishing for the rest of the day. The replacement had happened to come by and inquire about the possibility of such an outing. In view of the late hour, the captain charged the replacement $400 and stayed out two hours beyond the customary return time. The original customer's failure to appear until noon was due to the fact that he had been trying to charter another boat across the bay at a lower rate and had gotten lost after he was unsuccessful in getting such a charter.

Which of the following is an accurate statement concerning the rights of the parties?

(A) The captain can retain the $200 paid by the customer, because it would be difficult for the captain to establish her actual damages and the sum appears to have been a reasonable forecast in light of anticipated loss of profit from the charter.

(B) The captain is entitled to retain only $50 (10% of the contract price) and must return $150 to the customer.

(C) The captain must return $100 to the customer in order to avoid her own unjust enrichment at the customer's expense.

(D) The captain must return $100 to the customer, because the liquidated-damage clause under the circumstances would operate as a penalty.

[Q2086]

126. A man and a woman, who were cousins, acquired title in fee simple to a property, as equal tenants in common, by inheritance from their aunt. During the last 15 years of her lifetime, the aunt had allowed the man to occupy an apartment in the house on the property, to rent the other apartment in the house to various tenants, and to retain the rent. The man made no payments to the aunt, and since the aunt's death 7 years ago, he has made no payments to the woman (his cousin). For those 22 years, the man has paid the real estate taxes on the property, kept the building on the property insured, and maintained the building. At all times, the woman has lived in a distant city and has never had anything to do with the aunt, the man, or the property.

Recently, the woman needed money for the operation of her business and demanded that the man join her in selling the property. The man refused.

The period of time to acquire title by adverse possession in the jurisdiction is 10 years. There is no other applicable statute.

The woman brought an appropriate action against the man for partition. The man asserted all available defenses and counterclaims.

In that action, the court should

(A) deny partition and find that title has vested in the man by adverse possession.

(B) deny partition, confirm the tenancy in common, but require an accounting to determine if either the woman or the man is indebted to the other on account of the rental payment, taxes, insurance premiums, and maintenance costs.

(C) grant partition and require, as an adjustment, an accounting to determine if either the man or the woman is indebted to the other on account of the rental payments, taxes, insurance premiums, and maintenance costs.

(D) grant partition to the woman and the man as equal owners, but without an accounting.

[Q3025]

127. A testator owned a tract of land in fee simple. By will duly admitted to probate after his death, the testator devised the land to "any wife who survives me with remainder to such of my children as are living at her death."

The testator was survived by his widow and by three children, who were an accountant, a lawyer, and a doctor. Thereafter, the lawyer died and by will duly admitted to probate devised his entire estate to his friend. The accountant and the doctor were the lawyer's heirs at law.

Later the widow died. In an appropriate lawsuit to which the accountant, the doctor, and the friend are parties, title to the land is at issue.

In such lawsuit, judgment should be that title to the property is in

(A) the accountant, the doctor, and the friend, because the earliest vesting of remainders is favored and reference to the surviving wife's death should be construed as relating to time of taking possession.

(B) the accountant, the doctor, and the friend, because the provision requiring survival of children violates the Rule Against Perpetuities since the surviving wife might have been a person unborn at the time of writing of the will.

(C) the accountant and the doctor, because the lawyer's remainder must descend by intestacy and is not devisable.

(D) the accountant and the doctor, because the remainders were contingent upon surviving the life tenant.

[Q2187]

128. The defendant belonged to a sorority at a college. Members of the sorority who paid a rent of $100 per semester were entitled to a double-occupancy bedroom in the sorority house. Although house residents shared kitchen and dining room facilities, the bedrooms were not communal and were normally kept locked by their occupants. With the knowledge of its members, the sorority kept duplicates of all keys so that copies could be made in the event that a resident lost her key.

A cheerleader who was a member of the sorority suspected, based on the stream of visitors to the defendant's room at all hours of the day and night, that the defendant was selling marijuana. One weekend, when she knew that the defendant had gone home to visit her parents, the cheerleader called the police and told them of her suspicions and the facts that had given rise to them. In response to her call, two officers immediately came to the sorority house to interview the cheerleader. During the course of their conversation, the cheerleader stated that she was the defendant's roommate, and offered to let them into the defendant's room. In fact, someone else, not the cheerleader, was the defendant's roommate. The key which the cheerleader used to open the door was actually one of the duplicates kept by the sorority. Upon entering, the police officers saw a tobacco pipe containing traces of marijuana residue on a coffee table in the middle of the room. The defendant was subsequently prosecuted for possession of marijuana. Prior to trial, she made an appropriate motion to suppress the use of the pipe and its contents as evidence.

(A) Overruled, because the cheerleader had apparent authority to permit the entry into the room.

(B) Overruled, because the police had probable cause to believe that they would find marijuana in the room.

(C) Sustained, because the police did not have a warrant to search the room and the cheerleader did not have authority to let them search it.

(D) Sustained, because the police did not have probable cause to believe that they would find marijuana in the room.

[Q5073]

129. A lawyer worked steadily on a case for a client over five-year period, with the

billing agreed to be based on a particular amount charged per hour worked. The lawyer kept regular timesheets showing, for any day on which he worked on the matter, how long he worked and which of various activities (phone calls, letter-writing, etc.) he performed on that day. In the lawyer's suit against the client for non-payment, the lawyer did not offer into evidence the actual timesheets. Instead, in preparation for trial, the lawyer used the timesheets to create a summary showing, for each week, how much time the lawyer spent on each of the activity types. Then, at trial, the lawyer offered these weekly summaries, together with his testimony about how he had prepared them. If the client properly objects, the judge should hold that the summaries are

(A) inadmissible for any purpose, because the underlying timesheets from which they were prepared were not offered into evidence

(B) inadmissible as substantive evidence, but usable as non-admitted materials to refresh the lawyer's present recollection

(C) admissible as substantive evidence of hours worked, if the underlying timesheets were made available to the client prior to trial

(D) admissible as substantive evidence only if the underlying timesheets were lost through no fault of the lawyer

[Q6002]

130. At the defendant's murder trial, the defendant calls, as his first witness, a man to testify that the defendant has a reputation in their community as a peaceable and truthful person. The prosecutor objects on the ground that the witness's testimony would constitute improper character evidence. The court should

(A) admit the testimony as to peaceableness, but exclude the testimony as to truthfulness.

(B) admit the testimony as to truthfulness, but exclude the testimony as to peaceableness.

(C) admit the testimony as to both character traits.

(D) exclude the testimony as to both character traits.

[Q3164]

131. City police officers shot and killed the plaintiff's friend as he attempted to escape arrest for an armed robbery he had committed. The plaintiff brought suit in federal district court against the city police department and the city police officers involved, seeking only a judgment declaring unconstitutional the state statute under which the police acted. That newly enacted statute authorized the police to use deadly force when necessary to apprehend a person who has committed a felony. In his suit, the plaintiff alleged that the police would not have killed his friend if the use of deadly force had not been authorized by the statute.

The federal district court should

(A) decide the case on its merits, because it raises a substantial federal question.

(B) dismiss the action, because it involves a nonjusticiable political question.

(C) dismiss the action, because it does not present a case or controversy.

(D) dismiss the action, because the Eleventh Amendment prohibits federal courts from deciding cases of this type.

[Q1133]

132. The defendant was an alcoholic who frequently experienced auditory hallucinations that commanded him to engage in bizarre and sometimes violent behavior. He generally obeyed their commands. The hallucinations appeared more frequently when he was intoxicated, but he sometimes experienced them when he had not been drinking. After the defendant had been drinking continuously for a three-day period, an elderly woman began to reproach him about his drunken condition, slapping him on the face and shoulders as she did so. The defendant believed that he was being unmercifully attacked and heard the hallucinatory voice telling him to strangle his assailant. He did so, and she died.

If the defendant is charged with second degree murder, his best chance of acquittal would be to rely on a defense of

(A) intoxication.

(B) lack of malice aforethought.

(C) self-defense.

(D) insanity.

[Q4040]

133. A landowner owned Blackacre, which was improved with a dwelling. A neighbor owned an adjoining unimproved lot suitable for constructing a dwelling. The neighbor executed and delivered a deed granting to the landowner an easement over the westerly 15 feet of the lot for convenient ingress and egress to a public street, although Blackacre did abut another public street. The landowner did not then record the neighbor's deed. After the landowner constructed and started using a driveway within the described 15-foot strip in a clearly visible manner, the neighbor borrowed $10,000 cash from a bank and gave the bank a mortgage on the neighbor's property. The mortgage was promptly and properly recorded. The landowner then recorded the neighbor's deed granting the easement. The neighbor subsequently defaulted on her loan payments to the bank.

The recording act of the jurisdiction provides: "No conveyance or mortgage of real property shall be good against subsequent purchasers for value and without notice unless the same be recorded according to law."

In an appropriate foreclosure action as to the neighbor's land, brought against the neighbor and the landowner, the bank seeks, among other things, to have the landowner's easement declared subordinate to the bank's mortgage, so that the easement will be terminated by completion of the foreclosure.

If the landowner's easement is NOT terminated, it will be because

(A) the recording of the deed granting the easement prior to the foreclosure action protects the landowner's rights.

(B) the easement provides access from Blackacre to a public street.

(C) the landowner's easement is appurtenant to Blackacre and thus cannot be separated from Blackacre.

(D) visible use of the easement by the landowner put the bank on notice of the easement.

[Q3010]

134. A grantor who owned a parcel conveyed it by quitclaim deed as a gift to a woman, who did not then record her deed. Later, the grantor conveyed the parcel by warranty deed to a man, who paid valuable consideration, knew nothing of the woman's claim, and promptly and properly recorded. Next, the woman recorded her deed. Then the man conveyed the parcel by

quitclaim deed to his nephew as a gift. When the possible conflict with the woman was discovered, the nephew recorded his deed.

The parcel at all relevant times has been vacant unoccupied land.

The recording act of the jurisdiction provides:

"No unrecorded conveyance or mortgage of real property shall be good against subsequent purchasers for value without notice, who shall first record." No other statute is applicable.

The nephew has sued the woman to establish who owns the parcel.

The court will hold for

(A) the nephew, because the woman was a donee.

(B) the nephew, because the man's purchase cut off the woman's rights.

(C) the woman, because she recorded before the nephew.

(D) the woman, because the nephew was a subsequent donee.

[Q2163]

135. The plaintiff and the defendant own adjoining lots in the central portion of a city. Each of their lots had an office building. The defendant decided to raze the existing building on her lot and to erect a building of greater height. The defendant received all governmental approvals required to pursue her project. There is no applicable statute or ordinance (other than those dealing with various approvals for zoning, building, etc.).

The defendant constructed her new building without incident. However, when it was completed, the plaintiff discovered that the shadow created by the new higher building placed the plaintiff's building in such deep shade that her ability to lease space was diminished and that the rent she could charge and the occupancy rate were substantially lower. Assume that these facts are proved in an appropriate action the plaintiff instituted against the defendant for all and any relief available.

Which of the following is the most appropriate comment concerning this lawsuit?

(A) The plaintiff is entitled to a mandatory injunction requiring the defendant to restore conditions to those existing with the prior building insofar as the shadow is concerned.

(B) The court should award permanent damages, in lieu of an injunction, equal to the present value of all rents lost and loss on rents for the reasonable life of the building.

(C) The court should award damages for losses suffered to the date of trial and leave open recovery of future damages.

(D) Judgment should be for the defendant, because the plaintiff has no cause of action.

[Q1157]

136. The plaintiff, who is executor of her late husband's estate, has sued the defendant for shooting the husband from ambush. The plaintiff offers to testify that the day before her husband was killed, he described to her a chance meeting with the defendant on the street in which the defendant said, "I'm going to blow your head off one of these days."

The witness's testimony concerning her husband's statement is

(A) admissible, to show the defendant's state of mind.

(B) admissible, because the defendant's

statement is that of a party-opponent.

(C) inadmissible, because it is improper evidence of a prior bad act.

(D) inadmissible, because it is hearsay not within any exception.

[Q3045]

137. The plaintiff has sued the defendant for personal injuries arising out of an automobile accident. Which of the following would be ERROR?

(A) The judge allows the defendant's attorney to ask the defendant questions on cross-examination that go well beyond the scope of direct examination by the plaintiff, who has called the defendant as an adverse witness.

(B) The judge refuses to allow the defendant's attorney to cross-examine the defendant by leading questions.

(C) The judge allows cross-examination about the credibility of a witness even though no question relating to credibility has been asked on direct examination.

(D) The judge, despite the defendant's request for exclusion of witnesses, allows the plaintiff's eyewitness to remain in the courtroom after testifying, even though the eyewitness is expected to be recalled for further cross-examination.

[Q3153]

138. A pedestrian died from injuries caused when a driver's car struck him. The executor of the pedestrian's estate sued the driver for wrongful death. At trial, the executor calls a nurse to testify that two days after the accident, the pedestrian said to the nurse, "The car that hit me ran the red light." Fifteen minutes thereafter, the pedestrian died.

As a foundation for introducing evidence of the pedestrian's statement, the executor offers to the court a doctor's affidavit that the doctor was the intern on duty the day of the pedestrian's death and that several times that day the pedestrian had said that he knew he was about to die.

Is the affidavit properly considered by the court in ruling on the admissibility of the pedestrian's statement?

(A) No, because it is hearsay not within any exception.

(B) No, because it is irrelevant since dying declarations cannot be used except in prosecutions for homicide.

(C) Yes, because though hearsay, it is a statement of then-existing mental condition.

(D) Yes, because the judge may consider hearsay in ruling on preliminary questions.

[Q3147]

139. A federally owned and operated office building in the state of Red is heated with a new, pollution-free heating system. However, in the coldest season of the year, this new system is sometimes insufficient to supply adequate heat to the building. The appropriation statute providing the money for construction of the new heating system permitted use of the old, pollution-generating system when necessary to supply additional heat. When the old heating system operates (only about two days in any year), the smokestack of the building emits smoke that exceeds the state of Red's pollution-control standards.

May the operators of the federal office building be prosecuted successfully by Red authorities for violating that state's pollution control standards?

(A) Yes, because the regulation of

pollution is a legitimate state police power concern.

(B) Yes, because the regulation of pollution is a joint concern of the federal government and the state and, therefore, both of them may regulate conduct causing pollution.

(C) No, because the operations of the federal government are immune from state regulation in the absence of federal consent.

(D) No, because the violations of the state pollution-control standards involved here are so *de minimis* that they are beyond the legitimate reach of state law.

[Q1195]

140. A defendant is on trial for the murder of his father. The defendant's defense is that he shot his father accidentally. The prosecutor calls as a witness a police officer to testify that on two occasions in the year prior to this incident, he had been called to the defendant's home because of complaints of loud arguments between the defendant and his father, and had found it necessary to stop the defendant from beating his father.

The evidence is

(A) inadmissible, because it is improper character evidence.

(B) inadmissible, because the witness lacks firsthand knowledge of who started the quarrels.

(C) admissible to show that the defendant killed his father intentionally.

(D) admissible to show that the defendant is a violent person.

[Q3064]

141. Members of a religious group believe in Lucifer as their Supreme Being. The members of this group meet once a year on top of Mt. Snow, located in a U.S. National Park, to hold an overnight encampment and a midnight dance around a large campfire. They believe this overnight encampment and all of its rituals are required by Lucifer to be held on the top of Mt. Snow. U.S. National Park Service rules that have been consistently enforced prohibit all overnight camping and all campfires on Mt. Snow because of the very great dangers overnight camping and campfires would pose in that particular location. As a result, the park Superintendent denied a request by the group for a permit to conduct these activities on top of Mt. Snow. The park Superintendent, who was known to be violently opposed to cults and other unconventional groups had, in the past, issued permits to conventional religious groups to conduct sunrise services in other areas of that U.S. National Park.

The group brought suit in Federal Court against the U.S. National Park Service and the Superintendent of the park to compel issuance of the requested permit.

As a matter of constitutional law, the most appropriate result in this suit would be a decision that denial of the permit was

(A) invalid, because the free exercise clause of the First Amendment prohibits the Park Service from knowingly interfering with religious conduct.

(B) invalid, because these facts demonstrate that the action of the Park Service purposefully and invidiously discriminated against the group.

(C) valid, because the establishment clause of the First Amendment prohibits the holding of religious ceremonies on federal land.

(D) valid, because religiously motivated

142. A landowner died, validly devising his land to his wife "for life or until remarriage, then to" their daughter. Shortly after the landowner's death, his daughter executed an instrument in the proper form of a deed, purporting to convey the land to her friend. A year later, the daughter died intestate, with her mother, the original landowner's wife, as her sole heir. The following month, the wife remarried. She then executed an instrument in the proper form of a deed, purporting to convey the land to her new husband as a wedding gift.

    Who now owns what interest in the land?

    (A) The daughter's friend owns the fee simple.

    (B) The wife owns the fee simple.

    (C) The wife's new husband has a life estate in the land for the wife's life, with the remainder in the daughter's friend.

    (D) The wife's new husband owns the fee simple.

    [Q7023]

143. Under the terms of a written contract, a contractor agreed to construct for a homeowner a garage for $10,000. Nothing was said in the parties' negotiations or in the contract about progress payments during the course of the work. After completing 25% of the garage strictly according to the homeowner's specifications, the contractor assigned his rights under the contract to a banker as security for an $8,000 loan. The banker immediately notified the homeowner of the assignment. The contractor thereafter, without legal excuse, abandoned the job before it was half-complete. The contractor subsequently defaulted on the loan from the banker. The contractor has no assets. It will cost the homeowner at least $8,000 to get the garage finished by another builder.

    If the banker sues the homeowner for $8,000, which of the following will the court decide?

    (A) The banker wins, because the contractor-homeowner contract was in existence and the contractor was not in breach when the banker gave the homeowner notice of the assignment.

    (B) The banker wins, because the banker as a secured creditor over the contractor is entitled to priority over the homeowner's unsecured claim against the contractor.

    (C) The homeowner wins, because his right to recoupment on account of the contractor's breach is available against the banker as the contractor's assignee.

    (D) The homeowner wins, because his claim against the contractor arose prior to the contractor's default on his loan from the banker.

    [Q2032]

144. A landowner and a landscape architect signed a detailed writing in which the landscape architect agreed to landscape and replant the landowner's residential property in accordance with a design prepared by the architect and incorporated in the writing. The landowner agreed to pay $10,000 for the work upon its completion. The landowner's spouse was not a party to the agreement, and had no ownership interest in the premises.

    Shortly before the agreement was signed, the landowner and the architect orally agreed that the writing would not become binding on either party unless the landowner's spouse should approve the landscaping design. If the landowner's spouse disapproves the design and the landowner refuses to allow the architect to proceed with the work, is evidence of the oral agreement admissible in the architect's action against the landowner for breach of contract?

(A) Yes, because the oral agreement required approval by a third party.

(B) Yes, because the evidence shows that the writing was intended to take effect only if the approval occurred.

(C) No, because the parol evidence rule bars evidence of a prior oral agreement even if the latter is consistent with the terms of a partial integration.

(D) No, because the prior oral agreement contradicted the writing by making the parties' duties conditional.

[Q1044]

145. Public schools in a state are financed, in large part, by revenue derived from real estate taxes imposed by each school district on the taxable real property located in that district. Public schools also receive other revenue from private gifts, federal grants, student fees, and local sales taxes. For many years, the state has distributed additional funds, which come from the state treasury, to local school districts in order to equalize the funds available on a per-student basis for each public school district. These additional funds are distributed on the basis of a state statutory formula that considers only the number of students in each public school district and the real estate tax revenue raised by that district. The formula does not consider other revenue received by a school district from different sources.

The school boards of two school districts, together with parents and schoolchildren in those districts, bring suit in federal court to enjoin the state from allocating the additional funds from the state treasury to individual districts pursuant to this formula. They allege that the failure of the state, in allocating this additional money, to take into account a school district's sources of revenue other than revenue derived from taxes levied on real estate located there violates the equal protection clause of the Fourteenth Amendment. The complaint does not allege that the allocation of the additional state funds based on the current statutory formula has resulted in a failure to provide minimally adequate education to any child.

Which of the following best describes the appropriate standard by which the court should review the constitutionality of the state statutory funding formula?

(A) Because classifications based on wealth are inherently suspect, the state must demonstrate that the statutory formula is necessary to vindicate a compelling slate interest.

(B) Because the statutory funding formula burdens the fundamental right to education, the state must demonstrate that the formula is necessary to vindicate a compelling state interest.

(C) Because no fundamental right or suspect classification is implicated in this case, the plaintiffs must demonstrate that the funding allocation formula bears no rational relationship to any legitimate state interest.

(D) Because the funding formula inevitably leads to disparities among the school districts in their levels of total funding, the plaintiffs must only demonstrate that the funding formula is not substantially related to the furtherance of an important state interest.

[Q1073]

146. The defendant and the plaintiff had been friends for years, and worked in the same office. Ever since they were children, they had enjoyed playing "practical jokes" on each other. Frequently, they would spend hours together, laughing about the tricks they had played on each other. One day, planning to have some fun with the plaintiff, the defendant bought a large rubber spider from a toy store. Knowing that the plaintiff was horrified of spiders, the defendant came into work early, and placed the toy spider in the top drawer of the plaintiff's desk. Later, when the plaintiff arrived at work, he opened his top drawer to get out a letter opener and saw the rubber spider. Believing it to be real, and terrified that it would bite him, the plaintiff screamed in fear, fainted, and fell to the floor. As he fell, he struck his head on the corner of his desk, sustaining a serious fracture of the skull.

If the plaintiff asserts a claim for assault against the defendant for the injury which he sustained in the fall, which of the following arguments would be most effective in the defendant's defense?

(A) The plaintiff's fear of being bitten by a spider was not apprehension of a battery.

(B) A reasonable person in the plaintiff's position would not have become apprehensive at the sight of a spider.

(C) The plaintiff impliedly consented to the prank by engaging in a course of practical joking with the defendant.

(D) The defendant was not substantially certain that the plaintiff would be injured as a result of the joke.

[Q5112]

147. The defendant is charged with the murder of the victim. The prosecutor introduced testimony of a police officer that the victim told a priest, administering the last rites, "I was stabbed by [the defendant]. Since I am dying, tell him I forgive him." Thereafter, the defendant's attorney offers the testimony of a witness that the day before, when the victim believed he would live, he stated that he had been stabbed by Jack (not the defendant), an old enemy. The testimony of this witness is

(A) admissible under an exception to the hearsay rule.

(B) admissible to impeach the dead declarant.

(C) inadmissible because it goes to the ultimate issue in the case.

(D) inadmissible because it is irrelevant to any substantive issue in the case.

[Q4022]

148. A state statute requires each insurance company that offers burglary insurance policies in the state to charge a uniform rate for such insurance to all of its customers residing within the same county in that state. So long as it complies with this requirement, a company is free to charge whatever rate the market will bear for its burglary insurance policies.

An insurance company located in the state files suit in federal district court against appropriate state officials to challenge this statute on constitutional grounds. The insurance company wishes to charge customers residing within the same county in the state rates for burglary insurance policies that will vary because they would be based on the specific nature of the customer's business, on its precise location, and on its past claims record.

In this suit, the court should

(A) hold the statute unconstitutional, because the statute deprives the insurance company of its liberty or property without due process of law.

(B) hold the statute unconstitutional, because the statute imposes an undue burden on interstate commerce.

(C) hold the statute constitutional, because the statute is a reasonable exercise of the state's police power.

(D) abstain from ruling on the merits of this case until the state courts have had an opportunity to pass on the constitutionality of this state statute.

[Q2008]

149. When a homeowner became ill, he properly executed a deed sufficient to convey his home to his nephew, who was then serving overseas in the military. Two persons signed as witnesses to qualify the deed for recordation under an applicable statute. The homeowner handed the deed to his nephew's friend and said, "I want [the nephew] to have my home. Please take this deed for him." Shortly thereafter, the nephew's friend learned that the homeowner's death was imminent. One day before the homeowner's death, the nephew's friend recorded the deed. The nephew returned home shortly after the homeowner's death. The nephew's friend brought him up to date, and he took possession of the home. The homeowner died intestate, leaving a daughter as his sole heir. She asserted ownership of his home. The nephew brought an appropriate action against her to determine title to the home. The law of the jurisdiction requires only two witnesses for a will to be properly executed.

If the court rules for the nephew and against the daughter, what is the most likely explanation?

(A) The deed was delivered when the homeowner handed it to the nephew's friend.

(B) The delivery of the deed was accomplished by the recording of the deed.

(C) The homeowner's death consummated a valid gift causa mortis to the nephew.

(D) The homeowner's properly executed deed was effective as a testamentary document.

[Q7070]

150. A woman decided to steal a necklace that belonged to her neighbor. She knew where the neighbor kept the necklace because she had been in the neighbor's house on many occasions when the neighbor had taken off the necklace and put it away in a jewelry box in the bathroom. One night, the woman went to the neighbor's house. The neighbor was away and the house was dark. The woman opened the bathroom window, saw the jewelry box on the counter, and started to climb inside. As her leg cleared the window sill, the neighbor's cat let out a loud screech. Terrified, the woman bolted back outside and fled.

The crimes below are listed in descending order of seriousness. What is the most serious crime committed by the woman?

(A) Burglary.

(B) Attempted burglary.

(C) Attempted larceny.

(D) No crime.

[Q7027]

151. A state's code of civil procedure provides that no appeal may be prosecuted unless a notice of such appeal is mailed within twenty days after the entry of the final judgment which is being appealed. An appellee moves to dismiss an appeal on the

ground that the notice of appeal was not timely served. At a hearing on the motion to dismiss, a secretary in the office of the appellant's attorney testifies that he personally enclosed the notice of appeal in a properly addressed envelope which he then sealed. He states further that he placed the envelope in a basket marked "outgoing mail" in the office conference room at 2 p.m. on the eighteenth day after the judgment appealed from was entered. He states that as a matter of office routine the "outgoing mail" basket is emptied and its contents taken to the post office every day at 4 p.m. by another employee, although he does not personally know whether it was done on that particular day. The testimony should be

(A) excluded, since evidence of past conduct is not relevant to what was done on any particular day.

(B) excluded, unless some evidence is offered that the envelope which was deposited in the basket was actually mailed that day.

(C) admitted, only if the office employee who usually mails the contents of the "outgoing mail" basket testifies to what is customarily done.

(D) admitted, to prove that the notice of appeal was actually mailed on that day.

[Q5087]

152. The United States Department of the Interior granted the plaintiff the food and drink concession in a federal park located in the state of Purple. The plaintiff operated his concession out of federally owned facilities in the park. The federal statute authorizing the Interior Department to grant such concessions provided that the grantees would pay only a nominal rental for use of these federal facilities because of the great benefit their concessions would provide to the people of the United States.

The legislature of the state of Purple enacted a statute imposing an occupancy tax on the occupants of real estate within that state that is not subject to state real estate taxes. The statute was intended to equalize the state tax burden on such occupants with that on people occupying real estate that is subject to state real estate taxes. Pursuant to that statute, the Purple Department of Revenue attempted to collect the state occupancy tax from the plaintiff because the federal facilities occupied by the plaintiff were not subject to state real estate taxes. The plaintiff sued to invalidate the state occupancy tax as applied to him.

The strongest ground upon which the plaintiff could challenge the occupancy tax is that it violates the

(A) commerce clause by unduly burdening the interstate tourist trade.

(B) privileges and immunities clause of the Fourteenth Amendment by interfering with the fundamental right to do business on federal property.

(C) equal protection of the laws clause of the Fourteenth Amendment because the tax treats him less favorably than federal concessionaires in other states who do not have to pay such occupancy taxes.

(D) supremacy clause of Article VI and the federal statute authorizing such concessions.

[Q2150]

153. An ordinance of a city requires that its mayor must have been continuously a resident of the city for at least five years at the time he or she takes office. The plaintiff, who is thinking about running for mayor in an election that will take place next year, will have been a resident of the

city for only four and one-half years at the time the mayor elected then takes office. Before he decides whether to run for the position of mayor, the plaintiff wants to know whether he could lawfully assume that position if he were elected. As a result, the plaintiff files suit in the local federal district court for a declaratory judgment that the five-year-residence requirement is unconstitutional and that he is entitled to a place on his political party's primary election ballot for mayor. He names the chairman of his political party as the sole defendant but does not join any election official. The chairman responds by joining the plaintiff in requesting the court to declare the residence requirement invalid.

In this case, the court should

(A) refuse to determine the merits of this suit, because there is no case or controversy.

(B) refuse to issue such a declaratory judgment, because an issue of this kind involving only a local election does not present a substantial federal constitutional question.

(C) issue the declaratory judgment, because a residency requirement of this type is a denial of the equal protection of the laws.

(D) issue the declaratory judgment, because the plaintiff will have substantially complied with the residency requirement.

[Q2153]

154. At the defendant's trial for theft, a man, called as a witness by the prosecutor, testified to the following: (1) that from his apartment window, he saw thieves across the street break the window of a jewelry store, take jewelry, and leave in a car; (2) that the witness' wife telephoned the police and relayed to them the license number of the thieves' car as the witness looked out the window with binoculars and read it to her; and (3) that the witness has no present memory of the number, but that immediately afterward he listened to a playback of the police tape recording giving the license number (which belongs to the defendant's car) and verified that she had relayed the number accurately.

Playing the tape recording for the jury would be

(A) proper, because it is recorded recollection.

(B) proper, because it is a public record or report.

(C) improper, because it is hearsay not within any exception.

(D) improper, because the witness' wife lacked firsthand knowledge of the license number.

[Q3040]

155. At 11:00 p.m., a husband and wife were accosted in the entrance to their apartment building by the defendant, who was armed as well as masked. The defendant ordered the couple to take him into their apartment. After they entered the apartment, the defendant forced the wife to bind and gag her husband and then to open a safe which contained a diamond necklace. The defendant then tied the wife up and fled with the necklace. He was apprehended by apartment building security guards. Before the guards could return to the apartment, but after the defendant was arrested, the husband, straining to free himself, suffered a massive heart attack and died.

The defendant is guilty of

(A) burglary, robbery, and murder.

(B) robbery and murder only.

(C) burglary and robbery only.

156. A customer ate a spicy dinner at a restaurant on Sunday night. He enjoyed the food and noticed nothing unusual about the dinner.

Later that evening, the customer had an upset stomach. He slept well through the night, went to work the next day, and ate three meals. His stomach discomfort persisted, and by Tuesday morning he was too ill to go to work.

Eventually, the customer consulted his doctor, who found that the patron was infected with a bacterium that can be contracted from contaminated food. Food can be contaminated when those who prepare it do not adequately wash their hands.

The customer sued the restaurant for damages. He introduced testimony from a health department official that various health code violations had been found at the restaurant both before and after the customer's dinner, but that none of the restaurant's employees had signs of bacterial infection when they were tested one month after the incident.

The restaurant's best argument in response to the customer's suit would be that

(A) no one else who ate at the restaurant on Sunday complained about stomach discomfort.

(B) The restaurant instructs its employees to wash their hands carefully and is not responsible if any employee fails to follow these instructions.

(C) The customer has failed to establish that the restaurant's food caused his illness.

(D) The customer assumed the risk of an upset stomach by choosing to eat spicy food.

[Q3090]

157. Which of the following is most likely to be found to be a strict liability offense?

(A) A city ordinance providing for a fine of not more than $200 for shoplifting.

(B) A federal statute making it a felony to possess heroin.

(C) A state statute making it a felony to fail to register a firearm.

(D) A state statute making the sale of adulterated milk a misdemeanor.

[Q4036]

158. In a civil action, the plaintiff sued a decedent's estate to recover damages for injuries she suffered in a collision between her car and one driven by the decedent. At trial, the plaintiff introduced undisputed evidence that the decedent's car swerved across the median of the highway, where it collided with an oncoming car driven by the plaintiff. The decedent's estate introduced undisputed evidence that, prior to the car's crossing the median, the decedent suffered a fatal heart attack, which she had no reason to foresee, and that, prior to the heart attack, the decedent had been driving at a reasonable speed and in a reasonable manner. A statute makes it a traffic offense to cross the median of a highway.

In this case, for whom should the court render judgment?

(A) The decedent's estate, because its evidence is undisputed.

(B) The decedent's estate, because the plaintiff has not established a prima facie case of liability.

(C) The plaintiff, because the accident was of a type that does not ordinarily happen in the absence of negligence on the actor's part.

(D) The plaintiff, because the decedent crossed the median in violation of the statute.

[Q7059]

159. A landowner orally gave his neighbor permission to share the use of the private road on the landowner's land so that the neighbor could have more convenient access to the neighbor's land. Only the landowner maintained the road. After the neighbor had used the road on a daily basis for three years, the landowner conveyed his land to a grantee, who immediately notified the neighbor that the neighbor was not to use the road. The neighbor sued the grantee seeking a declaration that the neighbor had a right to continue to use the road.

Who is likely to prevail?

(A) The grantee, because an oral license is invalid.

(B) The grantee, because the neighbor had a license that the grantee could terminate at any time.

(C) The neighbor, because the grantee is estopped to terminate the neighbor's use of the road.

(D) The neighbor, because the neighbor's use of the road was open and notorious when the grantee purchased the land.

[Q7098]

160. A landowner owned a piece of land in fee simple of record on January 10. On that day, a bank loaned the landowner $50,000 and the landowner mortgaged the property to the bank as security for the loan. The mortgage was recorded on January 18.

The landowner conveyed the property to an investor for a valuable consideration on January 11. The bank did not know of this, nor did the investor know of the mortgage to the bank, until both discovered the facts on January 23, the day on which the investor recorded his deed from the landowner.

The recording act of the jurisdiction provides: "No unrecorded conveyance or mortgage of real property shall be good against subsequent purchasers for value without notice, who shall first record." There is no provision for a period of grace and there is no other relevant statutory provision.

The bank sued the investor to establish that its mortgage was good against the property.

The court should decide for

(A) the investor, because he paid valuable consideration without notice before the bank recorded her mortgage.

(B) the investor, because the bank's delay in recording means that she is estopped from asserting her priority in time.

(C) the bank, because the investor did not record his deed before the mortgage was recorded.

(D) the bank, because after the mortgage to it, the landowner's deed to the investor was necessarily subject to the mortgage.

[Q1054]

161. A vendor owned a tract of land in fee simple. The vendor and a vendee entered into a written agreement under which the vendee agreed to buy the property for $100,000, its fair market value. The agreement contained all the essential terms of a real estate contract to sell and buy, including a date for closing. The required

$50,000 down payment was made. The contract provided that in the event of the vendee's breach, the vendor could retain the $50,000 deposit as liquidated damages.

Before the date set for the closing in the contract, the vendee died. On the day that a woman was duly qualified as administratrix of the estate of the vendee, which was after the closing date, the administratrix made demand for return of the $50,000 deposit. The vendor responded by stating that he took such demand to be a declaration that the administratrix did not intend to complete the contract and that the vendor considered the contract at an end. The vendor further asserted that he was entitled to retain, as liquidated damages, the $50,000. The reasonable market value of the property had increased to $110,000 at that time.

The administratrix brought an appropriate action against the vendor to recover the $50,000. In answer, the vendor made no affirmative claim but asserted that he was entitled to retain the $50,000 as liquidated damages as provided in the contract.

In such lawsuit, judgment should be for

(A) the administratrix, because the provision relied upon by the vendor is unenforceable.

(B) the administratrix, because the death of the vendee terminated the contract as a matter of law.

(C) the vendor, because the court should enforce the express agreement of the contracting parties.

(D) the vendor, because the doctrine of equitable conversion prevents termination of the contract upon the death of a party.

[Q3119]

162. A doctor, a resident of the city of Greenville in the state of Green, is a physician licensed to practice in both Green and the neighboring state of Red. The doctor finds that the most convenient place to treat her patients who need hospital care is in the publicly owned and operated municipal hospital of the city of Redville in the state of Red, which is located just across the state line from Greenville. For many years the doctor had successfully treated her patients in that hospital. Early this year she was notified that she could no longer treat patients in the Redville hospital because she was not a resident of Red, and a newly adopted rule of the Redville hospital, which was adopted in conformance with all required procedures, stated that every physician who practices in that hospital must be a resident of Red.

Which of the following constitutional provisions would be most helpful to the doctor in an action to challenge her exclusion from the Redville hospital solely on the basis of this hospital rule?

(A) The bill of attainder clause.

(B) The privileges and immunities clause of Article IV.

(C) The due process clause of the Fourteenth Amendment.

(D) The ex post facto clause.

[Q3190]

163. A hardware distributor located on the West Coast gave its customer, a hardware retailer who was relocating to the East Coast, the following signed "letter of introduction" to a hardware manufacturer based on the East coast:

> This will introduce you to my good friend and former customer, who is a retailer and will be seeking to arrange the purchase of hardware inventory

from you on credit. If you will let him have the goods, I will make good any loss up to $25,000 in the event of his default.

The retailer presented the letter to the manufacturer, who then sold and delivered $20,000 worth of hardware to the retailer on credit. The manufacturer promptly notified the distributor of this sale.

Which of the following is NOT an accurate statement concerning the arrangement between the distributor and the manufacturer?

(A) It was important to enforceability of the distributor's promise to the manufacturer that it be embodied in a signed writing.

(B) By extending the credit to the retailer, the manufacturer effectively accepted the distributor's offer for a unilateral contract.

(C) Although the distributor received no consideration from the retailer, the distributor's promise is enforceable by the manufacturer.

(D) The distributor's promise is enforceable by the manufacturer whether or not the manufacturer gave the distributor seasonable notice of the extension of credit to the retailer.

[Q2174]

164. A landholder was land-rich by inheritance but money-poor, having suffered severe losses on bad investments, but still owned several thousand acres of unencumbered timberland. He had a large family, and his normal, fixed personal expenses were high. Pressed for cash, he advertised a proposed sale of standing timber on a choice 2,000-acre tract. The only response was an offer by a logger, the owner of a large, integrated construction enterprise, after inspection of the advertised tract. The logger offered to buy, sever, and remove the standing timber from the advertised tract at a cash price 70% lower than the regionally prevailing price for comparable timber rights. The landholder, by then in desperate financial straits and knowing little about timber values, signed and delivered to the logger a letter accepting the offer.

If, before the logger commences performance, the landholder's investment fortunes suddenly improve and he wishes to get out of the timber deal with the logger, which of the following legal concepts affords his best prospect of effective cancellation?

(A) Bad faith.

(B) Equitable estoppel.

(C) Unconscionability.

(D) Duress.

[Q3082]

165. A city operates a cemetery pursuant to a city ordinance. The ordinance requires the operation of the city cemetery to be supported primarily by revenues derived from the sale of cemetery lots to individuals. The ordinance further provides that the purchase of a cemetery lot entitles the owner to perpetual care of the lot, and entitles the owner to erect on the lot, at the owner's expense, a memorial monument or marker of the owner's choice, subject to certain size restrictions. The ordinance requires the city to maintain the cemetery, including mowing the grass, watering flowers, and plowing snow, and provides for the expenditure of city tax funds for such maintenance if revenues from the sale of cemetery lots are insufficient. Although cemetery lots are sold at full fair market value, which includes the current value of perpetual care, the revenue from the sale of such lots

has been insufficient in recent years to maintain the cemetery. As a result, a small amount of city tax funds has also been used for that purpose.

A group of city taxpayers brings suit against the city challenging the constitutionality of the city ordinance insofar as it permits the owner of a cemetery lot to erect a religious memorial monument or marker on his or her lot.

Is this suit likely to be successful?

(A) No, because only a small amount of city tax funds has been used to maintain the cemetery.

(B) No, because the purpose of the ordinance is entirely secular, its primary effect neither advances nor inhibits religion, and it does not foster an excessive government entanglement with religion.

(C) Yes, because city maintenance of any religious object is a violation of the establishment clause of the First Amendment as incorporated into the Fourteenth Amendment.

(D) Yes, because no compelling governmental interest justifies authorizing private persons to erect religious monuments or markers in a city-operated cemetery.

[Q1138]

166. A landowner was hunting rattlesnakes on his land with a pistol when he saw a hunter carrying a shotgun and attempting to enter the owner's land by crawling under the barbed wire fence which surrounded it. The owner waited until the hunter had gotten past the fence and then approached the hunter, telling him that he was trespassing and ordering him to leave. The hunter said, "I only want to shoot some birds. I got a right to do that if I want to, don't I?" After the hunter said this, the owner placed his hand on the hunter's chest and pushed him gently backward, repeating his demand that the hunter leave. The hunter shoved the owner away from him and pointed his shotgun at the owner, saying, "Nobody pushes me, Mister." The owner immediately drew his pistol from the holster on his belt and fired at the hunter, striking him in the arm and causing him to drop his shotgun.

If the hunter asserts a claim against the owner for battery, the court should find for

(A) the owner, if he reasonably believed that no lesser force would safely cause the hunter to leave his property.

(B) the owner, if he reasonably believed that no lesser force would safely prevent the hunter from firing the shotgun at him.

(C) the hunter, because the owner made the first use of force.

(D) the hunter, because the owner did not use force against him until the hunter's entry onto the realty was complete.

[Q5052]

167. A landowner and a prospective buyer, standing on a parcel owned by the landowner, orally agreed to its sale and purchase for $5,000, and orally marked its bounds as "that line of trees down there, the ditch that intersects them, the fence on the other side, and that street on the fourth side."

In which of the following is the remedy of reformation most appropriate?

(A) As later reduced to writing, the agreement by clerical mistake included two acres that are actually beyond the fence.

(B) The buyer reasonably thought that two acres beyond the fence were included in the oral agreement but the landowner did not. As later reduced to writing, the agreement included the two acres.

(C) The buyer reasonably thought that the price orally agreed upon was $4,500, but the landowner did not. As later reduced to writing, the agreement said $5,000.

(D) The buyer reasonably thought that a dilapidated shed backed up against the fence was to be torn down and removed as part of the agreement, but the landowner did not. As later reduced to writing, the agreement said nothing about the shed.

[Q1128]

168. A state has a statute providing that an unsuccessful candidate in a primary election for a party's nomination for elected public office may not become a candidate for the same office at the following general election by nominating petition or by write-in votes.

A woman sought her party's nomination for governor in the May primary election. After losing in the primary, the woman filed nominating petitions containing the requisite number of signatures to become a candidate for the office of governor in the following general election. The chief elections officer of the state refused to certify the woman's petitions solely because of the above statute. The woman then filed suit in federal district court challenging the constitutionality of this state statute.

As a matter of constitutional law, which of the following is the proper burden of persuasion in this suit?

(A) The woman must demonstrate that the statute is not necessary to achieve a compelling state interest.

(B) The woman must demonstrate that the statute is not rationally related to a legitimate state interest.

(C) The state must demonstrate that the statute is the least restrictive means of achieving a compelling state interest.

(D) The state must demonstrate that the statute is rationally related to a legitimate state interest.

[Q1122]

169. A skiing retailer, in a telephone conversation with a glove manufacturer, ordered 12 pairs of vortex-lined ski gloves at the manufacturer's list price of $600 per dozen "for delivery in 30 days." The manufacturer orally accepted the offer, and immediately faxed to the ski shop this signed memo: "Confirming our agreement today for your purchase of a dozen pairs of vortex-lined ski gloves for $600, the shipment will be delivered in 30 days." Although the retailer received and read the manufacturer's message within minutes after its dispatch, she changed her mind three weeks later about the purchase and rejected the conforming shipment when it timely arrived.

On learning of the rejection, does the manufacturer have a cause of action against the retailer for breach of contract?

(A) Yes, because the gloves were identified to the contract and tendered to the retailer.

(B) Yes, because the manufacturer's faxed memo to the retailer was sufficient to make the agreement enforceable.

(C) No, because the agreed price was $600 and the retailer never signed a writing evidencing a contract with the manufacturer.

(D) No, because the retailer neither paid for nor accepted any of the goods tendered.

[Q2185]

170. In a criminal trial, the evidence showed that the defendant's neighbor tried to kill the defendant by stabbing him. The defendant ran to his room, picked up a gun, and told his neighbor to back off. The neighbor did not, but continued her attack and stabbed him in the arm. The defendant then shot the neighbor twice. The neighbor fell to the floor and lay quietly moaning. After a few seconds, the defendant fired a third shot into the neighbor. The jury found that the neighbor died instantly from the third shot and that the defendant was no longer in fear of being attacked by her.

    The defendant could properly be convicted of which of the following degrees of criminal homicide, if any?

    (A) Attempted murder only.

    (B) Manslaughter only.

    (C) Murder or manslaughter.

    (D) No degree of criminal homicide.

[Q7069]

171. After being fired from his job, the defendant drank almost a quart of vodka and decided to ride the bus home. While on the bus, he saw a briefcase he mistakenly thought was his own, and began struggling with the passenger carrying the briefcase. The defendant knocked the passenger to the floor, took the briefcase, and fled. The defendant was arrested and charged with robbery.

    The defendant should be

    (A) acquitted, because he used no threats and was intoxicated.

    (B) acquitted, because his mistake negated the required specific intent.

    (C) convicted, because his intoxication was voluntary.

    (D) convicted, because mistake is no defense to robbery.

[Q3007]

172. A clerical worker has been employed for the past two years in a permanent position in the Public Records Office of a county. The clerk has been responsible for copying and filing records of real estate transactions in that office. The clerk works in a nonpublic part of the office and has no contact with members of the public. However, state law provides that all real estate records in that office are to be made available for public inspection.

    On the day an attempted assassination of the governor of the state was reported on the radio, the clerk remarked to a coworker, "Our governor is such an evil man, I am sorry they did not get him." The clerk's coworker reported this remark to the clerk's employer, the county recorder. After the clerk admitted making the remark, the county recorder dismissed him stating that "there is no room in this office for a person who hates the governor so much."

    The clerk sued for reinstatement and back pay. His only claim is that the dismissal violated his constitutional rights.

    In this case, the court should hold that the county recorder's dismissal of the clerk was

    (A) unconstitutional, because it constitutes a taking without just compensation of the clerk's property interest in his permanent position with the county.

    (B) unconstitutional, because in light of the clerk's particular employment duties his right to express himself on a matter of public concern outweighed any legitimate interest the state might have had in discharging him.

    (C) constitutional, because the compelling

interest of the state in having loyal and supportive employees outweighs the interest of any state employee in his or her job or in free speech on a matter of public concern.

(D) nonjusticiable, because public employment is a privilege rather than a right and, therefore, the clerk lacked standing to bring this suit.

[Q2184]

173. A radio manufacturer and a retailer, after extensive negotiations, entered into a final, written agreement in which the manufacturer agreed to sell and the retailer agreed to buy all of the retailer's requirements of radios, estimated at 20 units per month, during the period January 1, 2004, and December 31, 2006, at a price of $50 per unit. A dispute arose in late December, 2006, when the retailer returned 25 undefective radios to the manufacturer for full credit after the manufacturer had refused to extend the contract for a second three-year period.

In an action by the manufacturer against the retailer for damages due to the return of the 25 radios, the manufacturer introduces the written agreement, which expressly permitted the buyer to return defective radios for credit but was silent as to the return of undefective radios for credit. The retailer seeks to introduce evidence that during the three years of the agreement it had returned, for various reasons, 125 undefective radios, for which the manufacturer had granted full credit. The manufacturer objects to the admissibility of this evidence.

The trial court will probably rule that the evidence proffered by the retailer is

(A) inadmissible, because the evidence is barred by the parol evidence rule.

(B) inadmissible, because the express terms of the agreement control when those terms are inconsistent with the course of performance.

(C) admissible, because the evidence supports an agreement that is not within the relevant statute of frauds.

(D) admissible, because course-of-performance evidence, when available, is considered the best indication of what the parties intended the writing to mean.

[Q1108]

174. Central City in the state of Green is a center for businesses that assemble personal computers. Components for these computers are manufactured elsewhere in Green and in other states, then shipped to Central City, where the computers are assembled. An ordinance of Central City imposes a special license tax on all of the many companies engaged in the business of assembling computers in that city. The tax payable by each such company is a percentage of the company's gross receipts.

The Green statute that authorizes municipalities to impose this license tax has a "Green content" provision. To comply with this provision of state law, the Central City license tax ordinance provides that the tax paid by any assembler of computers subject to this tax ordinance will be reduced by a percentage equal to the proportion of computer components manufactured in Green.

The plaintiff is a company that assembles computers in Central City and sells them from its offices in Central City to buyers throughout the United States. All of the components of its computers come from outside the state of Green. Therefore, the plaintiff must pay the Central City license tax in full without receiving any refund. Other Central City computer assemblers use components manufactured in Green in varying proportions and, therefore, are entitled to partial reductions of their Central City license tax payments.

Following prescribed procedure, the plaintiff brings an action in a proper court asking to have Central City's special license tax declared unconstitutional on the grounds that it is inconsistent with the negative implications of the commerce clause.

In this case, the court should rule

(A) against the plaintiff, because the tax falls only on companies resident in Central City and, therefore, does not discriminate against or otherwise adversely affect interstate commerce.

(B) against the plaintiff, because the commerce clause does not interfere with the right of a state to foster and support businesses located within its borders by encouraging its residents to purchase the products of those businesses.

(C) for the plaintiff, because any tax on a company engaged in interstate commerce, measured in whole or in part by its gross receipts, is a per se violation of the negative implications of the commerce clause.

(D) for the plaintiff, because the tax improperly discriminates against interstate commerce by treating in-state products more favorably than out-of-state products.

[Q3114]

175. The defendant was prosecuted for armed robbery. At trial, the defendant testified in his own behalf, denying that he had committed the robbery. On cross-examination, the prosecutor intends to ask the defendant whether he had been convicted of burglary six years earlier.

The question concerning the burglary conviction is

(A) proper if the court finds that the probative value for impeachment outweighs the prejudice to the defendant.

(B) proper, because the prosecutor is entitled to make this inquiry as a matter of right.

(C) improper, because burglary does not involve dishonesty or false statement.

(D) improper, because the conviction must be proved by court record, not by question on cross-examination.

[Q4044]

176. After a liquor store was robbed, the police received an anonymous telephone call naming a store employee as the perpetrator of the robbery. Honestly believing that their actions were permitted by the U.S. Constitution, the police talked one of the employee's neighbors into going to the employee's home with a hidden tape recorder to engage him in a conversation about the crime. During the conversation, the employee admitted committing the robbery. The employee was charged in state court with the robbery. He moved to suppress the recording on the grounds that the method of obtaining it violated his constitutional rights under both the state and federal constitutions. Assume that a clear precedent from the state supreme court holds that the conduct of the police in making the recording violated the employee's rights under the state constitution, and that the exclusionary rule is the proper remedy for this violation.

Should the court grant the employee's motion?

(A) No, because the employee's federal constitutional rights were not violated, and this circumstance overrides any state constitutional provisions.

(B) No, because the police were acting in the good-faith belief that their actions were permitted by the federal Constitution.

(C) Yes, because the making of the recording violated the state constitution.

(D) Yes, because use of the recording would violate the neighbor's federal constitutional rights.

[Q7086]

177. A vendee entered into a valid written contract to purchase a large tract of land from a vendor for its fair market value of $50,000. The contract was assignable by the vendee. The vendee duly notified the vendor to convey title jointly to the vendee and "Charles," Charles being the vendee's friend whom the vendee had not seen for many years.

When the vendee learned that Charles would have to sign certain documents in connection with the closing, she prevailed upon her brother to attend the closing and pretend to be Charles. The vendee and her brother attended the closing, and the vendor executed an instrument in the proper form of a deed, purporting to convey the property to "[the vendee] and Charles, as tenants in common." The brother pretended that he was Charles, and he signed Charles's name to all the required documents. The vendee provided the entire $50,000 consideration for the transaction. The deed was promptly and properly recorded.

Unknown to the vendee or her brother, Charles had died several months before the closing. Charles's will, which was duly probated, devised "all my real estate to my nephew" and the residue of his estate to the vendee.

The vendee and the nephew have been unable to agree as to the status or disposition of the property. The nephew brought an appropriate action against the vendor and the vendee to quiet legal title to an undivided one-half interest in the property.

The court should hold that legal title to the property is vested

(A) all in the vendor.

(B) all in the vendee.

(C) one-half in the vendee and one-half in the vendor.

(D) one-half in the vendee and one-half in the nephew.

[Q2114]

178. In a civil trial for professional malpractice, the plaintiff sought to show that the defendant, an engineer, had designed the plaintiff's flour mill with inadequate power. The plaintiff called an expert witness who based his testimony solely on his own professional experience but also asserted, when asked, that the book Smith on Milling Systems was a reliable treatise in the field and consistent with his views. On cross-examination, the defendant asked the witness whether he and Smith were ever wrong. The witness answered, "Nobody's perfect." The defendant asked no further questions. The defendant called a second expert witness and asked, "Do you accept the Smith book as reliable?" The second witness said, "It once was, but it is now badly out of date." The plaintiff requested that the jury be allowed to examine the book and judge for itself the book's reliability.

Should the court allow the jury to examine the book?

(A) No, because the jury may consider only passages read to it by counsel or witness.

(B) No, because the plaintiff's expert in testifying did not rely on the treatise but on his own experience.

(C) Yes, because an expert has testified that the treatise is reliable.

(D) Yes, because the jury is the judge of the weight and credibility to be accorded both written and oral evidence.

[Q7005]

179. A homeowner owned a large poisonous snake which had been defanged and was kept in a cage. A storm damaged the homeowner's house and the snake's cage, allowing it to escape. During the cleanup after the storm, a volunteer worker came across the snake. The worker tried to run away from the snake and fell, breaking his arm.

In a suit by the worker against the homeowner based on strict liability in tort to recover for his injury, will the worker prevail?

(A) No, because the snake's escape was caused by a force of nature.

(B) No, because the worker should have anticipated an injury during his volunteer work.

(C) Yes, because the homeowner did not take adequate precautions to secure the snake.

(D) Yes, because the worker's injury was the result of his fear of the escaped snake.

[Q7075]

180. A retailer ordered from a produce wholesaler 500 bushels of No. 1 Royal Fuzz peaches, at a specified price, "for prompt shipment." The wholesaler promptly shipped 500 bushels, but by mistake shipped No. 2 Royal Fuzz peaches instead of No. 1. The error in shipment was caused by the negligence of the wholesaler's shipping clerk.

Which of the following best states the retailer's rights and duties upon delivery of the peaches?

(A) The wholesaler's shipment of the peaches was a counteroffer and the retailer can refuse to accept them.

(B) The wholesaler's shipment of the peaches was a counteroffer but, since peaches are perishable, the retailer, if it does not want to accept them, must reship the peaches to the wholesaler in order to mitigate the wholesaler's losses.

(C) The retailer must accept the peaches because a contract was formed when the wholesaler shipped them.

(D) Although a contract was formed when the wholesaler shipped the peaches, the retailer does not have to accept them.

[Q1141]

181. Bill and Chuck hated Vic and agreed to start a fight with Vic and, if the opportunity arose, to kill him. Bill and Chuck met Vic in the street outside a bar and began to push him around. Ray and Sam, who also hated Vic, stopped to watch. Ray threw Bill a knife. Sam told Bill, "Kill him." Chuck held Vic while Bill stabbed and killed him.

On a charge of murdering Vic, Sam is

(A) not guilty, because his words did not create a "clear and present danger" not already existing.

(B) not guilty, because mere presence and oral encouragement, whether or not he has the requisite intent, will not make him guilty as an accomplice.

(C) guilty, because, with the intent to have

Bill kill Vic, he shouted encouragement to Bill.

(D) guilty, because he aided and abetted the murder through his mere presence plus his intent to see Vic killed.

[Q4013]

182. The plaintiff was crossing the street on foot when she was struck by a delivery van owned by the defendant restaurant, and driven by a deliveryman who worked as an employee of the defendant and who was in the process of making a delivery. Following the accident, the deliveryman was charged with reckless driving and pleaded not guilty. At the trial on the charge of reckless driving, the deliveryman testified in his own defense. He stated that at the time of the accident, he had taken his eyes off the road to look for the address of the place to which he had to make his delivery, and that as a result he didn't see the plaintiff crossing the street.

The plaintiff subsequently brought an action against the restaurant under the theory of *respondeat superior* for personal injuries resulting from the deliveryman's negligence. At the trial of this action, the plaintiff proved that the deliveryman remained in the restaurant's employ until the deliveryman died from causes not related to the accident. The plaintiff then offered into evidence a transcript of the deliveryman's testimony at the reckless driving trial. Upon objection by the restaurant's attorney, the transcript should be

(A) admitted, under the prior testimony exception to the hearsay rule.

(B) admitted, under the past recollection recorded exception to the hearsay rule.

(C) admitted as a vicarious admission, under the public record exception to the hearsay rule.

(D) excluded as hearsay, not within any exception to the hearsay rule.

[Q5040]

183. An associate professor in the pediatrics department of a local medical school was denied tenure. He asked a national education lobbying organization to represent him in his efforts to have the tenure decision reversed. In response to a letter from the organization on the professor's behalf, the dean of the medical school wrote to the organization explaining truthfully that the professor had been denied tenure because of reports that he had abused two of his former patients. Several months later, after a thorough investigation, the allegations were proven false and the professor was granted tenure. He had remained working at the medical school at full pay during the tenure decision review process and thus suffered no pecuniary harm.

In a suit for libel by the professor against the dean of the medical school, will the professor prevail?

(A) No, because the professor invited the libel.

(B) No, because the professor suffered no pecuniary loss.

(C) Yes, because the dean had a duty to investigate the rumor before repeating it.

(D) Yes, because the dean's defamatory statement was in the form of a writing.

[Q7050]

184. The plaintiff sued the defendant for personal injuries suffered in a train-automobile collision. The plaintiff called an eyewitness, who testified that the train was going 20 miles per hour. The defendant then offered the testimony of an experienced police accident investigator who described his extensive training and

experience in examining high-speed accidents including ones involving trains. The investigator explained that he examined the physical evidence, including the types of damage inflicted on the metal structure of the car, and that such physical evidence is typically relied upon by investigators trying to determine the speed at which a collision occurred. The investigator then stated that it was his opinion that the train was going between 5 and 10 miles per hour at the moment of the collision.

This testimony by the investigator is

(A) improper, because there cannot be both lay and expert opinion on the same issue.

(B) improper, because the investigator is unable to establish the speed with a sufficient degree of scientific certainty.

(C) proper, because the investigator has demonstrated sufficient expertise to express an opinion on speed.

(D) proper, because the plaintiff first introduced opinion evidence as to speed.

[Q3117]

185. A proposed federal statute would prohibit all types of discrimination against black persons on the basis of their race in every business transaction executed anywhere in the United States by any person or entity, governmental or private.

Is this proposed federal statute likely to be constitutional?

(A) Yes, because it could reasonably be viewed as an exercise of Congress's authority to enact laws for the general welfare.

(B) Yes, because it could reasonably be viewed as a means of enforcing the provisions of the Thirteenth Amendment.

(C) No, because it would regulate purely local transactions that are not in interstate commerce.

(D) No, because it would invade the powers reserved to the states by the Tenth Amendment.

[Q2101]

186. A bright nine-year-old child attended a day care center after school. The day care center was located near a man-made duck pond on the property of a corporation. During the winter, the pond was used for ice skating when conditions were suitable. At a time when the pond was only partially frozen, the child sneaked away from the center and walked out onto the ice covering the pond. The ice gave way, and the child fell into the cold water. He suffered shock and would have drowned had he not been rescued by a passerby. At the time of the incident, the pond was clearly marked with signs that stated, "THIN ICE - NO SKATING." When the child left the day care center, the center was staffed with a reasonable number of qualified personnel, and the center's employees were exercising reasonable care to ensure that the children in their charge did not leave the premises. The jurisdiction follows a rule of pure comparative negligence.

In a suit brought on the child's behalf against the corporation, who is likely to prevail?

(A) The child, because the corporation owes a duty to keep its premises free of dangerous conditions.

(B) The child, because the pond was an attractive nuisance.

(C) The corporation, because the danger of thin ice may reasonably be expected to be understood by a nine-year-old child.

(D) The corporation, because the day care center had a duty to keep the child off the ice.

[Q7093]

187. In a personal injury case, the plaintiff sued a retail store for injuries she sustained from a fall in the store. The plaintiff alleged that the store negligently allowed its entryway to become slippery due to snow tracked in from the sidewalk. When the plaintiff threatened to sue, the store's manager said, "I know that there was slush on that marble entry, but I think your four-inch-high heels were the real cause of your fall. So let's agree that we'll pay your medical bills, and you release us from any claims you might have." The plaintiff refused the offer. At trial, the plaintiff seeks to testify to the manager's statement that "there was slush on that marble entry."

Is the statement about the slush on the floor admissible?

(A) No, because it is a statement made in the course of compromise negotiations.

(B) No, because the manager denied that the slippery condition was the cause of the plaintiff's fall.

(C) Yes, as an admission by an agent about a matter within the scope of his authority.

(D) Yes, because the rule excluding offers of compromise does not protect statements of fact made during compromise negotiations.

[Q7058]

188. A buyer mailed a signed order to a seller that read: "Please ship us 10,000 widgets at your current price." The seller received the order on January 7 and that same day mailed to the buyer a properly stamped, addressed, and signed letter stating that the order was accepted at the seller's current price of $10 per widget. On January 8, before receipt of the seller's letter, the buyer telephoned the seller and said, "I hereby revoke my order." The seller protested to no avail. The buyer received the seller's letter on January 9. Because of the buyer's January 8 telephone message, the seller never shipped the goods.

Under the relevant and prevailing rules, is there a contract between the buyer and the seller as of January 10?

(A) No, because the order was an offer that could be accepted only by shipping the goods; and the offer was effectively revoked before shipment.

(B) No, because the buyer never effectively agreed to the $10 price term.

(C) Yes, because the order was, for a reasonable time, an irrevocable offer.

(D) Yes, because the order was an offer that the seller effectively accepted before the buyer attempted to revoke it.

[Q3194]

189. A husband and wife took their 12-year-old son to a political rally to hear a controversial United States senator speak. The speaker was late, and the wife stepped outside to smoke a cigarette. While there, she saw a man placing what she believed to be a bomb against a wall at the back of the building. She went back inside and told her husband what she had seen. Without alerting anyone, they took their son and left. Some 20 minutes later, the bomb exploded, killing eight persons and injuring 50. In the jurisdiction, murder in the first degree is defined as an intentional homicide committed with premeditation

and deliberation; murder in the second degree is defined as all other murder at common law; and manslaughter is defined as either a homicide in the heat of passion arising from adequate provocation or a homicide caused by gross negligence or reckless indifference to consequence.

As to the deaths of the eight persons, what crime, if any, did the wife commit?

(A) Manslaughter.

(B) Murder in the first degree.

(C) Murder in the second degree.

(D) No crime.

[Q7026]

190. The personnel director of an investment company told a job applicant during an interview that the company was worth millions of dollars and that the company's portfolio would triple in the next several months. The applicant was very excited about the company's prospects and accepted an offer to work for the company. Two days later, the applicant read in the newspaper that the investment company had filed for bankruptcy reorganization. As a result of reading this news, the applicant suffered severe emotional distress but he immediately found another comparable position.

Is the applicant likely to prevail in his action for negligent misrepresentation?

(A) No, because the applicant did not suffer any physical injury or pecuniary loss.

(B) No, because the personnel director's statement was purely speculative.

(C) Yes, because the applicant relied on the personnel director's misrepresentations about the investment company.

(D) Yes, because the personnel director should have foreseen that his misrepresentations would cause the applicant to be upset.

[Q7040]

191. A trucker was driving a truckload of gravel over a highway in a rural part of the state, when through no fault of her own, one of the tires on her truck blew out, causing the truck to go out of control. The truck overturned, spilling the gravel onto the land of a private landowner that was adjacent to the road. The trucker, who was unhurt, returned later with another truck and a tractor equipped with a power shovel. Using the power shovel, the trucker scooped up the spilled gravel and loaded it onto the other truck.

If the landowner asserts a claim against the trucker for trespass to land, the court should award the landowner a judgment for

(A) nominal damage only.

(B) all damage resulting from the spilling of gravel onto the landowner's land.

(C) only the damage caused by the trucker's removal of the gravel from the landowner's land.

(D) no damage.

[Q5075]

192. [The basic facts are the same as in Question 186, but the question asked here is different.] A bright nine-year-old child attended a day care center after school. The day care center was located near a man-made duck pond on the property of a corporation. During the winter, the pond was used for ice skating when conditions were suitable. At a time when the pond was only partially frozen, the child sneaked away from the center and walked out onto the ice covering the pond. The ice gave way, and the child fell into the cold water. He suffered shock and would have

drowned had he not been rescued by a passerby. At the time of the incident, the pond was clearly marked with signs that stated, "THIN ICE - NO SKATING." When the child left the day care center, the center was staffed with a reasonable number of qualified personnel, and the center's employees were exercising reasonable care to ensure that the children in their charge did not leave the premises. The jurisdiction follows a rule of pure comparative negligence.

In a suit brought on the child's behalf against the day care center, who is likely to prevail?

(A) The child, because he left the center while he was under the center's care.

(B) The child, because the day care center is located near a pond.

(C) The day care center, because it was not negligent.

(D) The day care center, because the child was a trespasser.

[Q7094]

193. A contractor agreed to build a power plant for a public utility. A subcontractor agreed with the contractor to lay the foundation for $200,000. The subcontractor supplied goods and services worth $150,000, for which the contractor made progress payments aggregating $100,000 as required by the subcontract. The subcontractor then breached by refusing unjustifiably to perform further. The contractor reasonably spent $120,000 to have the work completed by a third party.

The subcontractor now sues the contractor for the reasonable value of benefits conferred, and the contractor counterclaims for breach of contract.

Which of the following should be the court's decision?

(A) The subcontractor recovers $50,000, the benefit conferred on the contractor for which the subcontractor has not been paid.

(B) The subcontractor recovers $30,000, the benefit the subcontractor conferred on the contractor minus the $20,000 in damages incurred by the contractor.

(C) The contractor recovers $20,000, the excess over the contract price that was paid by the contractor for the performance it had bargained to receive from the subcontractor.

(D) Neither party recovers anything, because the subcontractor committed a material, unexcused breach and the contractor received a $50,000 benefit from the subcontractor for which the subcontractor has not been paid.

[Q3145]

194. The defendant had been arraigned on a charge of burglarizing a home. He was assigned a public defender and pleaded not guilty, but because he was unable to post bail, was in jail awaiting trial. An undercover police officer was ordered by his commanding officer to pose as a prisoner and was placed in the same cell as the defendant. The undercover officer was instructed not to question the defendant about the charge against him. While they were in the cell together, the defendant told the undercover officer that he had committed the burglary with which he was charged.

If the defendant's attorney objects to the testimony of the undercover officer regarding the statement which the defendant made to him in the cell, the objection should be

(A) sustained, because the statement was made to a police officer in the absence of and without the consent of the defendant's attorney.

(B) sustained, because the undercover officer entrapped the defendant into making the statement.

(C) overruled, if the undercover officer was placed in the defendant's cell pursuant to a warrant.

(D) overruled, because the defendant made the statement voluntarily.

[Q5021]

195. In a writing signed by both parties on December 1, a buyer agreed to buy from a seller a gasoline engine for $1,000, delivery to be made on the following February 1. Through a secretarial error, the writing called for delivery on March 1, but neither party noticed the error until February 1. Before signing the agreement, the buyer and seller orally agreed that the contract of sale would be effective only if the buyer should notify the seller in writing not later than January 2 that the buyer had arranged to resell the engine to a third person. Otherwise, they agreed orally, "There is no deal." On December 15, the buyer entered into a contract with a third person to resell the engine to the third person at a profit.

On December 16, the buyer notified the seller by telephone of the buyer's resale agreement with the third person, and explained that a written notice was unfeasible because the buyer's secretary was ill. The seller replied, "That's okay. I'll get the engine to you on February 1, as we agreed." Having learned, however, that the engine had increased in value about 75% since December 1, the seller renounced the agreement on February 1.

If the buyer sues the seller on February 2 for breach of contract, which of the following concepts best supports the buyer's claim?

(A) Substantial performance.

(B) Nonoccurrence of a condition subsequent.

(C) Waiver of condition.

(D) Novation of buyers.

[Q2052]

196. A chemical engineer had no financial interest in or connection with a particular chemical company. The engineer noticed that the company's most recent publicly issued financial statement listed, as part of the company's assets, a large inventory of a certain special chemical compound. This asset was listed at a cost of $100,000, but the engineer knew that the ingredients of the compound were in short supply and that the current market value of the inventory was in excess of $1,000,000. There was no current public quotation of the price of the company's stock. The book value of the company's stock, according to the statement, was $5 a share; its actual value was $30 a share.

Knowing these facts, the engineer offered to purchase from a seller (an individual who had no connection with the company) at $6 a share the 1,000 shares of the company's stock owned by the seller. The seller and the engineer had not previously met. The seller sold the stock to the engineer for $6 a share.

If the seller asserts a claim based on misrepresentation against the engineer, will the seller prevail?

(A) Yes, because the engineer knew that the value of the stock was greater than the price she offered.

(B) Yes, if the engineer did not inform the seller of the true value of the inventory.

(C) No, unless the engineer told the seller that the stock was not worth more than

$6 a share.

(D) No, if the company's financial statement was available to the seller.

[Q4045]

197. Congress passed a statute directing the United States Forest Service, a federal agency, to issue regulations to control campfires on federal public lands and to establish a schedule of penalties for those who violate the new regulations. The statute provided that the Forest Service regulations should "reduce, to the maximum extent feasible, all potential hazards that arise from campfires on Forest Service lands." The Forest Service issued the regulations and the schedule of penalties directed by Congress. The regulations include a rule that provides for the doubling of the fine for any negligent or prohibited use of fire if the user is intoxicated by alcohol or drugs.

Which of the following is the best argument for sustaining the constitutionality of the Forest Service's rule providing for the fines?

(A) The executive branch of government, of which the Forest Service is part, has inherent rule-making authority over public lands.

(B) The rule is issued pursuant to a valid exercise of Congress's power to delegate rule-making authority to federal agencies.

(C) The rule is justified by a compelling governmental interest in safeguarding forest resources.

(D) The rule relates directly to law enforcement, which is an executive rather than legislative function, and hence it does not need specific congressional authorization.

[Q7036]

198. A father and his adult daughter encountered an old family friend on the street. The daughter said to the friend, "How about lending me $1,000 to buy a used car? I'll pay you back with interest one year from today." The father added, "And if she doesn't pay it back as promised, I will." The friend thereupon wrote out and handed to the daughter his personal check, payable to her, for $1,000, and the daughter subsequently used the funds to buy a used car. When the debt became due, both the daughter and the father refused to repay it, or any part of it.

In an action by the friend against the father to recover $1,000 plus interest, which of the following statements would summarize the father's best defense?

(A) He received no consideration for his conditional promise to the friend.

(B) His conditional promise to the friend was not to be performed in less than a year from the time it was made.

(C) His conditional promise to the friend was not made for the primary purpose of benefiting himself (the father).

(D) The loan by the friend was made without any agreement concerning the applicable interest rate.

[Q1089]

199. A retailer faxed the following signed message to his long-time widget supplier: "Urgently need blue widgets. Ship immediately three gross at your current list price of $600." Upon receipt of the fax, the supplier shipped three gross of red widgets to the retailer, and faxed to retailer the following message: "Temporarily out of blue. In case red will help, am shipping three gross at the same price. Hope you can use them."

Upon the retailer's timely receipt of both the shipment and the supplier's fax, which of the following best describes the rights and duties of the retailer and the wholesaler?

(A) The retailer may accept the shipment, in which case he must pay the wholesaler the list price, or he must reject the shipment and recover from the wholesaler for total breach of contract.

(B) The retailer may accept the shipment, in which case he must pay the wholesaler the list price, or he may reject the shipment, in which case he has no further rights against the wholesaler.

(C) The retailer may accept the shipment, in which case he must pay the wholesaler the list price, less any damages sustained because of the nonconforming shipment, or he may reject the shipment and recover from the wholesaler for total breach of contract, subject to the wholesaler's right to cure.

(D) The retailer may accept the shipment, in which case he must pay the wholesaler the list price, less any damages sustained because of the nonconforming shipment, or he may reject the shipment provided that he promptly covers by obtaining conforming widgets from another supplier.

[Q2111]

200. A wife was extremely hot-tempered and very possessive of her husband. She frequently flew into a hysterical rage if he even looked at another woman. One evening the husband and wife were in a bar when they began arguing. Wanting to hurt the wife, and knowing that it would infuriate her, the husband asked a young woman, who was sitting at the next table, to dance with him. The young woman accepted, but as she and the husband began to dance, the wife became enraged and ran at them, striking the husband over the head with a wine bottle. Later that night, the husband died of a head injury resulting from the blow. The wife was charged with murder, but her lawyer argued that the jury should be given a charge of voluntary manslaughter. Should the wife's lawyer's request be granted?

(A) Yes, on the theory of deliberate provocation.

(B) Yes, because of the wife's extreme feelings of possessiveness regarding the husband.

(C) No, if the ordinary person in the wife's situation would not have become enraged by the husband's dancing with the young woman.

(D) No, on the theory of mistaken justification.

[Q5048]

ANSWERS
SELF-ASSESSMENT TEST
A.M. EXAM

Answer Key

Use this Answer Key to quickly identify the correct answer to each question.

(1) C	(16) A	(31) B	(46) A	(61) D	(76) C	(91) A
(2) B	(17) C	(32) B	(47) C	(62) B	(77) A	(92) B
(3) A	(18) C	(33) D	(48) B	(63) B	(78) D	(93) C
(4) C	(19) C	(34) D	(49) D	(64) C	(79) B	(94) B
(5) C	(20) D	(35) B	(50) C	(65) B	(80) C	(95) C
(6) B	(21) A	(36) B	(51) C	(66) A	(81) D	(96) A
(7) B	(22) B	(37) C	(52) D	(67) A	(82) A	(97) C
(8) B	(23) B	(38) B	(53) B	(68) A	(83) B	(98) B
(9) B	(24) C	(39) A	(54) C	(69) B	(84) B	(99) C
(10) B	(25) C	(40) C	(55) D	(70) D	(85) C	(100) C
(11) A	(26) D	(41) D	(56) A	(71) C	(86) C	
(12) C	(27) B	(42) C	(57) C	(72) D	(87) A	
(13) C	(28) C	(43) D	(58) A	(73) A	(88) A	
(14) D	(29) C	(44) B	(59) B	(74) A	(89) D	
(15) C	(30) A	(45) B	(60) A	(75) D	(90) B	

Note: In Criminal Law answers, references to "LaFave" are to Wayne LaFave, *Principles of Criminal Law* (Thomson/West, 2003), references to "LaFave Criminal Law" are to Wayne LaFave, *Criminal Law* Hornbook (Thomson/West, 2000, 3d Ed.), and references to "M.P.C." are to the Model Penal Code (A.L.I.). In Contracts answers, references to "Rest. 2d" refer to the *Second Restatement of Contracts*, and in Torts answers, such references refer to the *Second Restatement of Torts*. In Torts answers, references to "Dobbs" refer to Dan Dobbs, *The Law of Torts* Hornbook (Thomson/West, 2000). In Property answers, references to "A.L.P." are to *American Law of Property* (Little Brown, 6 vols., 1952).

1. **C** Where a defaulting plaintiff has rendered some performance of value to the defendant, but has not substantially performed, the plaintiff may not recover "on the contract." But she may recover on a *quasi-contract* or *quantum meruit* ("as much as he deserved") theory — the court uses its equity-like powers to prevent unjust enrichment of the defendant. If the farmer didn't have to pay anything, he'd be unjustly enriched (at least with respect to the two painted barns, putting aside his damage from not getting the agreed-upon painting of the third barn) by the "value" to him of the painting of two barns. So the court would start by awarding the painter this value. But then, the farmer would be entitled to be made whole for the damages to him from not getting all three barns painted for the agreed-upon $6,000. So the court would compute how much it would now cost the farmer to get that single barn painted. If that cost would be $2,000 or less, the farmer's damages would be zero. But if it would cost more, then the difference would be deducted from the painter's quasi-contract "value of the services of painting two barns" recovery.

    (A) is wrong because even though the painting of all three barns was an express condition of payment under the contract, the court can and would still award a quasi-contract recovery, as described above.

    (B) is wrong because the painter is only entitled to a quasi-contract recovery, not to recover "on the contract." So any formula keyed to the painter's anticipated "profit" is irrelevant — it's the value to the defendant, not the profit that would have been made by the breaching plaintiff, that is the starting point. (Profits that would have been made by the plaintiff are relevant only where it's the defendant, not the plaintiff, who breached.)

    (D) is wrong because this formula doesn't take into account the farmer's right to deduct damages for the painter's failure to paint the third barn. (The court might indeed use the increase in the value of the two painted barns as the measure of the "reasonable value" of the painter's services, but the court would deduct from this number the farmer's damages from the failure to paint the third barn.)
    [Q3020]

2. **B** Courts will usually not grant specific performance of an individual's duty to perform personal services, because of the difficulties in supervising the defendant's ongoing performance, and the distastefulness of ordering what amounts to involuntary servitude. Here, for instance, if the court grants an order compelling the carpenter to do the work at the contracted-for price and in the contracted-for time period, the court may have to make constant decisions about whether the carpenter is keeping up to the schedule and doing the work according to specifications, so that the court risks becoming enmeshed in burdensome project details, which the court probably will conclude is not a sensible use of judicial resources. Also, the court may have to imprison the carpenter if he doesn't perform, a consequence that seems somewhat like slavery.

    (A) is wrong because the requirements for laches have not been satisfied here. It is true that if a plaintiff who is seeking equitable relief unjustifiably "sleeps on his rights," the defense of laches may preclude recovery. But here, there seem to be two reasons why laches would not apply: (1) we are told that the homeowner made a "reasonable and *prolonged* effort" to find a substitute, suggesting that the homeowner spent most or all of the one-year gap between repudiation and suit in reasonable efforts to mitigate, making the gap not unjustifiable; and (2) there is no evidence that the carpenter has been prejudiced by the delay, a usual requirement for laches.

(C) is wrong as a statement of law: when a plaintiff suffers from the defendant's anticipatory repudiation, all standard contract remedies are typically available to him, even though the time for performance has not yet arrived. So a decree of specific performance may be issued, though typically the decree would not require performance until the contractually-specified time for it.

(D) is wrong as a statement of law. It is true that a decree of specific performance, like other equitable relief, will not be granted where damages would provide an adequate remedy. But the availability of nominal damages alone will typically not be an adequate remedy, and that is certainly the case here, where the homeowner's actual damages will be more than nominal.

[Q2141]

3. **A** First, this is hearsay: the declarant's statement "I killed him" is being offered to show that she did indeed kill him. But FRE 804(b)(3) (one of the declarant-unavailable exceptions) gives a hearsay exception for a statement by a now-unavailable witness which "was at the time of its making so far contrary to the declarant's pecuniary or proprietary interest, or so far tended to subject the declarant to civil or criminal liability . . . that a reasonable person in the declarant's position would not have made the statement unless believing it to be true." The woman's statement in the deposition qualifies, since: (1) her subsequent death of course makes her unavailable; (2) the statement, viewed as of the time she made it, potentially subjected her to such civil and criminal liability that she would be unlikely to have made it unless she believed it was true. 804(b)(3) adds a further requirement, that a statement "tending to expose the declarant to criminal liability and offered to exculpate the accused is not admissible unless corroborating circumstances clearly indicate the trustworthiness of the statement." Here, the fact that the woman was known to have quarreled with and disliked the victim, and the fact that the victim's family chose to bring civil suit against the woman, supply the required corroborating circumstances to indicate the statement's trustworthiness.

(B) is wrong because, although there is indeed an exception for former testimony given under oath at a trial or other proceeding, the exception applies only if "the party against whom the testimony is now offered . . . had an opportunity and similar motive to develop the testimony by direct, cross, or redirect examination." See FRE 804(b)(1). Since the "party against whom the testimony is now offered" is the government, the statement could qualify only if the government had the opportunity and similar motive to "develop" (i.e., undermine) the woman's testimony in the earlier civil suit; since the prosecution was not part of that suit, this requirement was not satisfied.

(C) is wrong because, while the statement is indeed hearsay, the declaration-against-interest exception applies, as described in Choice (A) above.

(D) is wrong because, although the Best Evidence Rule does indeed sometimes require an original, FRE 1003 says that "a duplicate is admissible to the same extent as an original unless (1) a genuine issue is raised as to the authenticity of the original or (2) in the circumstances it would be unfair to admit to duplicate in lieu of the original." There is no indication on these facts that either of these problems is present.

[Q6001]

4. **C** This is the correct choice, because the explosion was caused by a design defect in a part of the plant unrelated to the filter system designed by the engineer. The only plausible basis for the suit here would have to be negligence. (Although the making of explosive chemicals may have been an "abnormally dangerous activity" — triggering strict liability — the engineer was not herself carrying out that manufacturing activity, and only the person carrying out the ultrahazardous activity has strict liability for it.) To be liable in negligence, the engineer would have to have had a duty to avoid a particular type of harm, and then to have failed to use reasonable care in carrying out that

duty. If the engineer had worked on the design that contained the defect, she certainly could have been held liable in negligence. But since the engineer dealt only with the filtering system, she never undertook any duty to ascertain the safety of the other aspects of the plant design. Consequently, nothing she did (or didn't do) could possibly have constituted a failure to use reasonable care in the discharging of a duty.

(A) is wrong because the engineer does not become liable for a design defect merely by including that defect in her blueprints. The facts state that the engineer was retained to design a filter system. Her duty was to protect people from unreasonable risk of injury arising from her design. The only way to show the design for the filter system was to include the rest of the plant in which the filter system was to be installed. Showing the rest of the plant, including the design defect, does not make her liable for all injuries arising for all design defects in the plant, absent an affirmative requirement to review or inspect those other parts of the blueprints. There is no principle that would impose on an engineer such an affirmative duty to review the safety of parts of blueprints for which the engineer has had no responsibility.

(B) is wrong because joint and several liability does not apply on these facts. Where two or more tortious acts combine to proximately cause an indivisible injury to a plaintiff, each tortfeasor is jointly and severally liable for that injury. Under these facts the engineer committed no tort. Merely including a part of the defectively designed plant in her drawings absent a requirement that she knew or should have known of the defect does not make her liable in tort for the defect. Without the engineer's having committed a tort leading to Plaintiff's injury, there can be no joint and several liability.

(D) is wrong because the fact that Plaintiff brought suit against the engineer personally means that it doesn't matter whether the engineer was an independent contractor or not. Had Plaintiff brought suit against *the corporation*, then perhaps the engineer's status with the corporation — that is, whether she was an employee or an independent contractor — might be relevant to the corporation's liability. However, the facts state that Plaintiff brought the action against the engineer individually. The engineer's liability will depend solely on whether the engineer behaved negligently, and that would be so (or not so) regardless of whether the corporation employed her or merely engaged her.

[Q3032]

5. **C** A person only has standing to claim a search or seizure violated the Fourth Amendment when the evidence was obtained from a search or seizure which violated the person's "legitimate expectation of privacy." *Rakas v. Illinois* (1978). This means that even if the defendant owns the property, or is present when the search takes place, he will have no standing to challenge the search *unless* the search violated his legitimate expectation of privacy. Under the facts here, Defendant clearly had no legitimate expectation of privacy as to the back seat of the football player's car, or as to the heroin (which in any event was no longer his property). Thus, he cannot object to the validity of the search, even if it violated the constitutional rights of the football player.

(A) is wrong because the "plain view" doctrine would not be determinative under these facts. The plain view doctrine provides one means by which the police can conduct a warrantless search; it states that police can make a warrantless seizure when they are on the premises for lawful purposes, and they inadvertently discover evidence in plain view. (A) correctly states that since the heroin was under the rear seat, it was not in plain view. However, this choice ignores the central reason why the motion to suppress will be denied: the defendant has no standing to object to the search, since it was the football player's car that was searched, and the defendant had no privacy interest in it.

(B) is wrong because it ignores the central issue in the case: the defendant does not have standing to object to the search. If you chose this response, it's because you overlooked the fact that *the defendant* is objecting to a search of *the football player's* car, in which the defendant has no privacy interest. For some extra credit, let's look at how the case would come out if it was the football player who was on trial, and who was objecting that the search was excessive. In that event, the statement in (B) may or may not be correct — it turns on whether the football player was subjected to a full custodial arrest (as opposed to being given a plain traffic ticket without being taken to the police station). If he *was* arrested, the police would be entitled to then conduct a search of the entire passenger compartment (since the compartment is considered "within the suspect's control," even if he was away from the car when the search took place). That would make the search here valid. If, however, the police *didn't* intend to take the football player into custody, they could only "frisk" his person — making the search *invalid.*

(D) is wrong, because there's no evidence that the football player was subject to a full custodial arrest — the facts only say that the football player was stopped for speeding. Without a full custodial arrest, the police would have no right to perform a search incident to arrest. Furthermore, (D) ignores the central issue, which is that the defendant has no standing to object to the search.
[Q4049]

6. **B** This was a firm offer that met the requirements of UCC §2-205, since it was (1) by a merchant; (2) in a letter signed by the offeror; and (3) it promised that the offeror would sell all items at the catalog price for a year (a promise to hold the offer open). It's true that this promise of irrevocability didn't legally extend beyond three months (despite what it said), but the three months was enough to cover February.

(A) is wrong because, while the doctrine of promissory estoppel says that detrimental reliance by the offeree may render an offer temporarily irrevocable, here there is no indication that the lawyer detrimentally relied on the stationer's offer.

(C) is wrong because the UCC does not require consideration for an offer to be irrevocable. The whole point of §2-205's firm-offer provision is that qualifying offers by merchants will be irrevocable even though not supported by consideration.

(D) is wrong because, while the maximum period of irrevocability for firm orders under UCC §2-205 is three months, when an offer that otherwise meets the firm-offer requirements promises more than three months' irrevocability, the offer will nonetheless be irrevocable for three months.
[Q3028]

7. **B** The common-law "firefighters' rule" says that when firefighters or police officers are injured during the course of the job, they normally have no claim against the person whose conduct created the peril. Dobbs, §285. Not all states follow the firefighters' rule. But even among those that do, the doctrine is generally limited to risks that are inherent in, and special to, that particular occupation. Dobbs, §286. This limit means that the doctrine will not apply here because being struck by a car in normal traffic is not one of the special risks inherent to dangerous police work. So the driver can be held liable under ordinary negligence principles. (Also, many courts say that the firefighters' rule applies only where the negligently-created peril was *responsible for the officer's presence at the scene*, and that approach, too, would cause the rule not to apply here, since the officer was not responding to the risk caused by the driver and was instead present at the scene by coincidence.)

(A) is wrong because, although this answer correctly states that the driver's motion should be denied, it misstates the legal basis for this conclusion. The firefighters' rule, although named with reference to firefighters, also covers police officers. They, too, are public servants at risk of injury by the perils that they have been employed to confront.

(C) is wrong because but-for causation is not sufficient to support the firefighters' rule defense here. As further described in the analysis of choice (B) above, the firefighters' rule applies to bar liability only when the risk that materialized was one of the unique risks inherent to the officer's dangerous work. Here, the fact that the officer was returning from an emergency when she was struck was just a coincidence. So the driver could still be held liable for his negligence because being struck by a car in normal traffic is not one of the special risks inherent in dangerous police work.

(D) is wrong because it overstates the scope of the firefighters' rule. The firefighters' rule only bars claims for injuries that result from risks that are unique or special to the plaintiff's inherently dangerous work. Thus where, as here, the officer is injured on the job, but by a risk that was not part of what makes the officer's job inherently dangerous, the firefighters' rule will not apply, and the driver can be held liable under garden-variety negligence principles.

[Q7006]

8. **B** The tort of conversion is the interference with a person's possessory rights in a chattel that is so serious as to warrant that defendant pay full value for the chattel. Under these facts, the neighbor borrowed the homeowner's chain saw without permission, thereby interfering with the homeowner's possessory rights. The facts state that the saw broke (as opposed to becoming slightly damaged or in need of minor repair), so we can take this as a serious interference as opposed to a minor one. Under the law governing conversion, the neighbor is responsible for the full value of the saw (but can keep it). In other words, the law of conversion applies the rule, familiar from retailing, that "You break it, you own it."

(A) is wrong because it incorrectly states the damages for the tort of conversion. Here, "actual damages" would or might amount to less than the full value of the homeowner's chattel, the saw (since the saw could presumably be fixed for less than the value of the saw pre-breakage). The essence of conversion is that it is a "forced sale" of the chattel to the defendant. In other words, the homeowner is entitled to the full value of the saw before it was taken, not just the actual damage amount needed to return it to the condition it was in before the neighbor took it.

(C) is wrong because it incorrectly suggests a defense to the tort of conversion. The tort of conversion is the interference with a person's possessory rights in a chattel that is so serious as to warrant that defendant pay full value for the chattel. It is not a defense that the defendant was acting for plaintiff's benefit. Had the neighbor been using the saw to, say, save the homeowner's life in an emergency, the defense of necessity might apply. But here, where the neighbor was initially acting to further his own interests, and then "helping" the homeowner in a non-emergency situation, the defense would not apply.

(D) is wrong because an intent to keep the chattel is not a necessary element in conversion. A person who makes a temporary but serious interference with another's chattel, in a way that causes substantial damage to the chattel, has committed conversion despite his intended return (or indeed his actual return) of the chattel soon after the taking. (For instance, if D takes P's car for a joy ride and seriously damages it, the fact that D promptly returns the wrecked car to P is no defense.)

[Q3003]

9. **B** The plaintiff is offering the defendant's out-of-court statement to prove that the defendant was speeding. Since the statement is being offered to prove the truth of its assertion, the statement is hearsay. However, the statement will be admissible under the admission exclusion to the hearsay rule. FRE 801(d)(2)(A) gives a hearsay exclusion for a statement that is offered against a party and is "the party's own statement[.]" Since the statement was made by the defendant, and is being offered against the defendant, it meets the requirements of the just-quoted rule.

(A) is wrong because there is no basis on which to admit a prior inconsistent statement. The basic problem with the evidence here concerns hearsay, which is an out-of-court statement offered to prove the truth of its assertion. Here, if the defendant's out-of-court statement is offered to prove that the defendant was, in fact, speeding, the statement will have to be admissible *substantively* — that is, to prove that the defendant was, in fact, speeding. The out-of-court statement won't work as a substantively-admissible prior inconsistent statement, though, because although FRE 801(d)(1)(A) does give a hearsay exclusion for a prior statement of a testifying witness where the statement is "inconsistent with the declarant's testimony," that exclusion applies only where the prior statement was "given *under oath* subject to the penalty of perjury at a *trial, hearing or other proceeding, or in a deposition.*" Since the defendant's prior statement during the officer's investigation was not made under oath or at a proceeding or deposition, it doesn't qualify. A second problem is that the defendant isn't the testifying witness.

Now, let's examine whether the statement can be used simply to *impeach* the defendant (in other words, call into question his truthfulness), rather than to prove substantively that the defendant really was speeding. Here, the plaintiff's counsel is trying to impeach the defendant by "extrinsic" evidence (i.e., evidence that doesn't come from the mouth of the impeached witness). But FRE 613(b) says that "Extrinsic evidence of a prior inconsistent statement by a witness is not admissible unless the witness is afforded an opportunity to explain or deny the same[.]" Since the plaintiff's counsel already had the defendant on cross and dismissed him without asking him about the prior statement, counsel has failed to comply with this rule, so the statement can't be used for impeachment except under the admission theory discussed in Choice (B).

(C) is wrong because the absence of a foundation doesn't matter here. That's because the statement is admissible as an admission by a party opponent under FRE 801(d)(2)(A), and admissions do not need any foundation to qualify under that Rule.

(D) is wrong because it fails to realize that the testimony will be admissible as an admission, for the reasons discussed in Choice (B) above.

[Q4015]

10. **B** This is the standard of relevance applied by the judge in determining admissibility under FRE 401. Under that rule, evidence is relevant if it has "any tendency to make the existence of any fact that is of consequence to the determination of the action more probable or less probable than it would be without the evidence."

(A) is wrong because the test for admissibility is whether the judge believes that the evidence is probative, not whether a reasonable jury could believe it to be so. This is established by FRE 104(a).

(C) is wrong because the judge determines admissibility and the jury determines sufficiency. It would be impossible for a party to build a case if every piece of evidence had to be sufficient to prove the point in dispute.

(D) is wrong because the preponderance standard is applied by the jury to all of the evidence admitted. It is not applied by the court to determine whether a particular piece of evidence can be considered by the jury on the ultimate question. Thus, this answer confuses the standard of proof used by the jury with the standard of admissibility used by the judge.

[Q7078]

11. **A** This is basically a problem involving "concurrence" — the examiners are thinking (maybe hoping) you'll reason, "The requisite intent no longer existed at the time of the explosion, therefore the requirement of concurrence between act and mental state has not been satisfied." It's true that "concurrence" is required. But in the case of a crime defined in terms of a particular result (like murder), the requisite concurrence is between *mental state and act, not* between *mental state and result*. In other words, at the moment D does the act that brings about the result, D must be actuated by the appropriate intent; it doesn't matter whether D still has that intent when the result finally occurs. Here, the "act" was the setting of the bomb. When the defendant planted the bomb, he was actuated by an intent to kill the CEO. The fact that before the bomb went off (producing death as a result) he had changed his mind is irrelevant.

There's a further element to worry about: the fact that an unintended victim (the vice president), not the intended victim (the CEO), was killed. But this makes no difference either, under the familiar doctrine of transferred intent, by which, if the type of harm intended is the type that results, the fact that a different victim ended up suffering that harm is irrelevant. Lastly, the fact that the security guard had the opportunity to avoid the harm but failed to do so is irrelevant — the defendant intended to bring about a death by bomb, and his act was the but-for cause of that death by bomb, so the fact that some other actor failed in a chance to avoid the harm makes no difference. And that's true even if the failure by the other person amounted to negligence.

(B) is wrong because under the analysis in Choice (A), two things prevent this choice from being correct: (1) the defendant's intent is measured as of the moment he planted the bomb (and the fact that by the time of death he no longer intended to kill anyone is irrelevant); and (2) the defendant's intent to kill the CEO is deemed "transferred" to the vice president.

(C) is wrong because, under the analysis in Choice (A), two things prevent this choice from being correct: (1) the defendant's intent is measured as of the moment he planted the bomb (and the fact that by the time of death he no longer intended to kill anyone is irrelevant); and (2) the fact that the security officer had a good opportunity to avoid the harm does not prevent the defendant's act from being the legal cause of the harm.

(D) is wrong because the defendant is guilty of murder, not just attempted murder. Under the analysis in Choice (A), the fact that the security officer had a good opportunity to avoid the harm does not prevent the defendant's act from being the legal cause of the harm. And that's true even if the security guard's failure amounted to negligence. The defendant's act of planting the bomb was clearly a "but-for" cause of the death, and was so closely connected with the death that it was certainly a "legal" or "proximate" cause of that death. (The fact that the guard's negligence may have *also* been a proximate cause [and a but-for cause] won't save the defendant from guilt for the death.) Since the defendant caused the death by an act that was intended to cause the death, he's guilty of murder, not just attempted murder.

[Q3133]

12. **C** The Full Faith & Credit (FF&C) clause prohibits state courts from re-litigating cases in which the courts of another state have rendered final judgment. Even if the first court should have applied the second court's laws under standard conflict rules, the FF&C clause bars the second court from re-hearing the case. (If the State B courts had not had jurisdiction over the man, and the jurisdiction issue had not been litigated or waived, the FF&C clause might not bar the State A courts from hearing the new suit. But the facts tell us that the man "defended" on the merits, thus waiving any claim he might have had that the State B courts lacked jurisdiction over him.) Accordingly, the court in State A was required to dismiss the suit.

(A) is incorrect, because the FF&C clause prevents the court in State A from relitigating the merits, and the fact that the woman drove the car to State A has no effect on the constitutional analysis.

(B) is, similarly, wrong because the location of the car has no effect on the constitutional analysis.

(D) is wrong because the movement of the car across state lines did not create a federal question.

[Q7051]

13. **C** The covenant of warranty requires defense only against suits that turn out to be meritorious. The covenant of warranty includes a promise by the covenantor to defend on behalf of the covenantee any lawful or reasonable claims of title by a third party. So if the grantee had lost the suit, she could have recovered her legal costs (and the value of the property) from the grantor. But ironically, by winning against the neighbor, the grantee lost her right to recover from the grantor. When the grantee won versus the neighbor, she established that the neighbor's claim was without merit. At that point, the grantor had no obligation to reimburse her for defending this now-known-to-be-valueless claim.

(A), (B), and (D) are wrong because each is, in some way, inconsistent with the above analysis. ((D) is also incorrect as a matter of law, because the neighbor cannot elect to sue either the grantor or the grantee — the grantee presently claims to have title to the property, so she, not the grantor, is the proper target for the neighbor's suit.)

[Q3159]

14. **D** The mother's will had the effect of giving the property to the son and the daughter as tenants in common, with a undivided one-half interest going to each. (A conveyance "to *A* and *B*," without further specification, creates a tenancy in common with equal shares.) At the time the creditor got his money judgment against the son, that judgment became a lien only against real property owned by the son, and the son's real property consisted of his undivided one-half interest. When the partition by judicial sale occurred, the son's interest in the property became sole ownership of one-half of the proceeds, and the creditor's lien became a lien solely on that share of the proceeds.

Choices (A), (B), and (C) are wrong because they are inconsistent with the above analysis.

[Q1066]

15. **C** Unless the sale contract specifies otherwise, the seller's title is not required to be marketable until the date set for the closing. The fact that there is an outstanding mortgage on the property, therefore, does not entitle the buyer to cancel the contract, as long as the seller has the right and probable ability to pay off the mortgage at the closing.

(A) is wrong because the fact that the mortgage was granted for pre-existing obligations (as opposed, say, to being a purchase money mortgage) is irrelevant to the issue of whether the seller's title is marketable. For instance, if the seller were not paying off the mortgage at the closing, the mortgage would indeed be an encumbrance rendering title unmarketable, even though it was granted to secure the seller's pre-existing obligation to the mortgagee.

(B) is wrong because the doctrine of equitable conversion is used to pass the risk of loss to the buyer under a purchase contract, and has nothing to do with whether the seller's title is marketable.

(D) is wrong because a purchaser's "real reason" (i.e., motive) for refusing to close is irrelevant to whether the purchaser has the right to so refuse. For example, if the seller's title had been unmarketable, the buyer would have been entitled to refuse to close even though her real reason for refusing was something entirely unrelated to the quality of the seller's title.

[Q2081]

16. **A** A landowner who causes a substantial, unreasonable interference with a neighbor's use or enjoyment of his property without a valid defense is liable for private nuisance. Most courts apply this rule in the case of watercourses, holding that an upstream owner may not completely block the flow of water if this would unreasonably interfere with a downstream owner's use and enjoyment of the latter's property.

(B) is wrong because the neighbor's desire to affect the vacationer's property is not an element of the tort of private nuisance. As described in the treatment of Choice (A) above, private nuisance is the unreasonable interference with another's use and enjoyment of the latter's property. Choice (B) is wrong mostly because it fails to factor in whether there has been an unreasonable interference with the vacationer's use and enjoyment of his property. For instance, if the damming was the only way to avoid flooding of the neighbor's property, and the harm it posed to the vacationer's use and enjoyment was very small, a court would conclude that the damning was not "unreasonable," and the vacationer would lose, even though the neighbor "intended" (in the sense of knowing with substantial certainty) that the vacationer's property would be "affected" (in the sense that water would no longer flow through it).

(C) is wrong because the tort nuisance covers use and *enjoyment*, not just use. A landowner who causes a substantial, unreasonable interference with a neighbor's use or enjoyment of his property without a valid defense is liable for private nuisance. The fact that the vacationer never goes "close" to the stream is not inconsistent with her having sustained an unreasonable interference with her "use and *enjoyment*" of her property. For instance, it's very possible that the vacationer used to like to view, from an upstairs window, the stream running through her property, and that she now has much less pleasure from the waterless view. Consequently, her "use and enjoyment" have been substantially impaired, even though in a narrow sense she never "made use" of the stream.

(D) is wrong because compliance with this type of statute would not preclude liability for nuisance. A landowner who causes a substantial, unreasonable interference with a neighbor's use or enjoyment of his property without a valid defense is liable for private nuisance. Many nuisances are not in violation of any particular law, since "positive law" (statutes, ordinances, and the like) do not purport to be the sole source of legal obligations. (For instance, a factory might get all required local permits, but might still be a private nuisance because it's unreasonably loud and noisy). Therefore, the fact that the dam satisfied the relevant affirmative laws when it was built does not foreclose the possibility of a successful nuisance suit.

[Q3041]

17. **C** If the driver was negligent, then a suit based on ordinary negligence could succeed, since the driver's negligence would have placed the owner and the owner's child in the zone of danger, and then caused emotional distress. So if the driver was negligent, the owner would prevail, making this aspect of Choice (C) correct. If the driver was not negligent, the owner's suit could of course not successfully be based on negligence. In that event, the suit would have to be based on trespass. However, trespass requires an intentional entry onto the plaintiff's property. Here, where the driver came onto the owner's property only as the result of a skid, the required "intentional entry" would not be found. (By the way, even if the driver intentionally chose to enter onto the owner's property to avoid hitting the child, the doctrine of private necessity would supply a defense to trespass.)

(A) is wrong because the fact that the entry was unauthorized does not settle the issue of whether the driver is liable. As further explained in the analysis of Choice (C) above, the driver could be liable only if negligent. The fact that the entry was "unauthorized" doesn't prove that driver was negligent. For instance, if the driver's behavior leading up to the moment he hit the brakes was non-negligent (e.g., he wasn't speeding, and was paying proper attention), the fact that the entry was not authorized by the owner would be irrelevant, and indeed the driver would not be liable in that scenario.

(B) is wrong because the presence of serious emotional distress is irrelevant if the driver violated no duty. The mere fact that the plaintiff suffered serious emotional distress does not make the defendant liable — the defendant must have violated some independent duty to the plaintiff. So the owner would have to establish either that: (1) the driver committed the tort of negligence (in which case severe emotional distress in the absence of physical injury would not be a barrier to recovery, given that the owner was in the "zone of danger"); or (2) the driver committed trespass. Since, as detailed in the treatment of Choice (C), neither of these torts is necessarily established by the facts, Choice (B)'s focus on the distress cannot be a complete answer to why or whether the owner would win.

(D) is wrong because the child's exercise of reasonable care is irrelevant to the outcome. First, let's assume the owner's suit is brought in negligence. If so, the fact that the child was or wasn't careful is irrelevant. If the child *was* careful, the driver still may or may not have behaved with reasonable care. If the child *wasn't* careful, the same is true — the driver might have been, or might have not been, careful. If the driver wasn't careful, the child's negligence would not prevent the driver's conduct from giving rise to liability — one of the common ways for a driver to be negligent is to fail to be attentive to other people's, especially children's, negligence. (Nor would the child's lack of care be imputed to the owner.) Now, let's assume that the owner's suit is brought in trespass.

Again, the fact that the child was or wasn't careful would be irrelevant. Either way, the driver's conduct was not an intentional and unprivileged entry onto the owner's premises (as described in Choice (C)). So Choice (D)'s focus on the carefulness of the child is completely irrelevant no matter what the legal theory of the owner's suit.

[Q3149]

18. **C** First, we need to consider whether the officer's initial entry into the apartment was a violation of the son's Fourth Amendment rights. An examination of a defendant's effects is a search if it is conducted under circumstances which violate the defendant's reasonable expectation of privacy. Ordinarily, a person has a reasonable expectation that an apartment which s/he has the exclusive right to occupy will remain private. And that's true even if the invasion of privacy is done by, or authorized by, the person's mother — the landlord may have lived in the building, and may have owned the unit, but her son was the exclusive occupant of the second-floor apartment. Therefore, the landlord did not have either apparent or actual authority to consent to a police search of that unit. Since the officer was a police officer, his entry into the space would probably be deemed to be governmental action, even though he was arguably on "private time" when he entered (since he acted as a police employee in noticing the stolen goods and seeking the warrant).

Given that the officer was conducting an illegal search of the son's apartment in the first instance, his reliance on illegally-obtained knowledge as the basis for receiving the warrant would taint the warrant — that is, the warrant would be viewed as poisonous fruit of the poisonous tree (the illegal entry). Since the warrant was invalid, any evidence obtained as a result of the execution of the warrant would also be excludable as poisonous fruit.

(A) is factually and legally wrong: since the warrant was obtained as a result of improperly-obtained initial information, the search done pursuant to that warrant was not legal as this choice asserts, and the fruits of that search must be excluded.

(B) is wrong as a matter of law: where the police officer who makes the discovery is in a position to make that discovery as the result of illegal conduct (here, the officer's initial entry into the apartment), the officer is indeed required to ignore the discovery, rather than using it as the basis for obtaining a warrant.

(D) is wrong because, although possession of stolen items is not by itself sufficient to permit the conclusion that the possessor was the thief, the evidence of that possession is certainly admissible as circumstantial evidence to be considered by the jury (assuming that the method of obtaining the evidence is not itself objectionable, as it is here).

[Q5080]

19. **C** This is a multiple-level hearsay problem: the hospital record is an out-of-court statement (the "outer" level), and it contains another out-of-court statement, namely, the plaintiff's statement that she fell when the ladder collapsed (the "inner" level). Since the inner level is being offered for the truth of the matter asserted therein (that the plaintiff fell when the ladder collapsed), both levels must meet some exclusion to the hearsay rule. (See FRE 805, saying that "hearsay included within hearsay is not excluded ... if *each part* of the combined statements conforms with an exception to the hearsay rule[.]") Fortunately for the plaintiff, FRE 803(4) and (6), taken together, permit the introduction of both levels. First, FRE 803(6) grants an exception for a "record ... of conditions ... made at or near the time ... from information transmitted by, a person with knowledge, if kept in the course of a regularly conducted business activity, and if it was the regular practice of that business activity to make the ... record[.]" Here, the various facets of this rule are satisfied since: (a) the hospital regularly made such patient-intake records; (b) the record here was made at or near the time of the patient's fall; (c) the information was "transmitted by a person with knowledge" (the plaintiff); and (d) the particular record was "kept in the course of a regularly conducted business activity" (the running of the hospital).

Next, 803(4) gives a hearsay exception for the plaintiff's own statement, since that statement was "made for the purposes of medical diagnosis or treatment and describing medical history, or past or present symptoms . . . or the inception or general character of the cause or external source thereof insofar as reasonably pertinent to diagnosis or treatment." That is, the plaintiff was trying to get treatment, and was describing her present symptoms, as well as the "cause or external source" of those symptoms (the falling ladder). So each level of the hospital record is supported by its own hearsay exception.

(A) is wrong because there is no need to exclude the portion about the ladder, due to the availability of the two hearsay exceptions discussed above.

(B) is wrong because the sentence is admissible under the two hearsay exceptions discussed in (C). It's true that 803(4)'s exception for "statements [made] for purposes of medical diagnosis or treatment" requires that the statement be "reasonably pertinent to diagnosis or treatment." But a terse statement about how an injury was caused — especially if not accompanied by any statements about fault — will generally satisfy the "reasonably pertinent" requirement, and the "ladder collapsed" statement here pretty clearly meets that requirement.

(D) is wrong because the statements in the record were not statements of opinion (and, indeed were not statements by the hospital personnel), so the fact that they were not made by experts in accident causation is irrelevant.

[Q5081]

20. **D** The man did not have the intent to sell cocaine, while the woman did. The prosecution of the woman poses the classic question of whether "factual impossibility" can be a defense. Factual impossibility is not a defense. That is, impossibility is no defense to an attempt prosecution in those cases where, had the facts been as D believed them to be, D would have had the mental state required for the substantive crime. Here, had the facts been as the woman believed (that the vials contained cocaine), the woman would have had the mental state required for the sale of cocaine. Therefore, she had the mental state for attempt. And, since she carried out the physical act of selling the substance, she meets the *actus reus* requirement for attempted drug sale as well.

On the other hand, the man does not have the mental state required for attempted sale of cocaine. The *mens rea* for an attempt to commit substantive crime X is the desire to commit acts which, if they were committed, would constitute the commission of crime X. Therefore, the *mens rea* for an attempt to sell drugs is the intent to sell drugs. Since the man didn't intend to sell drugs, he can't be liable for attempted sale of drugs.

(A), (B), and (C) are wrong because each is inconsistent with the analysis in (D) above.

[Q3002]

21. **A** The investor is strictly liable if the businessman's building did not contribute to the subsidence, but not liable otherwise. Every landowner is entitled to have his land receive the necessary physical support from adjacent and underlying soil. This right to lateral support is absolute — that is, once support has been withdrawn and injury occurs, the responsible person is liable even if he used utmost care (as the facts tell us the investor used). However, the absolute right to later support exists *only with respect to land in its natural state* — if D's excavation causes a cave-in on an adjacent parcel owned by P, P cannot win if the subsidence would not have occurred but for the weight of a structure on P's land. Choice (A) accurately states this rule.

(B) is wrong, because the businessman's right to lateral support was a basic right incident to his ownership of his own land, and did not need to be gained by adverse possession or prescription.

(C) is wrong, because an owner's inherent right to lateral support applies whether the land is "urban" or "rural."

(D) is wrong, because the investor's following the laws as to construction and use would not give her an excuse or a defense to her strict duty to provide lateral support.

[Q3087]

22. **B** Under the UCC, unless the contract provides otherwise, "payment is due at the time and place at which the buyer is to receive the goods." UCC §2-310(a). In other words, since the contract did not specify the time for payment, the UCC "gap filler" makes this a cash sale, with payment due when the goods are delivered. Furthermore, under §2-308(a), the place for delivery is "the seller's place of business..." So if the developer doesn't tender cash on March 1 at the retailer's place of business, the retailer has no duty to deliver the goods. (Nor is the developer entitled to wait until all 50 had been delivered — see the discussion of Choice (D) below).

(A) is wrong because delivery would not be to the developer's place of business. As noted above, under §2-308(a), unless the contract provided otherwise (which it didn't), the place for delivery was "the seller's place of business," not the buyer's.

(C) is wrong because payment was due concurrently with the retailer's delivery. As noted above, under UCC §2-310(a), unless otherwise agreed, "payment is *due at the time* and place at which the *buyer is to receive the goods*[.]" So the developer was required to pay C.O.D., and was not entitled to wait for a "reasonable time after ... delivery" as this choice recites.

(D) is wrong because it mistakes how deliveries in multiple lots work under the UCC. Under §2-307, unless otherwise agreed, "where the circumstances give either party the right to make or demand delivery in lots the price if it can be apportioned may be *demanded for each lot.*" Since the agreement here contemplates that delivery would occur separately for each of the two lots, and since the price can easily be apportioned (because the sets are usable independently of each other), the quoted provision applies. Therefore, the retailer was entitled to demand that payment for the first 25 sets be made at the time these sets were delivered.

[Q3103]

23. **B** The bank was the first grantee of both the note and the mortgage, so the bank is the owner unless the recording act somehow gave the investor superior title. When the bank promptly recorded the assignment to it of the note and mortgage, the bank complied with all requirements of the recording act. Therefore, no later assignment by the mortgage company to the investor (or anyone else) could take priority, under the recording act, over the assignment to the bank. The fact that the investor paid value for his assignment, and without actual notice of the prior assignment to the bank, doesn't change any of this — the investor is deemed to be on notice of what a proper record search would have indicated, and here a search on the mortgage company in the records would have disclosed the prior assignment to the bank. Similarly, the fact that the mortgage company kept possession of the note and mortgage after assigning these to the bank makes no difference; the investor as second grantee cannot take priority over a prior conveyance that was properly recorded.

(A), (C), and (D) are wrong because they are inconsistent with the above analysis.

[Q1123]

24. **C** Although the general rule is that a modification solely benefiting one party is unenforceable due to lack of consideration, there is a very important exception: if the modification is "*fair and equitable* in view of *circumstances not anticipated by the parties* when the contract was made," the modification will be binding without consideration. That is the case here: the large amount of rock was a "circumstance not anticipated by the parties when the contract was made," and the $20,000 seems to have been a fair estimate of the increased cost to the contractor in performing. Therefore, the fact that the contractor gave no consideration for the owner's promise to pay the extra $20,000 (the contractor merely promised to do what he was already obligated to do, i.e., build the warehouse and driveway) is irrelevant.

(A) is wrong because, although it is true that there was no consideration for the owner's promise to pay the additional $20,000, the absence of consideration does not matter for the reason explained in the discussion of choice (C).

(B) is wrong because the contractor's request for the extra $20,000 would not be deemed by a court to have been constituted duress. If no rock had been discovered, and the contractor had demanded the extra $20,000 merely because he knew that the owner was time-sensitive and vulnerable, this choice would probably be correct in result and reasoning. But because the facts make it clear that the $20,000 *was* merely an adjustment on account of the unanticipated cost of the excavating the rock, no duress will be found.

(D) is wrong because it gives the wrong explanation for the correct result. Even if the reasonable value of the contractor's total performance was $520,000 or greater, the contractor would not receive the extra $20,000 if the increase was due to the owner's desperation to have the project completed on time rather than due to an unanticipated circumstance (the rock) — in that case the requirement of consideration would render the modification unenforceable regardless of the "value" of the total performance.

[Q2004]

25. **C** There are certain kinds of duties that are non-delegable. In general a duty or performance is delegable unless the obligee has a substantial interest in having the delegator perform. Rest. of Contracts 2d §318(2). Contracts which call for the promisor's use of his own particular skills are normally not delegable. *Id.*, Comment c. Thus contracts involving artistic performances or professional services are generally not delegable. Here, the chef hired the decorator because of his own particular, personal decorating skills. Therefore, the rule that duties involving performance by a specified skilled person are not delegable applies. Thus, when the decorator sold his decorating business to the buyer, the chef was not obligated to permit the buyer to perform the chef-decorator contract, even though the buyer was also an experienced decorator of excellent repute.

(A) is wrong, because the contract was not delegable (for the reasons described above) whether the agreement contained a prohibition on delegation or not.

(B) is wrong because a contract involving the use of particular skills or artistic performances, such as the one here, is non-delegable even if the obligee receives assurances that the proposed delegate (here, the buyer) is able to complete the job, and no matter how superior the delegate's skills are.

(D) is wrong because the chef's participation would have been needed to effect a novation. If the obligee under the original contract (the person to whom the duty was owed) agrees to relieve the obligor of all liability after the delegation, a novation is said to have occurred. The effect of a novation is to substitute for the original obligor a stranger to the original contract. Here, the decorator's purported delegation to the buyer of his obligations did not effect a novation — for a novation to occur, the chef, the person to whom the decorator's duty of design was owed, would have had to agree to relieve the obligor, the decorator, of all liability.

[Q3072]

26. **D** The general rule about personal liability for mortgage payments as between present and future interests is that neither party has personal liability, except to the extent that party is receiving net operating income from the property. Since the son as remainderman gets no operating income from the property, he has no personal liability to make any mortgage payments. However, if neither he nor anyone else makes all required mortgage payments, the property will presumably be lost to foreclosure, in which case the son's remainder interest will be lost. Therefore, the son has the right (which he may well want to exercise), but not the obligation, to contribute his one-third share of whatever mortgage payments that the widow is unable or unwilling to make.

(A) is wrong because the holder of a future interest generally does not have the right to bring a partition action to compel the sale of the possessory estate (here, the widow's life estate).

(B) is wrong because it overstates the widow's obligation; the widow probably does have a personal obligation to pay her fairly-allocated share of the mortgage payments (based on the relative value of the widow's life estate versus the remainder), up to the amount of net income she's receiving, but this choice incorrectly suggests that she would be personally liable to pay the *entire* installments rather than just her share if the net income were large enough.

(C) is wrong because the son, as a remainderman, has no personal liability to make mortgage payments at all (since he is not getting any operating income out of which to pay them).

[Q1107]

27. **B** The action here would have to be brought in negligence (not, for instance, in strict liability, since there's no indication that the banana was defective). The only way the grocer could be found negligent is if it knew or should have known that the peel was on the ground, and had time to remove it before the customer passed by. There *are* slip-and-fall scenarios in which the mere fact that the accident happened is enough to trigger *res ipsa loquitur*. For instance, if the customer slips on an old and discolored peel, that might make for a case of res ipsa, since there is no way such a peel could be found on a grocer's floor without it having been present long enough for the grocer to have had a duty to remove it. But the condition of the peel here does not indicate that it has been on the ground for any significant period of time. Therefore, there is not enough evidence — either direct evidence or via the operation of *res ipsa* — to support a jury verdict that the store staff was negligent in failing to remove it before the customer's fall.

(A) is wrong because, while this answer correctly states that the judge should not let the case go to the jury, it misstates the legal basis for this conclusion. In slip-and-fall cases, even if a customer was negligent, he could recover some of his damages under a system of pure comparative negligence if a jury determined that the grocer was also negligent. So although it is true that the customer had an obligation to watch where he stepped, his failure to fulfill that obligation would not prevent the case from going to the jury.

(C) is wrong because it cites a mostly irrelevant fact. Strict products liability is not applicable here because the banana was not defective. So the suit would have to be based on negligence. While it's true that the plaintiff would have to show, by a preponderance of the evidence, that the peel came from a banana offered for sale by the grocer, such a showing would not be enough to entitle the plaintiff to get to the jury. Instead, the plaintiff would also have to show that it was more likely than not that the grocer behaved negligently by not removing the peel, and that's the piece that's missing on these facts.

(D) is wrong because foreseeability alone is not sufficient to establish that the grocer was negligent. The plaintiff must also offer evidence that the grocer fell below the standard of care, i.e., that he failed to adopt the precautions that a reasonably prudent person in his situation would adopt to avoid the foreseeable risk. There is no such evidence here, as explained in the discussion of Choice (B).

[Q7083]

28. **C** Although the state does some regulation of the insurance industry (for solvency), the state is not sufficiently involved with the operations of the insurance company here to satisfy the requirement — applicable to any equal protection claim — that there be "state action." Notice that the choice never uses the phrase "state action" — it's up to you to spot the state action issue and to notice that this choice's use of the phrase "not applicable to the actions of these ... companies" captures the state-action concept.

(A) is wrong for several reasons, including most basically the fact that it ignores the state-action requirement for any equal protection claim. (The fact that the *state police* are arguably failing to give equal protection is irrelevant, since the police aren't a party and aren't tightly associated with a party.)

(B) and (D) are wrong, similarly, because they too ignore the state-action requirement for equal protection claims. (If the state-action requirement were satisfied — if, for instance, the state expressly required burglary-insurance rates to be adjusted based on local crime rates — then (D) would be the best answer because it correctly expresses the idea that a governmental classification that does not involve a suspect class or fundamental right needs to be supported only by a rational basis.)

[Q1114]

29. **C** The doctrine of commercial impracticability can cover situations in which a pre-existing fact of which the parties were unaware at the time of contracting becomes known later, and renders performance impracticable. However, the impracticability defense will not apply where the party asserting it is found to have expressly or impliedly borne the risk of the event in question. Here, two facts strongly militate against the builder's being excused under the doctrine: (1) in any substantial excavation project, there is a very foreseeable risk of finding unexpectedly large rock deposits, and the more foreseeable the risk, the less likely it is to be excusable under the impracticability doctrine; and (2) the builder as a professional builder has more experience with the business risks involved in excavation than does a typical owner, so it makes economic sense to put the risk of an excavation-related surprise (or the burden of negotiating a clause dealing specifically with that risk) on the builder rather than on the owner.

(A) is wrong because, as described in the analysis of Choice (C), the doctrine of impracticability does not apply where the party seeking to use the doctrine is found to have impliedly borne the risk of the event in question, as the builder would be found to have done here.

(B) is wrong because, while mutual mistake might apply here just as impracticability might apply, the doctrine of mutual mistake will not apply where the party seeking to assert it would be found to have borne the risk of that type of mistake, and the builder would be found to have borne that risk here.

(D) is wrong because the builder would be found to have borne the risk of subsurface granite even if such granite was previously unknown in the vicinity of the construction site — as further explained in the analysis of Choice (C) above, a builder will normally be found to have borne the risk of unfavorable sub-surface conditions.

[Q1172]

30. **A** There are two issues here: (1) Was the stop of the car constitutional? and (2) If the answer to (1) is yes, was the search of the car a permissible adjunct to that arrest? As to (1), under the "good faith reliance" exception to the exclusionary rule, evidence that derives from an initial arrest, stop or search generally will not be suppressed where police reasonably held a good-faith but erroneous belief that the arrest, stop or search was authorized by a valid warrant. So, for instance, in facts much like these, the Supreme Court held in *Arizona v. Evans* (1995) that a good-faith-reliance exception to exclusionary rule applied where an arrest and resulting incidental search were based on an outstanding arrest warrant that should have been removed from the computer but still showed up as the result of a court employee's clerical error. In this case, the computer check on the license number of the driver's car revealed that there was an outstanding warrant for the driver's arrest based on unpaid parking tickets; the police had no reason to believe that the warrant was invalid, so the stop of the car and the arrest of the driver were justified on the good-faith-reliance exception of *Evans*.

As to (2), once the stop of the car and the arrest of the driver were established to be valid because of the police's good-faith reliance on the warrant, long-established law says that the police may, incident to the arrest, make a search of the car's entire passenger compartment, and the contents of any containers found in that compartment. *N.Y. v. Belton* (1981). So the police's search of the passenger compartment incident to the arrest, and their consequent discovery of the glassine bags, was valid.

(B) is wrong because, while this answer correctly states that the motion to suppress should not be granted, it misstates the legal basis for that conclusion. Absent a custodial arrest or probable cause, a traffic stop does not authorize a full-blown search of the passenger compartment. See *Knowles v. Iowa* (1998).

(C) is wrong because, as is further described in connection with Choice (A) above, when the police make an arrest in reasonable reliance on erroneous information that an arrest warrant is outstanding, they may make a search incident to that arrest, the fruits of which will not be inadmissible on account of the exclusionary rule. So while it is technically true that "no lawful arrest" could be made on the basis of the warrant here, it does not follow that the evidence from the search was inadmissible.

(D) is wrong because neither probable cause nor reasonable suspicion was required, since the search was incident to an arrest. It is true that the arrest warrant turned out to be invalid, but evidence generally will not be suppressed where, as in this case, police reasonably held a good-faith belief that their actions leading to its discovery were authorized by a valid warrant. See the more extensive discussion of this issue in Choice (A) above.

[Q7042]

31. **B** The driller's "proposal" was not an offer, because it could not be accepted by the unilateral act of the recipient (since by its terms it could not become a contract until it was not only signed by the developer, the recipient, but also signed by the driller). When the developer signed the form and and returned it to the driller, the developer was making an offer on the terms described in the form. The driller could have accepted the offer by signing, but didn't in fact sign. However, when the driller started work, his conduct of doing the work described in the form, at the appropriate place, constituted an acceptance by conduct. This acceptance-by-conduct included a promise (albeit an implied one) to complete the work as described in the offer document (the form that the driller didn't sign).

(A) is wrong because, although it lists the correct result, it explains it on an incorrect legal theory. The driller's form could not be an offer, because the provision requiring both signatures meant that the unsigned form as dispatched by the driller did not empower the recipient (the developer) to unilaterally complete the deal (i.e., accept) by signing. Therefore, the developer's signature created an offer, not an acceptance. (And acceptance did not occur until the driller accepted by conduct.)

(C) is wrong because, although the driller never accepted by signature, he did accept by his conduct of starting the well drilling.

(D) is wrong because it misstates the effect of the driller's commencement of performance. That commencement of performance served as an acceptance of the contract, and thereby obligated the driller to complete his side of the deal.

[Q1041]

32. **B** This is a classic case of protectionism: the in-state retailers have persuaded the legislature to strengthen the in-staters' economic position vis-a-vis out-of-state retailers (since small in-state retailers now get an advantage that small out-of-state retailers don't get, and get an unearned cost-equality with large out-of-state retailers). So out-of-state retailers are being discriminated against (treated less favorably by virtue of their out-of-state status). This sort of protectionism is virtually a per se violation of the dormant commerce clause, and is certainly an undue burden on commerce.

(A) is wrong because economic regulation that does not involve a suspect class or fundamental right (and the regulation here involves neither) will receive only mere-rationality review under the due process clause, and the measure here would pass that review.

(C) is wrong because the privileges and immunities of "national" (as opposed to state) citizenship are guaranteed by the Fourteenth Amendment, Sec. 1; that P&I clause would not protect the plaintiffs because only a few rights have been recognized as rights of national citizenship for purposes of the clause (e.g., the right to travel physically from state to state, to move from state to state, and to vote in national elections), and the right of an out-of-stater to be free of economic discrimination is not one of them. (The plaintiffs might win with an argument based on Art. *IV*'s P&I clause, which protects against discrimination by a state against out-of-staters; however, that clause doesn't protect the rights of "national citizenship," but rather, the rights of state citizenship.)

(D) is wrong because economic regulations that do not involve a suspect or semi-suspect class or fundamental right receive only easy-to-satisfy mere-rationality review under the equal protection clause, and the statute here would pass that review (since the legislature could reasonably have believed that its citizens would fare better, overall, if small local retailers were not at a disadvantage to large out-of-state retailers.)

[Q1190]

33. **D** Intentional force that exceeded the player's consent would be an offensive contact constituting a battery. An action for battery has three elements: (1) defendant's act bringing about a harmful or offensive contact with plaintiff's person; (2) defendant's intent to bring about such contact or to create the apprehension of immediate contact; and (3) causation. For the plaintiff to prevail in an action for battery he'd have to prove an offensive contact. Roughness up to the level to which the players as a group impliedly consented would not be deemed harmful or offensive. But consent would not be a defense if the defendant intentionally used more than the consented-to level of force.

(A) is wrong because what is at issue is not the fact of intentional contact, but the level of contact consented to by the players in the game. Apparent consent is that which a reasonable person would infer from plaintiff's conduct. Thus, for example, somebody who voluntarily engages in a body contact sport impliedly consents to the normal contacts inherent in playing it. If the defendant intended to strike the plaintiff, but in a way that was consistent with the play of the game, then the plaintiff's consent would be found to be implied by his participation in the game and his use of the same tactics.

(B) is wrong because it ignores the significance of the plaintiff's consent. What would otherwise be a harmful or offensive contact will not be actionable if it was consented to. Because the plaintiff's participation in the rough game, and his use of the same tactics, would be found to constitute implied consent to a certain level of roughness, the mere fact that the defendant intended to cause, say, an offensive contact that was consistent with the general game-play would not expose him to liability.

(C) is wrong because it ignores the possibility that the defendant may have exceeded the scope of the players' implied consent. It's true that if the defendant acted merely with the same level of roughness as previously manifested by various players in the game (including the plaintiff), the plaintiff would be deemed to have consented to it. But the defendant may have used more than the level of force to which plaintiff would be found to have consented. In that event, the implied-consent doctrine wouldn't apply, and the defendant could be liable.

[Q3017]

34. **D** FRE 412, the federal "rape shield" provision, applicable to civil and criminal cases "involving alleged sexual misconduct," puts tight limits on evidence of an alleged victim's past sexual behavior and sexual predisposition. Except for a few narrow exceptions, evidence is inadmissible if offered either to "prove that any alleged victim engaged in other sexual behavior" or to "prove any alleged victim's sexual predisposition." Both the testimony and the court record here are evidence of the alleged victim's "other sexual behavior" and/or "sexual predisposition." Therefore, they're inadmissible under FRE 412 unless they fall within one of that rule's narrow exceptions. In criminal cases, the main exceptions are for (1) conduct with the defendant offered to support a defense of consent (covered in FRE 412(b)(1)(B)), and (2) conduct with others offered to show that the

defendant was not the source of semen or the victim's injury (covered in FRE 412(b)(1)(A)). Since the defendant is relying on an alibi defense rather than on a consent defense, the first of these exceptions doesn't apply. Since the defendant is not offering the victim's history of prostitution to show that he was not the source of semen or of the victim's injuries, the second exception doesn't apply. So both pieces of evidence are excluded by FRE 412.

(A), (B) and (C) are each inconsistent with the above analysis and thus wrong.

[Q5030]

35. **B** The Supreme Court has repeatedly held that even if a city is using its zoning powers to limit or prohibit a speech-related activity, the regulation is acceptable if the city is reasonably targeting the secondary effects of that speech (e.g., crime or lower property values) rather than targeting the expressive content of that speech. See, e.g., *Erie v. Pap's A.M.* (2004) (city may completely ban "nude dancing" to combat the bad secondary effects of such). Since the government is targeting the secondary effects rather than the message, the regulation is to be evaluated based on the test for content-neutral time, place and manner regulations, which as this choice suggests makes such regulations valid as long as they are designed to serve a substantial governmental interest and do not unreasonably limit alternative avenues of expression. Since the interest in preventing blight is "substantial," and since adult uses are permitted in alternative venues (areas zoned commercial), these requirements are easily satisfied.

(A) is wrong because it falsely asserts that the city may use its zoning powers to forbid particular messages based on their content. Such a content-based regulation would have to be strictly scrutinized, and would almost certainly be struck down.

(C) is wrong because it badly misstates the law: cities may indeed use their zoning regulations to prevent operators of adult theaters and the like from choosing their location, as long as the city is acting reasonably to combat the perceived negative secondary effects of the business, rather than out of distaste for the content of the messages transmitted by the business.

(D) is wrong because it exactly misstates present law; cities may (not "may not") "zone property in a manner calculated to protect property from the likely adverse secondary effects of adult theaters and bookstores." *Erie v. Pap's, supra.*

[Q2193]

36. **B** In general, evidence of a defendant's character or disposition is inadmissible for the purpose of proving that he acted in a particular way on a particular occasion. See FRE 404(a), first sentence. But 404(b) qualifies this rule by saying that "evidence of other crimes, wrongs, or acts ... may, however, be admissible for other purposes, such as ... absence of mistake or accident[.]" Since the defendant has claimed that he was "unaware that there was cocaine hidden in [the statue's] base," the fact that he was previously convicted of (knowingly) smuggling cocaine hidden in the base of another brass statue tends to prove absence of mistake or accident, and is thus admissible.

(A) is wrong because, although FRE 406 permits evidence of habit to be used as circumstantial evidence that on a particular occasion the defendant's conduct was consistent with his habit, such habit evidence requires a showing that the actor in question *consistently* acts in a particular way, and one prior experience is not sufficient to establish a habit.

(C) is wrong because, although evidence of a defendant's previous conduct is inadmissible if offered against him for some purposes, it may be admissible if offered against him for others. (C) is therefore overinclusive — for instance, it does not correctly reflect that the defendant's previous conduct here tends to prove absence of mistake, as discussed in (B) above.

(D) is wrong because, although FRE 609(b) indeed says that evidence of a prior conviction is not usually admissible for the purpose of impeaching a witness if the conviction occurred more than ten years prior to the trial at which it is offered, the defendant's prior conviction is not being offered to impeach his credibility, but rather to establish absence of mistake.

[Q5136]

37. **C** A deed must be delivered to be valid. Delivery is a question of intent. The words of the landowner included "this is yours," showing the necessary intent to strip himself of dominion and control over the deed and to immediately transfer the title. In addition, handing the deed to the grantee raises a rebuttable presumption of delivery. Recording the deed is not required and thus the request not to record the document until later was irrelevant so long as delivery was present. Once the deed was delivered in the initial encounter, the friend's false statement that he had destroyed the deed did not reverse the deed's effect, since that lie did not meet the requirements for a valid re-conveyance. (Indeed, even if the friend had in fact destroyed the deed, this wouldn't have changed the fact that the friend was the owner, since a grantee's destruction of a deed does not constitute a conveyance back to the original grantor.)

(A) is incorrect, because the deed to the friend was delivered to him when the landowner handed over the deed; neither the death of the landowner nor the friend's subsequent recording of the deed had any effect on the deed's validity.

(B) is incorrect, because delivery occurred at the time the deed was handed to the friend with the words "this is yours," and the subsequent misrepresentation that the friend made that he had destroyed the deed has no effect on the prior valid delivery.

(D) is incorrect, because recording a document has no effect on its validity. The deed to the friend was valid because it was in the proper form and was delivered to him, and his subsequent recording of the deed had no effect on his claim of ownership (though it would provide constructive notice to other later claimants).

[Q7009]

38. **B** The city here is engaging in economic regulation, and no suspect class or fundamental right is involved. The "even plausibly justifiable" standard is a good summary of the extreme deference that courts give to government choices in the economic-regulatory area where no suspect class or fundamental right is at issue. Grandfather schemes in which people with longtime track records of pursuing an activity are treated more favorably than newcomers to that activity are a good illustration of classifications that are very likely to be upheld.

(A) is wrong because it incorrectly applies strict scrutiny; strict scrutiny would be appropriate for a regulation that intentionally disfavored a suspect class (e.g., persons of a particular race) or substantially impaired a fundamental right (e.g., the right to vote), but the classification here does not do either of these things.

(C) is wrong because the grandfather scheme here would not be found to be so "tenuous" or "underinclusive" as to fail the easy-to-satisfy rational-basis test.

(D) is wrong as a statement of law; so long as no suspect class or fundamental right is impaired, grandfather clauses are usually found valid, and are certainly not "per se violations" of equal protection.

[Q1021]

39. **A** The key point is that Congress can use its commerce powers to regulate even entirely *intrastate* transactions, on the theory that such transactions are being regulated as part of a broader regulation of interstate transactions, and excluding purely intrastate transactions from the overall scheme would be unwieldy. So, for instance, Congress here can forbid a farmer's sale, at a roadside stand adjacent to his farm, of a tomato that he had raised, where the farmer sprayed a cancer-causing substance produced inside that same state onto the tomato — even though this is an entirely intrastate transaction, it is still a "commercial" transaction, and can be regulated pursuant to Congress's broader interstate-commerce regulatory scheme.

(B) is wrong for several reasons; most importantly, the Fourteenth Amendment protects only against various conduct (e.g., denials of equal protection and due process) involving "state action," and while Congress has the power to enforce that Amendment by appropriate legislation, Congress here is not focused on attempting to prohibit any state from violating the Amendment.

(C) is wrong because there is no general congressional power to "provide for the general welfare"; there is only a power to *tax and spend* for the general welfare.

(D) is similarly incorrect because there is no general congressional power to "promote science and the useful arts"; there is only the limited power in Art. I, Sec. 8, Cl. 8 to "promote the progress of science and useful arts" by "securing for limited times to authors and inventors the exclusive right to their respective writings and discoveries" (i.e., the power to issue *patents* and *copyrights*).

[Q1026]

40. **C** The Supreme Court has held that a threat communicated with the intent to intimidate the recipient, like the communication in this case, is not protected by the free speech clause of the First Amendment. If the state had singled out only certain types of threats (e.g., ones based on race), there might be a First Amendment problem, but the statute here bans *all* threats of violence, so it is content-neutral and thus acceptable.

(A) is incorrect, because as explained above, threats of violence with intent to intimidate are not protected by the First Amendment, and that's true even if the speaker never acted (and indeed never intended to act) on the threat.

(B) is incorrect because it misstates the legal basis for the correct conclusion that the man may be punished: intimidating threats of violence may be proscribed regardless of whether the threatener was committing a trespass.

(D) is incorrect because the Supreme Court has never held that racially motivated threats can violate the Thirteenth Amendment's prohibition of involuntary servitude.

[Q7095]

41. **D** The conveyance to the son was a gift of a fee simple subject to the condition precedent that the son get a college degree prior to turning 30. Until the son got the degree, the conveyance did not create any present possessory interest in him (and the possessory interest remained in the landowner, with an executory interest in the daughter ready to spring out of the landowner if the son turned 30 without getting the degree). Therefore, the classmate continued to be a tenant of the landowner, not of the son, with the result that the son did not have the right to terminate the classmate's tenancy or oust him.

(A) is wrong because the phrase "upon the condition precedent..." in the landowner-to-son conveyance made the gift a fee simple subject to a condition precedent, not a fee simple subject to divestment. (If the gift had read, "to my son and his heirs, but if my son turns 30 without having obtained a college degree, then to my daughter," then the son *would* indeed have had a fee simple subject to divestment, and the son would have won the case, making this choice correct.)

(B) is wrong because a conveyance by the owner will not normally terminate a tenancy, even where the conveyance is a transfer of a fee simple absolute or a fee simple subject to divestment; furthermore, in this case the conveyance was of a fee simple subject to a condition precedent, so it was even further from terminating the classmate's tenancy.

(C) is wrong because the fact that the permission to occupy was both oral and rent-free establishes that it was a tenancy at will (or else a license); therefore, it could be terminated at any time by either party acting unilaterally. Consequently, although this choice correctly states the result that the classmate wins, it does not correctly state the reason this is so.

[Q1173]

42. **C** Although Congress, when it spends, must spend "for the general welfare," this test is extremely easy to satisfy — as the choice correctly states, all that is required is that the spending be "reasonably deemed to serve the general welfare," and that it not violate some specific constitutional ban (e.g., the Establishment Clause's ban on spending for the purpose of advancing religion). Since Congress could rationally have believed that rewarding the "best universities" would promote the country's general welfare, and that determining the "ten best" by this kind of vote was a rational way to go about attaining that end, the spending is constitutional.

(A) is wrong because the statute here is an acceptable exercise of legislative delegation: Congress has made it reasonably clear to the Dept. of Education what they are to do, and how they are to do it, so there is no "unconstitutional delegation" despite the fact that non-federal officials will be somehow involved in the process.

(B) is wrong, because when a governmental classification does not involve a suspect or semi-suspect class or fundamental right, equal protection requires only a rational relation between the means chosen and a legitimate governmental objective, and the means and end here meet this easy-to-satisfy standard. (To put it another way, limiting the money to the "top ten," and picking the top ten this way, are *not* "arbitrary and capricious" methods.)

(D) is wrong because the mere fact that Congress' use of its spending power is being challenged does not make the matter a nonjusticiable political question.

[Q2145]

43. **D** This is the best response, because without the showing of "rough proportionality" specified in this choice, the ordinance violates the Takings clause. *Dolan v. City of Tigard* (1994) holds that when a city conditions a building permit on some "give back" by the owner, there must be a "rough proportionality" between the burdens on the public that the building permit would bring about, and the benefits to the public from the give-back. There's nothing in the facts to suggest that the city ever made the required showing here. (Indeed, the facts tell us that city officials presented no evidence of any sort, so they certainly didn't produce evidence either about the size of the public burden from allowing the coffeehouse or the size of the corresponding benefit from the new child care facility they were requiring here.)

(A), (B), and (C) are all wrong because they misstate the burden of proof and the standard. When a city demands a "give back" in return for approving construction, the city, not the owner, bears the burden of proof as to rough proportionality (and this burden is probably somewhere between the easy-to-satisfy "rational relation" test of Choice (A) and the strict scrutiny of Choice (D)).

[Q3162]

44. **B** The company's promise was not supported by consideration, since the worker didn't confer any benefit to the company, or undergo any legal detriment, in exchange for the promise. (See Choice (A) for more details about why this is so.) However, the doctrine of promissory estoppel applies to make the company's promise enforceable even without consideration.

Rest. 2d §90(a) says that "A promise which the promisor should *reasonably expect to induce action or forbearance* on the part of the promisee or a third person and which *does induce* such action or forbearance is *binding if injustice can be avoided* only by enforcement of the promise." This section applies here. It was reasonably foreseeable to the company that when it made the "you'll get a pension if you retire" offer to the worker, he would or might rely on it by retiring, rather than staying on or taking another job. The promise then did in fact induce the foreseeable reliance: the worker relied by not only retiring but by buying the RV and not taking another position somewhere else. Furthermore, that reliance has made the worker unemployable elsewhere, so that without enforcement of the promise the worker won't have any means of support. Consequently, all the requirements of promissory estoppel are satisfied, making the promise enforceable despite the lack of consideration. Notice, by the way, that *neither the correct choice nor any other choices here mentions the doctrine of promissory estoppel.* That's typical of MBE fact patterns where the correct answer is promissory estoppel: the examiners try to allude to the doctrine without mentioning it explicitly, because they believe that mentioning it will tip you off and make the question too easy.

(A) is wrong because the fact that the Board did not bargain to have the worker retire prevented there from being consideration for the pension promise. A promise or act (here, the worker's retirement) can be consideration for a counter-promise only if the promise or act was "bargained for or given in exchange" for the counter-promise. So here, the worker's retirement would be consideration for the promise of a pension if and only if the Board bargained for that retirement, or received it in exchange for the promise. But here, there is no indication that the Board was bargaining for his retirement, or that it promised the pension in exchange for that retirement. (Apparently the company didn't care too much whether the worker stayed on the job or retired, as evidenced by the fact that the resolution said that the pension would be payable whenever the worker, at his own option, made the decision to retire.) Consequently, the worker's retirement was not consideration for the company's pension promise, making Choice (A) wrong. (In reality, the promise is enforceable even without consideration, as described in Choice (B).)

(C) is wrong because, although the promise of a pension was an otherwise-unenforceable promise to make a gift, it became enforceable under the doctrine of promissory estoppel once the worker relied on it to his detriment.

(D) is wrong because, while it's true that the company could simply have fired the worker at any time without any pension payments or other payments, once the company made its promise to pay a pension and the worker reasonably relied on it, the fact that the worker was an at-will employee ceased to matter — the doctrine of promissory estoppel made the promise binding.
[Q3169]

45. **B** An accomplice is one who, with the intent that the crime be committed, aids, counsels, or encourages the principal before or during the commission of the crime. The young man's friends should be acquitted as accomplices to manslaughter because the facts make clear they did not intend that the young man murder the woman, nor did they do anything during the young man's attack to aid, counsel or encourage him. Only after the crime was complete, when the woman fell to the ground, did they urge the young man to flee. Nor does the fact that the friends did nothing to help the woman — when assistance to her during the beating could conceivably have prevented the death — make any difference. Except in special circumstances (none of which applies here) a witness to a crime has no affirmative duty to intervene to prevent the crime or aid the victim, even if this could be easily done. Therefore, failing to render such assistance cannot give rise to criminal liability.

(A) is wrong because the young man's friends could be found guilty of being accomplices even if the young man was not convicted. An accomplice is one who, with the intent that the crime be committed, aids, counsels, or encourages the principal before or during the commission of the crime. Under the modern view of accomplice liability, the fact that the principal has not yet been convicted of the substantive crime does not bar trial and conviction of the accomplices. If the principal were actually *acquitted*, this might bar prosecution, but that's not what happened here — a mistrial would not in most jurisdictions bar the prosecution of the alleged accomplices.

(C) is wrong because urging the young man to flee was not a form of aid or counsel before or during the crime. An accomplice is one who, with the intent that the crime be committed, aids, counsels, or encourages the principal *before or during* the commission of the crime. The young man's friends should be acquitted because to be accomplices they would have to have, before or during the assault on the victim, aided, counseled or encouraged the young man in the attack, with the intent that the attack be committed. By definition, they could not be accomplices merely by urging the young man to flee after the crime was completed.

(D) is wrong because as a general matter no legal duty is imposed on any person to affirmatively act for the benefit of others. Absent one of several types of legal relationships between two parties (e.g., one put the other in peril), no legal duty is imposed on one person to affirmatively act for the benefit of the other. None of those legal relationships existed here. Therefore, the young man's friends had no duty to intervene to prevent the young man's attack. Consequently, they cannot be made criminally liable for that failure to intervene, whether on an accomplice theory or any other.

[Q3070]

46. **A** While the facts here don't state it explicitly, the child's claim had to be in strict liability, since she recovered from the toy company for the engineer's improper design. (If the child's claim had been for negligence, the toy company could only have been held liable for its *own* negligence, not the engineer's improper design.) Indemnity applies to strict products liability in such a way that subsequent suppliers (those closer to the ultimate user) can seek indemnity from those earlier in the supply chain, so that whoever was responsible for the defect is ultimately liable for it. Thus when a secondary "downstream" tortfeasor (here, the toy company) pays a judgment due to the tort of the primary "upstream" tortfeasor (here, the engineer), the secondary tortfeasor can recover indemnity — full reimbursement — from the primary tortfeasor.

(B) is wrong because it mischaracterizes the facts. Joint tortfeasors are tortfeasors who act "in concert" (with an express or implied agreement) to produce a single result. Under these facts, the engineer and the toy company didn't act in concert; it was the engineer's improper design that created the risk. As a result, they weren't joint tortfeasors. Even if they *were,* this *wouldn't* mean that the toy company would prevail against the engineer – at most, in some states he could recover from the engineer some portion of the damages as "contribution." And contribution would not match up with these facts, under which the toy company's claim is based on *indemnity,* as opposed to contribution.

(C) is wrong because its conclusion doesn't follow from its premise. When a "downstream" seller (one closer to the ultimate user) incurs strict liability for a defective product, that seller is entitled to indemnity from the upstream person who introduced the defect by, for instance, creating a defective design. (See the further discussion of the indemnity mechanism in Choice (A) above.) So this choice reaches the wrong conclusion from the correct premise: because the toy company was strictly liable (but not a primary tortfeasor), it *can* recover from the engineer.

(D) is wrong because in a strict product liability case, a downstream party does not lose its right to indemnification from an upstream party (as further described in Choice (A) above) by the mere fact that the downstream party could have discovered the defect by a reasonable inspection and did not do so. That is, the party who introduced the defect — here, the engineer — has to ultimately foot the bill, and can't escape the bill by the fact that the party seeking indemnity failed to catch the introducer's error.

[Q4052]

47. **C** The buyer's status as a bona fide purchaser (BFP) entitled her to priority over the lawyer. One who purchases from the record owner of property is eligible for the protection of the recording act, as against someone else who previously took from that same record owner and did not properly record. Here, at the time the buyer took, the lawyer was the record owner (in fee simple), and the child was a "prior transferee" from the lawyer. (That is, the lawyer created an interest in the child by the trust document, and this interest was created prior to the conveyance to the buyer). So the buyer is in a position to use the recording act to gain protection against the child as prior transferee from the same grantor (the lawyer). To get the benefit of the recording act, the buyer had to be a BFP; that is, she had to have (1) taken her position for value, and (2) been without notice (actual, constructive, or inquiry) of the prior instrument at the time she took. The buyer meets requirement (1) because the facts tell us that she "paid the fair market value"; and she meets requirement (2)

because the facts tell us that she "had no knowledge of the written agreement between the grantor and the lawyer" (and that written agreement *is* the prior grant).

Choice (A) is wrong because it ignores the effect of the recording act. It may be true as a general principle that "a successor in title to the trustee takes title subject to the grantor's trust." But this is subject to the rule that a bona fide purchaser (BFP) from the trustee will take free of the unrecorded instrument by which the BFP's grantor created the trust. (If this were not true, no one could ever safely buy property — there would always be the risk that the grantor had secretly created a trust encumbering the property.)

Choice (B) is wrong because trusts creating equitable interests *are* subject to the recording act. A beneficiary's interest in a trust is indeed, as this choice suggests, an equitable interest. (The trustee has legal title.) But this choice is false in stating that equitable interests are not subject to recording acts. Because the instrument creating the trust was never recorded, the trust was not in the chain of title and the buyer did not have inquiry notice of the trust (letting her take the property as a BFP). The fact that the trust was not "authenticated to be eligible for recordation" (i.e., not witnessed or notarized) doesn't help the child as grantee — it was up to him to make sure that the document was authenticated and then to record it, if he wanted not to take the risk of being undone by a later transfer by his grantor.

Choice (D) is wrong because a trust *was* created. It's true that the lawyer may initially have had a fee simple. But once he signed the written trust document with the grantor, he was in effect creating a new interest in the property, a trust for the benefit of the child. The fact that the grantor had no title at the time this trust was executed is irrelevant (the lawyer could simply have decided on his own to create a trust for the child).

[Q3005]

48. **B** Where the language of the recording act is ambiguous about whether judgment creditors are covered (e.g., where, as here, "purchasers for value" are what are covered), most courts have interpreted the statute so as not to cover the judgment creditor. There is no guarantee that a court would interpret the statute in this anti-creditor way, but that's at least a possibility, and of the four choices this is the most likely explanation for an anti-creditor result. (Remember, you're not asked to say how the case will come out — you're merely asked to say what the most likely rationale will be *if* the case is decided for the buyer.)

Choice (A) is wrong because the doctrine of equitable conversion has nothing to do with any issue presented by this question. Equitable conversion, where the court chooses to apply it, makes a vendor under a land-sale agreement the "equitable seller," and the vendee the "equitable buyer." The main consequence of the doctrine's application is that risk of loss passes to the buyer upon the signing of the contract, even though the seller still holds the legal title.

Choice (C) is wrong, because the seller's possession would not suggest the seller had sold the property to the buyer. Under a recording statute like the one here, a subsequent bona fide purchaser (i.e., a person who gives valuable consideration and has no actual or constructive notice of the prior instrument) prevails over a prior grantee who failed to record. If the creditor was trying to become covered by the recording act, and *the buyer* had been in possession at the time the creditor filed her lien, the fact that the buyer (not the seller, who was the record owner) was in possession at the date of lien filing might have been enough to cause the buyer to lose, since this possession might have put her on inquiry notice that the seller was perhaps no longer the owner. But the fact that *the seller* was still in possession didn't put the buyer on notice of anything, so it's irrelevant on these facts.

Choice (D) is wrong, because recording acts protect the second, not the first, purchaser in certain circumstances. Here, it would be the creditor (who can argue that she "purchased" by filing her lien), not the buyer, who is trying to get the protection of the recording act. It is the person seeking the protection of the recording act (the second purchaser), not the person resisting application of the act (the first purchaser) who needs to be "without notice." So here, the notice status of the creditor might well matter (if the recording act otherwise applied to judgment lien creditors). But the notice status of the buyer, the first "purchaser," does not matter at all.

[Q3123]

49. **D** The FRE (like the common law) provide that evidence that a person carried or did not carry liability insurance is not admissible on the issue of whether that person acted negligently. (See FRE 411, first sent.) This rule bars such evidence when it is offered by a plaintiff to suggest that because the defendant was insured, the defendant was probably careless. However, the rule does not apply where the evidence is offered for some other purpose, "such as proof of agency, *ownership, or control* ..." (FRE 411, second sent.) That's what's happening here — the evidence is being used to show that because the defendant bought a liability policy on the plane, he had ownership or control of it.

(A) is wrong because the terms of the policy are not at issue, only the policy's existence. The Best Evidence Rule (B.E.R.) states that in proving the terms of a writing or a recording, where the terms are material, the original must be produced. Here, the B.E.R. would apply if the terms of the insurance policy were in question. But the terms are not in question here and are not material — Witness' testimony involves only the existence of the policy, not its terms, so the B.E.R. does not apply.

(B) is wrong because it misstates the rule. The rule against proof of liability insurance is not a general rule against "proof of insurance where insurance is not itself the issue" (as this choice asserts). Instead, the rule prohibits proof of a liability policy's existence when offered to prove negligence (and that rule applies here, as Choice (D) asserts).

(C) is wrong because such evidence is offered to suggest the defendant was probably careless. FRE 411, first sentence, says that "Evidence that a person was or was not insured against liability is not admissible upon the issue whether the person acted negligently or otherwise wrongfully." Since this choice suggests that an insured plane owner would be less likely to properly maintain the plane, it's a method of asserting the defendant's negligence, and thus flies squarely in the face of FRE 411.

[Q3136]

50. **C** For the pedestrian to recover, she will have to show negligence on the part of the car owner. The pedestrian has two shots at this: (1) negligence per se; and (2) garden-variety negligence. As to negligence per se, before the standard of care in a statute can be the basis for a claim of negligence per se, it must be the case that the ordinance was drafted at least in part for the purpose of protecting against the particular hazard that occurred. Rest. 2d, §286(d). This requirement is not satisfied here, because we're told that the purpose of the statute was solely to expedite the flow of car traffic, not to protect against the formation of the ice. With respect to garden-variety negligence, the pedestrian has simply come forward with no evidence that the accident was caused (i.e., the ice was caused) by any failure on the part of the car owner to use reasonable care under the circumstances. (Indeed, if the car owner had complied with the statute by washing the car in a private driveway instead of the street, this would not have reduced the risk of accumulating ice on pedestrian walkways and might even have increased that risk.) Accordingly, the car owner's motion should be granted.

(A) is wrong because negligence creating the risk of an icy surface cannot be inferred from the mere fact that the car owner allowed the water to accumulate; the cold snap was "sudden and unexpected." Because there is no reasonable inference of negligence and no evidence of negligence (the statute is irrelevant because it does not speak to the risk that materialized in this case), the car owner's motion should be granted.

(B) is wrong because the statutory violation is not even evidence of negligence here. The statute was not enacted to reduce the risk of accumulating ice on the public walkways. Indeed, if the car owner had complied with the statute by washing the car in a private driveway, this would not have reduced the risk of accumulating ice on pedestrian walkways and might even have increased that risk. Therefore, violation of the statute has no probative value on the issue of whether the car owner was negligent.

(D) is wrong because, as is discussed further in Choice (C) above, the statute was enacted solely to reduce a particular safety risk (congested traffic lanes) that neither materialized nor caused the pedestrian's injury, so the negligence per se doctrine does not apply, and the statutory violation is irrelevant.

[Q7020]

51. **C** The expanded use of the easement here — especially the parking along the driveway at all hours — probably does represent excessive use going beyond the intended scope of the easement. However, a court would almost certainly limit the remedy to an injunction against further violations, or to damages for the two past violations, and would not order a forfeiture of the easement. That's because forfeitures are drastic remedies, and will be awarded in excessive-use situations only if no other remedy will be adequate, which would not be the case for the violations here.

(A) is wrong because, while the order has indeed probably excessively expanded their use of the easement, the court would not order the easement forfeited as a remedy, for the reasons stated above.

(B) is wrong for the same reason as (A).

(D) is wrong because a court would not grant the neighbor the extreme remedy of forfeiture whether or not she had used self-help.

[Q2021]

52. **D** Assault occurs when, with the intent to induce such apprehension, the defendant induces in the plaintiff a reasonable apprehension that a harmful or offensive contact with the plaintiff will occur. When the defendant makes the plaintiff fear for a harmful or offensive bodily contact upon a third person, this does not constitute assault of the plaintiff no matter how closely connected the plaintiff and the third person are. Rest. 2d, §26. Since the mother did not fear contact with herself, she was not assaulted.

(A) is wrong because the defendant's conduct did not induce the mother to apprehend contact with herself.

(B) is wrong because the doctrine of transferred intent does not apply on these facts. Transferred intent can apply in an assault case, where D intends to put X in fear of imminent contact, and in fact puts P in fear that P will suffer such a contact — D has assaulted P. Rest. 2d, §32(2). But the doctrine doesn't apply here for two reasons: (1) the defendant did not intend to cause an apprehension of harmful contact in the scout (or any person); and (2) the mother was not in fact put in fear of a contact with herself.

(C) is wrong because it cites a fact that is irrelevant. If the defendant's conduct had given the mother reason to apprehend contact with herself, this would be assault of the mother, and it would not matter whether she had perceived contact with her daughter the scout.

[Q5018]

53. **B** In the absence of congressional action, the state rule here probably would be a violation of the dormant Commerce Clause (what the question calls the "negative implications of the commerce clause"), because it discriminates against out-of-state growers. But Congress may use its commerce power to permit states to discriminate against interstate commerce. The federal statute here explicitly authorizes states to enact state-of-origin labeling requirements on imported citrus fruit.

(A) is incorrect, because the balancing argument would work only if: (1) Congress had not enacted a statute authorizing the state regulation at issue; and (2) the state law did not discriminate against interstate commerce. In this case, however, neither of these conditions is satisfied: Congress *has* authorized state-of-origin labeling requirements on imported citrus fruit, and the state law *is* discriminatory.

(C) is incorrect, because the state law *does* discriminate against out-of-state citrus growers, in that the law requires that all citrus fruit "imported" into the state be stamped with the state of origin, while the law imposes no such requirement on citrus fruit grown within the state.

(D) is incorrect, because although this argument correctly paraphrases the burden on the state to justify a law that discriminates against interstate commerce, the argument would be less likely to succeed than the "Congress authorized it" argument: in the absence of Congressional authorization, the burden on a state to justify its discriminatory regulation is a heavy one, and states only rarely succeed in carrying it. Here, the availability of less-discriminatory alternatives (e.g., requiring in-state growers, not just out-of-staters, to stamp the state's two-letter code on the fruit) makes it unlikely that the state would win with this argument.
[Q7084]

54. **C** Since all the incidents of unconsciousness occurred within three months after the accident and nearly three years ago, it was probably reasonable for the defendant to believe that they would not occur again. If she entertained that belief, and if it was reasonable, she cannot be said to have knowingly disregarded the plain and strong likelihood of harm as required by the statute. Although it is not certain that a court would come to that conclusion, (C) contains the only argument listed which could possibly support the defendant's defense.

(A) is incorrect because if the defendant did knowingly disregard the plain and strong likelihood of further blackouts, it would not matter what caused them.

(B) is incorrect because the crime, if any, took place when the defendant drove in knowing disregard (etc.), and so would have already been committed by the time the defendant passed out.

(D) is incorrect because the statute does not require knowledge that death or serious injury will result, but only knowledge that there is strong likelihood that it will.
[Q5050]

55. **D** Under the UCC, a purported acceptance document will not be prevented from operating as a true acceptance even though it states terms that are additional to or different from those in the offer. UCC §2-207(1). Therefore, the wholesaler's form with the "We are please to accept" language on it operated as an acceptance even though it contained an additional term (the liability cap). On the other hand, the liability cap was an "additional" term (i.e., a term dealing with a subject that was not covered in the retailer's offer). When the offeror and offeree are both merchants, §2-207(2) says that an additional term is to be construed as a "proposal for addition to the contract," and becomes part of the contract unless (1) "the offer expressly limits acceptance to the terms of the offer" (which didn't happen here), (2) the additional term "materially alter[s]" the contract, or (3) the offeror promptly notifies the offeree that the offeror objects to the additional term. Here, event (2) has occurred: a liability cap would almost certainly be considered by a court to be a "material alteration" of an offer that did not contain any cap. Therefore, a contract was formed but it did not include the liability cap.

(A) is wrong because, as explained in more detail in Choice (D) above, while the liability-limitation clause was indeed a material alteration of the offer, this fact did not prevent the wholesaler's form from constituting an acceptance. (The wholesaler's form meshed sufficiently with the retailer's offer form, and contained sufficient words of acceptance, that it was a "definite ... expression of acceptance" under §2-207(1) even though it contained the additional term.)

(B) is wrong because a contract was formed as soon as the wholesaler sent its form, and whether the retailer eventually did or did not expressly consent to the liability-limitation clause wouldn't matter to the issue of whether a contract was formed. (As explained in the discussion of Choice (D), the liability-limitation clause, since it was a material alteration, didn't become part of the contract even if the retailer remained silent.)

(C) is wrong because, while it correctly says that a contract is formed, it is incorrect in stating that the liability-limitation clause would become part of the contract. It's true that a liquidation-of-damages clause can, if the parties agree on it and it is reasonable, be enforced under the UCC. But such a clause won't enter the contract unless the parties somehow agree on the clause, and here, because the proposed clause was a material alteration, the retailer won't be presumed to have agreed from the mere fact that the clause was present on the wholesaler's acceptance and the retailer remained silent.

[Q2034]

56. **A** Murder is the unjustified killing of a human being with malice aforethought. "Malice aforethought" is a term of art that covers a number of possible mental states, including an intent to cause great bodily harm to a human being. A defendant "intends" a particular consequence if she desires it or knows to a substantial degree of certainty that it will occur. Since the defendant desired that the exposure to Terminate would cause great bodily harm (blindness) to the co-worker, she will be deemed to have intended to cause great bodily harm to a human being. Since the friend died, the defendant is guilty of his murder. (The doctrine of transferred intent applies — since the defendant had the requisite intent regarding the co-worker, her intent will be "transferred" to the person who actually died, the friend.)

(B) is wrong because engaging in an inherently dangerous activity, even intentionally, does not constitute one of the mental states that will suffice for murder. Engaging in an inherently dangerous activity is a tort concept (producing strict liability), but not a criminal-law concept.

(C) is wrong because the defendant's intent to cause great bodily harm to *any* human being is sufficient to make her guilty of murder in causing the death of the friend, by use of the doctrine of transferred intent (further described in choice (A) above).

(D) is wrong because, although the intent to kill is one of the mental states that will suffice for murder, it's not the only one. An intent to cause serious bodily harm will also suffice.

[Q5017]

57. **C** Art. III, Sec. 2, says that the federal judicial power extends "to controversies between two or more States." Art. III, Sec. 3 then says that "in all cases ... in which a State shall be a Party, the Supreme Court shall have original jurisdiction." That same article says that the Supreme Court's "appellate jurisdiction" shall be "with such exceptions, and under such regulations as the Congress shall make." There is no similar provision allowing Congress to make exceptions to (i.e., restrictions on) the Supreme Court's original jurisdiction, so Congress can't restrict the Supreme Court's original jurisdiction. Since a boundary dispute between two states is a dispute in which "a State shall be a party," since the Supreme Court has original jurisdiction over cases involving a party, and since Congress is not authorized to limit the Supreme Court's original jurisdiction, it follows that Congress cannot "adjudicate finally" (i.e., remove the Supreme Court's right to adjudicate) the boundary dispute.

Choice (A) is wrong because, under *Coleman v. Miller* (1939), the House and Senate together *do* have the right (indeed, the exclusive right) to determine whether a disputed state ratification of an amendment is valid.

Choice (B) is incorrect because the Senate *does* have the power to determine the eligibility of its members — Art. I, Sec. 5, Cl. 1 says that "each House shall be the judge of the Elections, Returns, and *Qualifications* of its own Members."

Choice (D) is wrong because Art. I, Sec. 7, Cl. 3 says that "Every Order, *Resolution*, or Vote to which the Concurrence of the Senate and House of Representatives may be necessary ... shall be presented to the President of the United States[.]" This clause implicitly gives each house the power to adopt resolutions; a resolution will not become law unless signed by the President, but the clause means that either house's adoption of a resolution is proper.

[Q1087]

58. **A** The carpenter is entitled to the contract price for the work done. The other items of damage are unrecoverable either because they were unforeseeable at the time the contract was made or because they were not caused by the breach.

(B) is wrong because the medical expenses are unrecoverable. That's true because even if the heart attack was caused by the breach (which would be difficult to establish), the medical expenses were unforeseeable to one in the homeowner's position at the time the contract was made.

(C) is wrong because the $2,000 for the loss of the bargain on the car was, similarly, unforeseeable to the homeowner at the time the contract to do the work was made; that car contract was a special circumstance, of which the homeowner had no notice, bringing the case within the *Hadley v. Baxendale* principle.

(D) is wrong because the carpenter is entitled only to the contract price for the work done. No unjust enrichment claim is viable on these facts, because an unjust enrichment claim cannot exceed the contract price when all of the work giving rise to the claim has been done and the only remaining obligation of the homeowner is the payment of the price.

[Q7099]

59. **B** The tape is admissible as a prior inconsistent statement offered to impeach the witness, but inadmissible substantively because of hearsay. First, let's consider the recording's admissibility for impeachment. FRE 613(b) implicitly allows use of extrinsic evidence to show that a witness has made a prior inconsistent statement. ("Extrinsic evidence of a prior inconsistent statement by a witness is not admissible unless the witness is afforded an opportunity to explain or deny the same and the opposite party is afforded an opportunity to interrogate the witness thereon, or the interests of justice otherwise require.") So here, once the witness said on the stand that the defendant had given a non-racial explanation for the firing, the witness' tape-recorded statement that the defendant had given a racial explanation was extrinsic evidence tending to show a prior inconsistent statement by the witness. Consequently, the statement was admissible for impeachment under FRE 613(b), since the witness was still on the stand (and thus had a chance to explain or deny the statement).

Now, let's consider substantive admissibility. Here, the tape recording is "hearsay within hearsay." The outer level is that the witness is making a recorded, and thus out-of-court, statement. The inner level is that the witness is repeating an admission made by the defendant. Here, the inner level is not inadmissible hearsay, because it falls within the exception for admissions introduced against the maker. See FRE 801(d)(2) (A statement is not hearsay if "The statement is offered against a party and is (A) the party's own statement...") But the outer level is hearsay that is not within any exception — the witness is making an out-of-court statement (the witness' words on the recording) offered to demonstrate the truth of the matter asserted (that the defendant made a certain admission to the witness). There is nothing in this statement ("The defendant told me he fired the plaintiff for racial reasons") that falls within any hearsay exception. Thus the statement can't come in for the substantive purpose of demonstrating that the defendant was racially motivated.

(A) is wrong because, as is described in the analysis of Choice (B), the recording is not admissible as "evidence of the defendant's racial motivation," which is a substantive (non-impeachment-of-the-witness) purpose.

(C) is wrong because, as is described in Choice (B), the statement is admissible for impeachment as a prior inconsistent statement of the witness.

(D) is wrong because no violation of the Constitution occurs when a person secretly records a conversation to which he is a party (and in any event, the witness was not a governmental actor, again preventing the recording from possibly being a constitutional violation).

[Q3026]

60. **A** Once a criminal defendant has asserted his right to have an attorney present, further interrogation in the absence of the attorney makes any incriminating statements by the defendant inadmissible. Since the defendant was questioned after asserting his right to counsel, the statement which he made in response to that questioning must be excluded.

(B) is wrong because even if the sheriff knew the defendant's whereabouts and lied to the lawyer, this would not affect the outcome. For example, in a roughly analogous case in which the police falsely told the defendant's lawyer that the defendant was not a suspect, and then did not tell the defendant that his lawyer was trying to contact him, the Court held that the defendant's waiver of his right to a lawyer after receiving the *Miranda* warnings was valid. *Moran v. Burbine* (1986). So here, if the defendant had not insisted on the right to a lawyer, the fact that the sheriff blocked the lawyer's access by lying about not knowing the defendant's whereabouts would not have made the defendant's waiver of his *Miranda* rights invalid.

(C) is wrong for the same reason that (B) is wrong: it was solely the defendant's decision to insist on a lawyer that made the subsequent interrogation unlawful. Once the defendant so insisted, his motion would win even if the sheriff lied to the lawyer about not knowing the defendant's whereabouts.

(D) is wrong because, once a defendant has requested counsel, the courts will be extremely reluctant to conclude that the defendant's later conduct constituted a waiver of his already-asserted right to consult a lawyer. As the Supreme Court has put it, "An accused ... having expressed his desire to deal with the police only through counsel, is not subject to further interrogation by the authorities until counsel has been made available to him, unless the *accused himself initiates* further communication, exchanges or conversations with the police." *Edwards v. Ariz.* (1981). Here, after the defendant requested counsel, his admission about growing marijuana came about in response to interrogation initiated by the police, not by the defendant. Therefore the bright-line no-waiver rule of *Edwards* applies, and the confession must be excluded as a violation of *Miranda*.

[Q5136]

61. **D** Since the tenant's judgment was only against the brother, the tenant's judgment lien was only against the brother's real property, not the sister's real property. That real property consisted of the brother's joint tenancy interest. At the moment of the brother's death, that joint tenancy interest ceased to exist, and there was nothing left for the judgment lien to be a lien against.

(A) is wrong because the basis for the tenant's judgment (and thus for his judgment lien) was the brother's having injured him in the fight; since this had nothing to do with the tenant's having been a tenant of both brother and sister, it did not create any lien against the sister's interest in the property.

(B) is wrong because it inaccurately characterizes the brother's interest: it was a joint tenancy, not an "undivided one-half interest" (a phrase that would be used to describe a tenancy in common). Therefore, the fact that the judgment was filed while the brother was still alive is irrelevant, because the brother's joint tenancy ceased to exist at the moment he died.

(C) is wrong because it cites an irrelevant factor; even if the sister had had actual notice of the judgment while the brother was still alive, there would be no lien after the brother died for the reasons described in the discussion of (D).

[Q1090]

62. **B** The setting up of a presidential advisory commission, such as the one here, falls within the President's executive powers — nothing in the facts indicates that the commission will have legislative or judicial powers, so the commission is a proper delegation by the President of his executive power. As to funding: Congress has the right to earmark specified federal monies to be spent as the President shall determine. Therefore, nothing about this arrangement violates any constitutional provision.

(A) is wrong, because the President does *not* have "plenary power to provide for the health, safety, and welfare of the people..." For instance, the President does not have power to spend federal money for what he determines to be the health needs of "the people." This answer ignores both the source of the President's authority (which is limited to the executive power, that is, the power to see that the laws are carried out) and the need for all funding to be appropriated by Congress.

(C) is wrong because it incorrectly states the effect of the Tenth Amendment. The Tenth Amendment states that the powers not delegated to the federal government by the Constitution, and not prohibited to the states, are reserved to the states. The Tenth Amendment has relatively little force today as a limit on federal power. (About the only force it has as a limit on federal powers is to prevent Congress from directly forcing the states to enact or enforce federal policies). The Amendment does not mean that the federal government may not exercise power over a "traditional state function." So the fact that vaccination has traditionally been a function handled by the states does not mean that the Tenth Amendment bars the federal government from taking action with respect to vaccinations.

(D) is wrong, because Congress does not need to authorize the creation of a temporary commission. An Advisory Commission on Vaccination is not a new federal agency — it is an advisory group, set up for a specific purpose and having a temporary existence. The President does not need Congressional approval to create such an organization. Nor has Congress prohibited its creation (which if it had happened might bar creation of the Commission), because as the facts state no federal statute authorizes or prohibits this action.

[Q3109]

63. **B** UCC §3-311 deals with the effect of a creditor's cashing of an "in full settlement" partial-payment check. To get the protection of §3-311 (i.e., to have the creditor's cashing of the check constitute full settlement), the debtor must show that: (1) the check or accompanying written communication contained a "conspicuous statement to the effect that the instrument was tendered as full satisfaction of the claim," (2) the underlying claim was either "unliquidated" or "subjected to a bona fide dispute," and (3) the debtor acted in good faith. Here, all of these requirements are met, since: (1) we're told that the check was "conspicuously marked, 'Payment in full' "; (2) the parties had a real dispute about whether the $5,000 initially quoted by the lawyer was merely a non-binding estimate or a binding cap; and (3) we're expressly told that the client's letter expressed his "good-faith belief" that the lawyer had quoted the $5,000 as a cap. Therefore, when the lawyer cashed the check, his doing so constituted an implied agreement to an accord and satisfaction of his claim, under §3-311. Note that this result would still occur even if the lawyer had placed a notation of protest or of reservation-of-rights on the check before cashing it.

(A) is wrong for two reasons: (1) the "rule of law" it purports to state about the risk of loss probably would not be accurate even in the absence of the lawyer's cashing the partial-payment check; and (2) under UCC §3-311, the cashing of that check constituted a settlement, for the reasons stated in the discussion of Choice (B) above.

(C) is wrong because it is not clear that the $5,000 figure quoted by the lawyer was merely an estimate — in the absence of the check-cashing, a court might well have found that the client reasonably understood the figure to be a firm cap (i.e., an upper bound) on the amount that the lawyer would charge, in which case the cap would have been deemed part of the contract.

(D) is wrong for two reasons: (1) there may indeed have been a specific agreement on the total amount of the lawyer's fee (the facts are indeterminate about whether this would be true, in the absence of the partial-check-cashing); and (2) when the lawyer cashed the check, the case became governed by UCC §3-311, not the parties' original agreement, whatever that was.

[Q2123]

64. **C** A conspiracy requires an agreement between at least two people, the intent to enter into such an agreement, and the intent to achieve the agreement's unlawful objective. Here, the woman didn't have the intent to enter into an agreement to steal food stamps, or the intent to steal food stamps; she only had the intent to buy stolen food stamps. As a result, she was not part of a conspiracy to actually steal the food stamps. Had she actually helped to plan or participated in or assisted the theft, these acts would be evidence of her agreement to take part in the conspiracy; but she didn't.

(A) is wrong because although it states a correct rule of law, the rule does not apply to these facts, and the choice arrives at an incorrect result. (A) states as a given that the woman has entered "the conspiracy." This statement overlooks the central issue under these facts: whether or not the woman actually entered the conspiracy *to steal* the stamps. A conspiracy requires an agreement, an intent to enter into such an agreement, and the intent to achieve the agreement's objectives. Here, the woman did not conspire to actually steal the food stamps, because she didn't intend to steal the food stamps and didn't agree to enter into a plan to effect the stealing of the food stamps.

(B) is wrong because it mischaracterizes the facts, and arrives at an incorrect result. The woman did not knowingly and willingly aid and abet the *theft;* she had no agreement regarding the theft, no intent to enter into such an agreement, and no intent to steal the food stamps. She merely agreed to buy stolen goods, and that wasn't aiding and abetting the theft. More specifically, there's no indication that the woman intended to aid and abet a theft that she believed had not yet occurred — her command to bring the goods over "right now" indicates, on the contrary, that she thought they had already been stolen.

(D) is wrong because it misstates the law. A conspiracy requires that there be an agreement between at least two people, but it doesn't require that they all be charged with conspiracy. Beyond the agreement requirement, conspiracy requires that the defendant have intended to enter such an agreement, and have the intent to achieve the agreement's unlawful objective (at common law, a conspiracy could alternatively involve a lawful ultimate act, to be done unlawfully). If you chose this response, you may have mistaken these facts for a situation where there are two parties to a conspiracy who are both charged with conspiracy, and one is acquitted. The rule under those circumstances is that the other could not be convicted, because it takes at least two guilty parties to have a conspiracy (likewise, with a conspiracy of three persons, and all three are charged with conspiracy, if two are acquitted, the third would have to be also). However, the facts here state that *only the woman has been charged.* Thus, the acquittal-based rule would not apply.

[Q4002]

65. **B** This choice correctly identifies the key factor which will exonerate the student: His mistake negates the necessary *mens rea* for burglary. The key here is to remember the elements of burglary, the defenses that apply, and apply them strictly. Common-law burglary requires the breaking and entering of the dwelling house of another, at night, with the intent to commit a felony therein. Most states broaden this to include entry at all times in all kinds of structures (thus eliminating the breaking, dwelling house, and nighttime requirements). Here, what the student's mistake — believing looking at the exam questions is criminal when, in fact, it isn't — does is to negate his *mens rea*. There's no burglary when a defendant breaks and enters to commit a non-felony. The defense that covers these facts is legal impossibility — that is, what he intended to do was not criminal. Since this negates the required intent for burglary, he'll be acquitted.

(A) is wrong because it does not correctly apply the burglary definition to these facts. At common law, burglary requires breaking and entering the dwelling house of another, at night, with intent to commit a felony therein. Under most modern statutes, entry at all times in all kinds of structures is covered (thus eliminating the breaking, dwelling house, and nighttime requirements). Thus, the crime is *complete* once the breaking and entering with the appropriate intent has taken place. It's not necessary that the person actually *commit* the felony therein — he need only *intend* to do so. Thus, choice (A)'s language about the student not completing the crime *cannot* be correct, since if he avoids liability for burglary, it cannot be on that basis. For the same reason, the statement about attempted burglary does not apply to these facts. Attempted burglary would apply under these facts, for instance, to the student being caught *just before* he broke into the professor's office (since attempt requires, at common law, proximity to the actual crime). In fact, what will exonerate the student is his mistaken belief that what he intended to do — look at exam questions — was a crime, as discussed in (B) above.

(C) is wrong because it does not apply to these facts, and arrives at the wrong result. If the student *had* the correct mental state, his breaking and entering would make him liable for burglary. At common law, burglary requires breaking and entering the dwelling house of another, at night, with the intent to commit a felony therein (most modern statutes broaden this to include entry at all times in all kinds of structures, thus eliminating the breaking, dwelling house, and nighttime requirements). Thus, the "mental state" to which (C) refers is *intent.* So the student had to have the intent to do act X inside the dwelling where, if he actually did act X, this would have been a felony. But since act X here (looking at exam papers) would not have been a felony, the student did not have the requisite "intent to commit a felony therein."

(D) is wrong because it misstates the facts – what's involved here is *legal* impossibility, not *factual* impossibility. Factual impossibility occurs when completion of the crime is impossible due to physical facts not known to the defendant, e.g., a pickpocket picking an empty pocket. As (D) correctly states, factual impossibility is no defense. However, what's involved here is *legal* impossibility, which arises when the defendant intends to do is an act that the defendant believes constitutes a crime but that is not in fact defined as a crime. Legal impossibility is a valid defense, and applies to these facts, as further discussed in Choice (B) above.
[Q4037]

66. **A** An assignment arises when a tenant transfers all or some of the leased premises to another for the remainder of the lease term, retaining no interest in the assigned premises. In this case, prior to the agreement with the friend, the tenant had privity of contract with the landlord because of the lease. The tenant also had privity of estate because the tenant was in possession of the apartment. Subsequently, an assignment arose when the tenant transferred the premises to the friend for the remainder of the lease term of nine months. The friend was then in privity of estate with the landlord as to all promises that run with the land, including the covenant to pay rent. (When the friend moved out, this did not end the privity of estate, because the friend did not assign to someone else, and simply abandoned the premises. See Rest. 2d (Landlord & Tenant), §16.1, Illustr. 24.) The tenant was not released by the landlord, however, and thus remained liable on privity of contract.

(B) is incorrect, because the friend entered privity of estate with the landlord when he received the assignment, and this privity of estate remained with the friend until the end of the lease because the friend made no assignment. Therefore, the friend remained liable on privity of estate for the period after he vacated. Furthermore, because the landlord never released the tenant, the tenant remained liable for the full $3,500 on privity of contract.

(C) is incorrect, because the landlord never released the tenant, thereby keeping the tenant liable on privity of contract based on the original lease. (There was no express release, and a release would not be implied merely because the landlord accepted rent from the friend.)

(D) is incorrect, because this choice assumes that the friend was a sublessee, which he was not. A sublease arises when a tenant transfers the right of possession to all or some of the leased premises to another for a time less than the remaining time of the lease, or when the tenant retains some other interest in the premises. Here, the tenant transferred all the remaining time of the lease to the friend and retained no other interest. Accordingly, this was an assignment and not a sublease. As an assignee, the friend was in privity of estate with the landlord as to all promises that run with the land, including the covenant to pay rent.

[Q7004]

67. **A** FRE 407 seeks to encourage safety precautions by prohibiting evidence of subsequent remedial measures from being used for the purpose of showing fault or defect. Such evidence may be admissible for other purposes, however. Here, the accountant had denied ownership of the vehicle. Since it is unlikely that anyone other than the owner would arrange to have the brakes overhauled, the testimony of the mechanic is relevant to establish the accountant's ownership and should, therefore, be admitted.

(B) is wrong because of the above-stated policy of encouraging safety precautions.

(C) is wrong because the evidence is being used to establish that the accountant was the owner of the vehicle, not to establish the condition of the brakes on any particular day. (Also, the condition of the brakes on the day after the accident is relevant to show their probable condition on the day of the accident — FRE 407 keeps out this evidence if offered to show fault or defect not because it's irrelevant, but because allowing it would discourage the taking of socially-valuable remedial measures.)

(D) is wrong because the evidence is being offered to establish ownership, a purpose that is not forbidden by FRE 407's rule against the offering of remedial measures to show fault or defect.

[Q5072]

68. **A** FRE 608(b) says that "Specific instances of the conduct of a witness, for the purpose of attacking or supporting the witness' credibility, other than conviction of crime as provided in rule 609, *may not be proved by extrinsic evidence.* They may, however, in the discretion of the court, if probative of truthfulness or untruthfulness, be *inquired into on cross-examination of the witness* (1) concerning the witness' character for truthfulness or untruthfulness..." The present use fits the second sentence of FRE 608(b): the giving of false testimony in a prior trial is obviously "probative of untruthfulness." And Choice's (A)'s limitation to matters "elicited from the expert on cross-examination" brings the situation into the second sentence (cross-examination) rather than the first sentence (extrinsic evidence).

(B) is wrong because, as described in Choice (A) above, the prior-bad-act evidence here can only be brought out on cross, making this choice wrong since it does not include this limitation. On the other hand, if the evidence *is* brought out on cross, it need not be supported by "clear and convincing" evidence. It's true that as a judge-made rule, the cross-examiner must have a "good faith basis" for believing that the false-testimony episode actually occurred. But such a good-faith basis, not the possession of clear-and-convincing-evidence, is all that is required for introducing the topic on cross.

(C) is wrong because the defendant's testimony, though "collateral," would be admissible if elicited on cross-examination. If the evidence were being offered "extrinsically" (e.g., by testimony from a different witness who witnessed the false testimony), this choice would be correct — see the first sentence of FRE 608(b), quoted in the discussion of Choice (A) above. But the evidence would be allowed to be brought up ("elicited") on cross of the expert himself, even though it relates solely to credibility rather than to a substantive issue in the case (and thus concerns a "collateral matter").

(D) is wrong, because evidence of a prior bad act by the witness demonstrating the witness' poor character for truthfulness does not fall within the general ban on proof of character traits to show action-in-conformity-therewith-on-the-present-occasion. Instead, FRE 608(b) imposes specific rules governing when such evidence is admissible — as described in Choice (A), such prior-acts-of-lying evidence may be brought out only on cross of the witness whose veracity is in question, not by means of "extrinsic evidence." Therefore, Choice (D) is an incorrect statement of both the rule and the outcome.

[Q3013]

69. **B** Although the state supreme court made a finding about what the state constitution required, this decision was not truly "independent" of federal constitutional law, because the facts make it clear that the state court was first determining what the federal constitution required, and only then concluding that the state constitution required the same thing. Therefore, the Supreme Court can and should correct the state court's error in federal constitutional law. Once the Supreme Court has done this, it should then remand in order to give the state court the opportunity to conclude, after further reflection, that the state constitution's ban on discriminatory legislation goes further than the federal ban.

Choice (A) is wrong as a pure matter of law: even where provisions of a state and the federal constitution contain identical language, the state court is always free to interpret the state constitution as imposing different requirements than the apparently-identical federal provision.

Choice (C) is wrong because, for the reasons described above, the state court's decision was not in fact based on an adequate and independent state ground.

Choice (D) is wrong as a pure matter of law: nothing prevents a state government from seeking review of the decisions of its own courts in the U.S. Supreme Court, as long as the decision poses some serious question of federal law.

[Q1010]

70. **D** The key here is that the defendant had no *intent* to kill or cause a serious injury. Murder is an unlawful killing with malice aforethought. "Malice aforethought" is a term of art, and can be satisfied by various mental states: (1) intent to kill; (2) intent to do serious bodily injury; (3) intent to commit one of various dangerous felonies (producing felony murder); or (4) acting with reckless disregard of the value of human life (producing "depraved-heart" murder). Depraved heart murder occurs where Defendant engages in conduct which, at the least, a reasonable man would realize creates an extremely high degree of risk to human life, and which results in death. Choice (D), with its language "without an intent to kill but with disregard of the consequences" coupled with an act highly dangerous to life, essentially reflects this rule.

(A) is wrong because it misapplies the doctrine of transferred intent. Under transferred intent, a person intending to commit a crime against one person, accidentally commits a crime against another. His intent will be "transferred" from the person he intended to harm to the person he *actually* harmed (e.g., D tries to shoot A to death and instead kills B). What's missing under these facts is the defendant's intent to kill in the first place – he doesn't intend to kill or even injure *anyone*. If anything, he intends for the children to run out of the way and *not* be injured. Since he has no criminal intent, it can't be transferred.

(B) is wrong because the felony is not sufficiently "independent" from homicide to be covered by the felony murder rule. The felony murder rule is as follows: Where a killing is committed during the course of certain "dangerous" felonies (or an attempt at such), the homicide is considered first degree murder, even though there is no intent to kill or cause great bodily harm. Such "dangerous" felonies typically include rape, kidnapping, mayhem, arson, robbery, and burglary. The dangerous felony must be reasonably "independent" of the killing. Assault with a deadly weapon would itself require an intent to do serious bodily harm or to kill, so the "independence" required by the felony murder rule would be lacking.

(C) is wrong because the reasoning it states is insufficient to convict the defendant of intentional killing. While intentional killing is sufficient for murder, intent must be one of two types: Either the actor must consciously desire a result, regardless of the likelihood his conduct will cause it; or, alternatively, he must know the result is practically certain to result from his conduct, regardless of whether he wants it to happen. Thus, under the facts in this question, the defendant would have to want to kill the children, or know he was practically certain to kill one if he drove toward them. Thus, (C) is incorrect in stating that knowing they were there and deliberately driving at them would be sufficient to convict the defendant — in addition, he'd have to know that driving at them would result in one being killed. In fact, the defendant believes they will run to get out of the way — he doesn't know he's practically certain to kill one.

[Q4035]

71. **C** This was an output contract, as well as a requirements contract. Under UCC §2-306(2), "A lawful agreement by either the seller or the buyer for exclusive dealing in the kind of goods concerned imposes unless otherwise agreed an obligation by the seller to use best efforts to supply the goods and *by the buyer to use best efforts to promote their sale.*" This was an exclusive-dealing contract (all requirements and output contracts are exclusive-dealing contracts); therefore, since the parties did not otherwise agree, §2-306(2) imposed on the bakery the "obligation ... to use best efforts to promote [the goods'] sale." When the bakery renounced the agreement without having even bought any buns yet, it breached this best-efforts-to-promote obligation.

(A) is wrong because, even though the bakery made no express promise to buy any of the manufacturer's buns, under §2-306(2) the bakery was implicitly obligated to make best efforts to promote the sale of buns so that the bakery would need some of them.

(B) is wrong because, under §2-306(1), "A term which measures the quantity by the output of the seller ... means such actual output ... as may occur in good faith[.]" This section has the effect of providing a quantity (or at least, a method for determining quantity), saving the output contract here from indefiniteness.

(D) is wrong because it does not speak to the main issue in the case. It's essentially true that both buyer and seller "impliedly assume the risk of price and demand fluctuations," but the question here is whether buyer could rely on the sudden reduction in its own customers' demand to escape the contract. UCC §2-306(2) in effect allocates this risk, by saying that the buyer in both a requirements and output contract must use good faith to promote sale of the goods, effectively negating the bakery's ability to discontinue the product line here without any promotional effort.

[Q1017]

72. **D** FRE 803(2) admits a hearsay statement that would otherwise be barred under Rule 802 where the statement "relat[es] to a startling event or condition made while the declarant was under the stress of excitement caused by the event or condition." In this case, the assault was a startling event, and the victim made the statement immediately after the beating, trying to identify the perpetrator. Thus, all the admissibility requirements of Rule 803(2), the excited utterance exception, are met.

(A) is wrong because, although the statement is hearsay, it is admissible under FRE 803(2), the excited utterance exception, as described in Choice (D) below.

(B) is wrong because the statement fits under the FRE 803(2)'s exception to the hearsay rule for excited utterances. Under the hearsay exceptions in Rule 803, there is no requirement that the declarant be made available to testify. In this case, the victim's statement would have been admissible even if she had not been available at trial. Nor is there any requirement that the declarant under an FRE 803 exception be asked about the hearsay statement.

(C) is wrong because, while the declarant does not have to die for a statement to be admissible as a dying declaration under FRE 804(b)(2), this statement fails to satisfy that exception for at least two reasons. First, the declarant has to be unavailable, as the dying declaration is one of the "declarant unavailable" exceptions of Rule 804. Here, the victim testified and so obviously is not unavailable. Second, a dying declaration is admissible only in homicide prosecutions and civil cases. This is a criminal case for aggravated assault.

[Q7037]

73. **A** A person who is engaged in the *business of selling products*, and who sells a *defective product*, is subject to liability for harm to persons or property caused by the defect. Rest. 3d (Prod. Liab.) §1. One type of defect is a *"design* defect." A design defect occurs "when the foreseeable risks of harm posed by the product could have been reduced or avoided by the adoption of a *reasonable alternative design* by the seller or other distributor, or a predecessor in the commercial chain of distribution, and the omission of the alternative design renders the product *not reasonably safe."* Rest. 3d (Prod. Liab.) §2(b). The plaintiff has made a prima facie showing that satisfies these requirements for strict liability, since a reasonable jury could find that: (1) the defendant was engaged in the business of selling or distributing cars; (2) the fact that the Rapido's motor may stall if the engine has not had an extended warm-up is a design defect since a reasonable alternative design (which didn't need an extended warmup to avoid stalling) was available and would have reduced this risk; (3) the omission of this alternative design made the car not reasonably safe; and (4) the defect (the stalling motor and ensuing accident) caused harm to the plaintiff (his shock, which resulted in a heart attack). The plaintiff can thus make her prima facie case, so the defendant's motion should be denied.

(B) is wrong because the "crashworthiness" of the car was not at issue on these facts. "Crashworthiness" in a vehicle is the attribute of being able to withstand a collision without posing an unacceptably large risk of injury to the passengers. Non-crashworthiness can certainly be a type of defect. However, on the facts as alleged by the plaintiff here, the injury to her occurred from the "shock of the crash," not from any failure of the vehicle to appropriately withstand the collision. (In other words, the facts indicate that even in a perfectly crashworthy vehicle, the plaintiff would probably have had the same shock and thus the same heart attack). Consequently, even if a reasonable jury could find that the vehicle was "defective" because it was non-crashworthy (something not at all clear on these facts), the jury would probably not be entitled to find that the defect of non-crashworthiness was the legal cause of the injury. In that event, the defendant would still win on its motion. So although the conclusion (the defendant loses on the motion) is correct, the explanation of why it loses is not correct.

(C) is wrong because it was foreseeable that cars with engines that stall could be in accidents, so the elderly man's failure to stop was not superseding. An intervening cause is a force that takes effect after the defendant's negligence and which contributes to that negligence in producing the plaintiff's injury. Some, but not all, intervening causes are sufficient to prevent the defendant's negligence from being considered the proximate cause of the injury. Intervening causes of this kind are usually called "superseding causes" because they supersede or cancel the defendant's liability. An intervening cause that was "foreseeable" as something that might combine with a defect to cause an injury will generally not be deemed to be superseding cause. Here, it was perfectly foreseeable that a car that stalled due to a defect would be extra likely to be hit from the rear. Therefore, being hit from the rear was a foreseeable (and thus non-superseding) intervening cause given a "defective-because-likely-to-stall" engine.

(D) is wrong because the defendant "takes the plaintiff as he finds him." Where the defendant's negligence causes an aggravation of plaintiff's existing physical or mental illness, defendant is liable for the damages caused by the aggravation, which is to say, the tortfeasor takes the victim as he finds him. So here, this rule means that the defendant cannot escape liability by arguing that a person of normal sensitivity would not have suffered a heart attack under these circumstances.

[Q3146]

74. **A** The case is governed by the UCC, since a trailer, though large, is still an item of personal property and thus constitutes "goods," the sale of which is covered by Article 2. To begin our analysis, if we assume that the contracted-for trailer was one with a spare tire, the buyer was permitted to reject the tendered trailer for lack of the tire. That's because §2-601 says that in a single-shot (non-installment) contract, "unless otherwise agreed ... if the goods or the tender of delivery fail *in any respect* to conform to the contract, the buyer may (a) reject the whole [.]" So no matter how minor the defect, the buyer was entitled to insist that it be cured before he was required to accept the trailer. But it does not follow that the defect entitled the buyer to cancel the contract. That's because §2-508(1) says that "where any tender or delivery by the seller is rejected because non-conforming and the time for performance has not yet expired, the seller may seasonably notify the buyer of his intention to cure and may then within the contract time make a conforming delivery." Here, the time for performance would not expire until the end of business on Monday, June 1, and the dealer was proposing to cure the problem on Monday, i.e., within the contract time. Therefore, the dealer met the notification requirement of §2-508(1), and had the right to try to make the actual cure up until the end of June 1.

(B) is wrong because, while §2-601 in theory applies the perfect tender rule — which would allow the buyer to reject and terminate immediately — that rule is subject to the seller's right under §2-508(1) to give notice of intent to cure within the contract period and to then make the cure.

(C) is wrong because the buyer was not required to accept the trailer on May 31, with the defect still uncured. And that was true no matter how easy and probable a timely cure appeared to be. Instead, the buyer was permitted to suspend his performance (i.e., his acceptance and payment), wait and see whether the dealer promptly cured the defect as promised, and if it didn't, make a final rejection.

(D) is wrong because the buyer was *not* required to accept the trailer given the defect, despite the fact that the defect did not substantially impair the trailer's value. If the tendered goods are defective, no matter how small the defect is (assuming it indeed amounts to a true "defect" as opposed to a permissible variation under relevant trade usage), the buyer may reject the goods if the defect is not cured. To put it another way, there is no doctrine of "substantial performance" with respect to the seller's obligations under a single-shot (non-installment) contract for the sale of goods.

[Q2106]

75. **D** The ownership and operation of ordinary buildings is not subject to the type of intense regulation that would permit inspections that were supported by neither a search warrant nor probable cause. *Camara v. Municipal Court* (1967). So this case does not fall within the special rule allowing warrantless and probable-causeless searches of heavily-regulated businesses like weapons dealers. But even a garden-variety regulatory scheme will allow regulators to conduct a search of the building to look for health and safety violations without probable cause to suspect that there are violations in any particular building, as long as the regulators first get a series of warrants covering each building to be inspected, and as long as the regulators seeking the warrants demonstrate merely that their inspections will be done pursuant to reasonable administrative standards. *Camara, supra*. So here, the fact that there was a warrant covering the defendant's building, when coupled with the fact that the inspections were being done pursuant to an organized attempt to enforce health and safety codes applicable to the neighborhood, sufficed to meet the requirements of the Fourth Amendment even though there was no probable cause to believe that the defendant's building had violations.

(A) is wrong because, even in the absence of probable cause to believe that health and safety violations exist in a particular building, a warrant to search it for such violations may be issued as part of reasonable standards-based efforts to enforce a generally-applicable regulatory scheme.

(B) is wrong because the existence of such a neighborhood-inspection scheme justifies the issuance of warrants like those issued here, rather than invalidating it.

(C) is wrong because it is a misstatement of law. The ownership and operation of ordinary buildings is not subject to the type of intense regulation that would permit inspections that were not supported by a search warrant (as would, for instance, operation of a weapons dealership). *Camara v. Municipal Court* (1967). So a warrant was required by the Fourth Amendment. However, as detailed in Choice (D), the warrant did not need to be supported by probable cause to believe that violations would be found in any particular building.

[Q5022]

76. **C** This choice is correct because the friend cannot be impeached on a collateral issue by extrinsic evidence. The manager's testimony is not relevant to any substantive issue in the case — it bears solely on the friend's credibility. Therefore, the matter is governed by FRE 608(b), which says in part that "Specific instances of the conduct of a witness, for the purpose of attacking or supporting the witness' credibility, other than conviction of crime as provided in Rule 609, may not be proved by extrinsic evidence." In other words, once a lawyer has completed cross-examination of a witness, he must be satisfied with whatever he could bring out on cross tending to show that the witness lied on a collateral matter (i.e., a matter not pertaining to the substantive issues in the case) — the lawyer may not introduce another witness, or document, to prove that the first witness lied. Here, the testimony of the manager is extrinsic evidence of specific conduct by the friend, offered for the purpose of attacking the friend's credibility. Therefore, it is barred by the just-quoted portion of 608(b).

(A) is wrong because there is no discretion to admit extrinsic evidence to impeach on a collateral issue. If the prosecutor had presented the friend with a document tending to show he had lied on his credit card application, *that* would be admissible in the judge's discretion, because the second sentence of Rule 608(b) says that "Specific instances of the conduct of a witness, for the purpose of attacking or supporting the witness' credibility ... may, however, in the discretion of the court, if probative of truthfulness or untruthfulness, be *inquired into on cross-examination* of the witness (1) concerning the witness' character for truthfulness or untruthfulness[.]" But since the testimony here is from witness 2 (the manager) about the credibility of witness 1 (the friend), it's extrinsic evidence governed by the first sentence of 608(b) (quoted in the discussion of Choice (C) above), not the sentence just quoted; therefore, the judge can't use her discretion to admit it.

(B) is wrong because, while the friend may have "opened the door" to being asked further questions about his application on cross, he did not (and could not) open the door to the use of extrinsic evidence to show he was lying. As the discussion of Choice (C) indicates, once a lawyer has completed cross-examination of a witness, he must be satisfied with whatever he could bring out on cross tending to show that the witness lied on a collateral matter (i.e., a matter not pertaining to the substantive issues in the case) — the lawyer may not introduce another witness, or document, to show that the first witness lied. So nothing the friend said could have "opened the door" to this type of extrinsic evidence.

(D) is wrong because whether the friend could have honestly misunderstood the form is irrelevant — the evidence is extrinsic evidence barred because it pertains to a collateral matter, as discussed in the analysis of Choice (C) above.

[Q3122]

77. **A** Defense of property is a defense to an intentional tort — one may use *reasonable* force to prevent trespass, or other interference with one's land or chattels. However, deadly force (i.e., force that is likely to cause death or serious bodily harm) cannot be used except to prevent an intrusion that is likely to cause death or serious injury to the inhabitants. When a property owner uses force indirectly, by means of an automatic mechanical device like the one here, the case is judged by the same standards as if the owner were acting directly. Consequently, if a live person in the owner's position would not reasonably have believed that the intruder posed a serious risk of death or seri-

ous injury to the inhabitants, use of the deadly-force mechanical device would not be privileged. By this standard, even though the salesman was an outright trespasser, because he did not pose a threat of death or serious bodily harm the homeowner was only entitled to use reasonable, non-deadly force to deter him.

(B) is wrong because even if the intent is only to deter, deadly force cannot be used against trespassers who do not pose a threat of death or serious injury to the inhabitants, as is more fully explained in the analysis of Choice (A).

(C) is wrong because deadly force cannot be used against non-dangerous trespassers, even if a warning is given. As is described more fully in the treatment of Choice (A), deadly force cannot be used against trespassers who do not pose a threat of death or serious injury to the inhabitants. This rule is true even if the owner gives a warning against entry. (In any event, the warning here did not even specify that serious force, posing the risk of bodily injury or death, would be used, so it's doubly unlikely to immunize the homeowner from liability.)

(D) is wrong because even if the homeowner did reasonably fear that intruders would come to harm him or his family, the salesman himself did not pose such a danger. When an owner uses an automatic mechanical device to protect against intruders, the situation is judged by the same standards as if the owner were personally applying the force. Therefore, the mechanical device can supply deadly force (force likely to cause death or serious bodily injury) only if the owner could do so personally on the particular occasion in question. An owner could use such deadly force only if the owner reasonably feared, in that particular situation, that the intruder posed a risk of death or serious bodily harm to the owner or other inhabitants. Here, one in the homeowner's position would have realized that the intruder was unlikely to pose such harm, and was instead a salesman. Since the homeowner would not have been entitled to use deadly force "by hand" against the salesman (e.g., by shooting him), he is not protected when his automatic device applies deadly force.

[Q3195]

78. **D** When the grantor conveyed Lot 1 to the investor, the grantor burdened Lot 2 with the covenant to reimburse the owner of Lot 1 for wall-repair expenses. This covenant was enforceable, and ran with the land on both the burden and benefit side. Even though more than 50 years have passed, no event has occurred (e.g., change of circumstances rendering fulfillment of the covenant's purposes impossible) that would cause the covenant to be extinguished, and the mere passage of time does not suffice to end the covenant. The fact that the covenant ran with the land on the benefit side means that the student as present owner of the benefited lot gets to enforce the covenant; this running of the benefit side occurs even though the deed to conveying the benefited parcel to the student did not mention the covenant or the wall (since mention of the covenant in the deed to the benefited lot is simply not a requirement). The running of the covenant on the burden side means that the obligation of payment attached to the grantor's son's interest in Lot 2. Therefore, the only way the student can lose is if his expenditures were not reasonable and customary (in which case they would not be covered by the terms of the covenant, even though the covenant is still enforceable).

(A) is wrong because nothing occurred to cause the doctrine of adverse possession to affect title to the benefited lot (Lot 1) while that lot was held by either the investor, the housewife, or the student. For instance, no action by any owner of Lot 2 could even arguably have constituted the requisite hostile, notorious, open, and continuous possession of the wall so as to wipe out the covenant governing repairs.

(B) is wrong because the fact that the investor's deed from the grantor for Lot 1 was not recorded had no effect on anyone who ever had an interest in Lot 2. It's true that the grantor, by conveying Lot 1 to the investor, simultaneously created a covenant burdening Lot 2, which was an interest in Lot 2. But a grantee's failure to record under a recording act has no effect on the rights as between the original grantor and grantee; therefore, in a contest between the grantor and the investor, the investor's failure to record his covenant against Lot 2 would not prevent the investor from recovering reimbursement from the grantor while the grantor still owned Lot 2. The interesting question is whether the investor's failure to record can be taken advantage of by the grantor's son as the grantor's successor. In other words, is the grantor's son a "subsequent purchaser without notice" who can take advantage of the fact that the deed creating the covenant never appeared in his chain of title? The answer is that because recording acts invariably protect only "purchasers for value," and because the son took by intestate succession (and thus did not give value for his interest), the son is *not* a purchaser for value and thus *cannot* take advantage of the recording act. (If the son had purchased for value and without notice of the covenant, he *would* have been free of the covenant on account of the investor's failure to record.)

(C) is wrong because the owner of a parcel benefited by an affirmative covenant does not lose the benefit merely because he did not act in reliance on the covenant's existence.

[Q2107]

79. **B** This is a somewhat tricky question because it's a hybrid — you need to know the relevant procedural rule as well as the substantive rule. First, procedure: As a general rule, if the evidence would justify a reasonable jury in convicting the defendant of a lesser offense (here, manslaughter), the issue should be submitted to the jury. By stating that whether the issue of manslaughter should go to the jury is based on what the jury could find, instead of what the judge believes the evidence shows, (B) correctly states this rule. Next, substance: the reasoning in (B) correctly identifies a basis on which the jury could find the defendant guilty only of manslaughter. Voluntary manslaughter is an unlawful killing committed under adequate provocation. Murder is an unlawful killing committed with malice aforethought. Thus, if the jury finds that an act by the other customer sufficiently provoked the defendant, it will find him guilty of voluntary manslaughter instead of murder. Being hit in the face with an umbrella is just the sort of thing that *could* be considered provocation sufficient to reduce the defendant's liability to manslaughter. A wrinkle in this problem is that the defendant, in a way, provoked the provocation by stealing the tip. But that's not relevant for the defendant's liability in *this* question (whereas it would be relevant to the customer's liability in attacking the defendant, since she would have a crime-prevention argument); see the analysis of Choice (D) for why.

(A) is wrong because it does not apply the correct rule for voluntary manslaughter. In order to be found liable for only voluntary manslaughter instead of murder, the jury would have to find that the defendant acted under provocation; that is, that he committed an unlawful killing with malice aforethought, but was provoked. If you chose (A), you probably did so because you confused the rule for voluntary manslaughter with that for depraved-heart murder, which is what (A) more or less states. Thus, if the jury found that the defendant acted with reckless indifference to the value of human life, but not with the intent to kill or seriously injure, it would *still* find him guilty of depraved-heart murder.

(C) is wrong because it arrives at an incorrect result, and does not allow the jury to find voluntary manslaughter, which is possible from these facts. In the jury's role as the finder of *facts,* the jury should be given the option to find any result which is plausible (i.e., that a reasonable jury could find beyond a reasonable doubt) on these facts. And voluntary manslaughter is such a result, because a reasonable jury could find that the defendant was sufficiently provoked to reduce murder to manslaughter. Thus, (C)'s statement that the defendant intended to kill or cause serious harm doesn't go far enough, because even if he *did* act with intent, if he did so under adequate provocation he'll only be liable for voluntary manslaughter.

(D) is wrong because it arrives at the wrong result, based on incorrect legal reasoning. The defendant's provoking the assault on himself would not prevent him from being found guilty of manslaughter. When a defendant would otherwise have the defense of self-defense (leading to outright acquittal), most states make available the doctrine of "imperfect self-defense." Under that doctrine, when the defendant intentionally kills another, he'll be liable for voluntary manslaughter if either he was the initial aggressor in a fight (and therefore not entitled to a self-defense claim), *or* he honestly but unreasonably believed deadly force was necessary. So the fact that the defendant arguably provoked the encounter — assuming that what the defendant did was indeed viewed as "being the aggressor" (which it probably wouldn't be, since the defendant merely stole, rather than being the first to use force) — wouldn't deprive him of the right to be convicted of voluntary manslaughter rather than murder.

[Q4038]

80. **C** Prior statements that are inconsistent with a witness's present testimony impeach the witness' credibility because they tend to show that the witness' trial testimony is not believable. The prior inconsistent statement was not made under oath, and so does not fit the exemption to the hearsay rule provided by FRE 801(d)(1)(A). There is no other hearsay exception that is satisfied under the facts. Therefore, the statement is admissible only to impeach the witness and not for its truth.

(A) is wrong because, under FRE 607, "[t]he credibility of a witness may be attacked by any party, including the party calling the witness."

(B) is wrong because the prior statement of the witness is inadmissible hearsay under FRE 802 only if offered to prove that the defendant was involved in the transaction. It is not hearsay if offered to impeach the witness whose trial testimony is inconsistent with it. This is because, whether true or not, the statement is probative to show that the witness is not credible—he said one thing at trial and said something else previously.

(D) is wrong because the first part of the statement is correct but the second part is incorrect. The prior inconsistent statement was not made under oath, and so does not fit the exemption to the hearsay rule provided by FRE 801(d)(1)(A). There is no other hearsay exception that is satisfied under the facts. Therefore the statement is admissible only to impeach the witness and not for its truth. Using the statement to prove the defendant's involvement would violate FRE 802, the hearsay rule.

[Q7019]

81. **D** First, we have to decide whether the landlord committed trespass. Trespass to land occurs when the defendant intentionally enters land in the "possession" of another. A tenant has possession of the premises, even though he does not have outright ownership. Conversely, a landlord of leased premises, even though she owns the premises, does not have possession of them. So the landlord here committed trespass when he entered the student's premises. As to remedies: there is evidence supporting compensatory damages (emotional distress, the removal of the faucets) and punitive damages (malicious intent, ill will). Because the lease is still in effect and the trespasses are repeated and ongoing, injunctive relief should also be available.

(A) is wrong because the student is in legal possession of the apartment and thus has an interest that can be vindicated in a trespass action, as further described in Choice (D) above.

(B) is wrong because: (1) damage is not necessary to establish a cause of action in trespass; and (2) in any case, the removal of the faucets was damage to the property.

(C) is wrong because these facts demonstrate a pattern of ongoing malicious behavior, so the law student is unlikely to be limited to compensatory damages. In addition to compensatory damages for emotional distress and the removal of the faucets, the student is entitled to punitive damages (demonstrated by the landlord's malicious intent and ill will). And because the lease is still in effect and the trespasses are repeated and ongoing, injunctive relief should also be available.

[Q7088]

82. **A** Incident to a lawful arrest in an arrestee's home, the officers executing the warrant may conduct a

"protective sweep" of all or part of the premises, if they have a "reasonable belief" that another person who might be dangerous to the officers may be present *in the areas swept. Maryland v. Buie* (1990). So here, the police had the right to search the house for accomplices. The Uzi, however, was found in a box on a closet shelf. Clearly the weapon was neither in plain sight nor in a place where a person could be found. Therefore, the protective-sweep exception doesn't apply. Since the search warrant covered only the brown suitcase (which the police had already seized), their search of the closet could not be justified on the grounds that they were executing the search warrant either.

(B) is wrong because the answer misstates the applicable law: the police had the right to search the house for accomplices. As is described in the analysis of Choice (A) above, the police had the right to check protectively for other persons. Therefore, this choice — since it says that no further search of the house was permitted once the suitcase was seized — is inconsistent with the officers' right to make the protective search (which may be made at any time that the police are still on the premises and are thus vulnerable to a sudden attack from someone who might be hiding).

(C) is wrong because the weapon was not in an area that could be searched. It's true that the police were lawfully in the bedroom (under their right to make a protective sweep — see Choice (A)). But while they were in the bedroom, the police were only permitted to look in places where a person might be hiding. They therefore weren't allowed to look in small boxes, as they did here.

(D) is wrong because, while the police knew that there might well be weapons in the house, they would have needed a warrant in order to look for such weapons at the top of the closet. There are two requirements that must be satisfied before a house may be searched for a particular item, unless there is some applicable exception: (1) probable cause to believe that the item will be found; and (2) a warrant to search for it. Here, since the facts tell us that the police had gotten reliable information that the singer and his accomplices "kept a small arsenal of weapons in [the singer's] home," requirement (1) was satisfied as to the weapons. But although the police procured a search warrant, that warrant did not cover the weapons, only the brown suitcase. Therefore, the fact that the police were already in the home, and the further fact that they had probable cause to believe that the weapons would or might be found, were not enough to permit them to look not either in the bedroom or in the closet. And while their need to make a "protective sweep" justified them in looking in the bedroom, this need did not, as described in the discussion of Choice (A), authorize them to search in a small box on a shelf, since no one could have been hiding there.

[Q3068]

83. **B** The woman's consent justified the officers' entry. When a person consents to the entry of law enforcement officers into an area as to which the person would otherwise have a justifiable expectation of privacy, that consent validates the police entry, and nullifies any need for either probable cause or a search warrant that may have existed prior to the consent. Once the police then make their consented-to entry, the "plain view" doctrine entitles them to seize any item whose contraband or evidentiary nature is obvious, as long as when they have the view the police are standing in a place where they have a right to be. *Harris v. U.S.* (1968). Since the woman consented to the officers' entry into her house, and since the officers spotted the heroin while standing in a place to which the consent applied, there could not have been either an illegal search or an illegal seizure.

(A) is wrong because, while this answer correctly states that the woman's motion to suppress the heroin should not be granted, it misstates the legal basis for this conclusion. Even assuming there was probable cause to search the home, a warrant would have been required for entry had the woman not consented. See, e.g., *Payton v. New York* (1980).

(C) is wrong because the search of the man, even assuming it was improper, did not violate the woman's rights and therefore provides no basis for suppressing evidence found in her house. That is, the woman did not have "standing" to assert a violation of the constitutional rights of a third party. Cf. *Minnesota v. Carter* (1998) (discussing standing requirements for third-party constitutional claims).

(D) is wrong because there is no requirement that officers inform individuals of their right to refuse consent. See *Schneckloth v. Bustamonte* (1973). Therefore, the consent was valid.

[Q7022]

84. **B** The remainder to "my niece, her heirs and assigns" was a remainder to the niece in fee simple. Since the niece was alive and identifiable at the time of the grantor's deed, the remainder to the niece was vested. A vested remainder can be left by will. Therefore, the remainder passed by the will to the boyfriend.

(A) is wrong because the remainder was never contingent, not even for an instant.

(C) is wrong because a vested remainder can be passed by will, and the will here devised the remainder to the boyfriend; therefore, the fact that the niece's cousin was the niece's heir at law is irrelevant.

(D) is wrong because the remainder here was vested, not contingent; therefore, the doctrine of destructibility of contingent remainders is irrelevant.

[Q1151]

85. **C** To establish a prima facie case for invasion of privacy by appropriation of plaintiff's picture or name, only one element needs to be proved: that there was an unauthorized use by defendant of plaintiff's picture or name for commercial advantage. Under these facts the actor consented to an amateur photographer taking his picture as he sat drinking Vineyard wine at a nightclub. He did not consent to the bottler's using his photo for commercial purposes. The bottler's advertisement in a nationally circulated magazine was intended for the bottler's commercial advantage.

(A) is wrong because the actor's consent was to the amateur photographer, not to the bottler's commercial use. To establish a prima facie case for invasion of privacy by appropriation of plaintiff's picture or name, only one element needs to be proved: that there was an unauthorized use by defendant of plaintiff's picture or name for commercial advantage. Here, the actor's consent was specifically to an amateur photographer. The scope of the actor's consent was to a single amateur photograph. He did not consent to the bottler's using that photograph for its commercial advantage. Therefore, his "consent" would not negate the bottler's liability.

(B) is wrong because public figures retain the right not to have their image utilized for commercial advantage. It's true that the actor was a well-known movie star and so would be considered a public figure. While this fact might conceivably be relevant in other kinds of invasion of privacy claims, or in some defamation claims, it is irrelevant to the claim here, as to which the only element that needs to be proved is that there was an unauthorized use by defendant of plaintiff's picture or name for commercial advantage. Therefore, the actor's status as a public figure does not exonerate the bottler.

(D) is wrong because a person's enjoyment of a product does not convey the rights to commercial use of an image of the person using the product. To establish a prima facie case for invasion of privacy by appropriation of plaintiff's picture or name, only one element needs to be proved: that there was an unauthorized use by defendant of plaintiff's picture or name for commercial advantage. Truth is therefore not a defense to this appropriation form of invasion of privacy. Thus although it's true that the actor enjoyed Vineyard wine, this fact did not give the bottler the right to make commercial use of the actor's image, or to say, for commercial purposes, that the actor liked the wine.

[Q3192]

86. **C** Under joint and several liability, the entire amount can be collected from any one of the defendants. That defendant, in turn, can seek to recover a proportional share of the damages from the other defendants. The fact that there is no imputed negligence means that the parents' lack of care

does not reduce the child's recovery.

(A) is wrong because, while this might be a correct computation of the driver's pro rata share of damages, it is not correct under comparative negligence with joint and several liability. Under joint and several liability, the entire amount can be collected from any one of the defendants. That defendant, in turn, can seek to recover a proportional (rather than a pro rata) share of the damages from the other defendants.

(B) is wrong because, although this answer would be correct if liability were only several, here liability is joint and several. Under joint and several liability, the entire amount can be collected from any one of the defendants. That defendant, in turn, can seek to recover a proportional share of the damages from the other defendants.

(D) is wrong because, while this might be the rule under a traditional contributory negligence regime where the negligence of the parent is imputed to the child and bars all recovery, it is not the rule under the regime here (no imputation, plus joint-and-several liability). Under joint and several liability, the entire amount can be collected from any one of the defendants. And with no imputing of liability, the parents' fault is not imputed to the child, so that parental fault does not reduce the child's recovery from the driver.

[Q7072]

87. **A** This choice is correct because evidence of intoxication might negate the requisite intent for both crimes. Voluntary intoxication evidence may be offered, when the defendant is charged with a crime that requires purpose or intent, to establish that the intoxication may have prevented the defendant from formulating the requisite intent. Each of the crimes charged here requires a particular intent. Assault requires an intent to cause bodily harm. Attempted murder requires an intent to kill. If the defendant was intoxicated, this fact might (would not necessarily, but might) indicate that he could not or did not form the required intent. Therefore, the evidence is relevant to both crimes, and must be admitted.

(B), (C), and (D) are all wrong because they are inconsistent with the above analysis.

[Q4007]

88. **A** The only plausible action would be for battery, the intentional infliction of a harmful or offensive bodily contact. Since it's clear that the passenger did not intend to make a "harmful" contact, the question is whether he intended to make an "offensive" contact. A bodily contact is offensive if and only if it "offends a reasonable sense of personal dignity." Rest. 2d, §19. The contact here does not meet this standard for offensiveness, because the woman gave no indication that she did not want to be subjected to the ordinary touches that are part of life in a crowded society. In the absence of such an indication from her, the passenger was entitled to believe that the woman implicitly consented to a light tap to get her attention, i.e., that such an attention-getting tap would not "offend a reasonable sense of personal dignity." Therefore, the passenger did not commit battery. (Nor did he commit negligence, since negligence requires an unreasonable risk of harm, which was not present in these circumstances when viewed from the perspective of the facts known to the passenger.)

(B) is wrong because, while this answer correctly states that the woman cannot prevail, it misstates the legal basis for this conclusion. It is true that if the woman was suing for *assault*, she would have to prove that she thought that she was about to be touched in order to win. But the elements of a *negligence* or a *battery* action could be established without any reference to whether she had an apprehension of this or any other sort, so the lack of apprehension cannot explain the fact of non-liability. (Instead, the non-liability for negligence or battery is due to the reasons given in choice (A) above.)

(C) is wrong because the fact that the touching was intentional does not make the touching actionable, either as battery or anything else. It's true that battery (the most likely tort on these facts) is the intentional infliction of a harmful or offensive bodily contact, so the fact that the passenger intentionally touched the woman sounds like it might lead to liability. But the defendant must not only intend the touching, he must intend a touching that, viewed from the perspective of one in his position, would be regarded as harmful or offensive. For the reasons given in choice (A), the passenger did not have cause to regard his touch as being harmful or offensive here.

(D) is wrong because serious injury is neither necessary nor sufficient to support either battery or negligence, although some damage would be required to recover in negligence. For battery, the defendant must not only make a touching that turns out to be harmful or offensive (which the touching here arguably was because of the resulting pain to the woman), the defendant must *intend* a touching that, viewed from the perspective of one in his position, would be regarded as harmful or offensive. Here, one in the passenger's position would not expect the touch to be either harmful or offensive, so the requirement of an "intentional or offensive touching" is not met.

[Q7063]

89. **D** The issue here is the validity of the school's gender-based classification, under which students who are mothers of an infant can use the day-care center but students who are fathers of an infant cannot. For such a gender-based classification, the court uses intermediate-level scrutiny, under which, as Choice (D) recites, the defendant (the government) bears the burden of showing that its classification is "substantially related" to the fulfillment of an "important governmental interest." [*Craig v. Boren* (1976)] Notice that the standard is the same for a male plaintiff who is disadvantaged by the classification as it would be for a female plaintiff who was disadvantaged.

(A) would be correct if the classification were one that did not involve a suspect or semi-suspect class or fundamental interest (e.g., a garden-variety economic or social-welfare regulation); but since gender is a semi-suspect category, the standard in choice (A) is insufficiently demanding.

(B) is incorrect mainly because, when the classification is based on gender, the use of semi-strict scrutiny means that the government bears the burden of persuasion. (Also, the key phrases "narrowly drawn as possible" and "substantial governmental interest" are not quite right).

(C) is wrong because, while it correctly places the burden of persuasion on the government defendant, this choice recites the standard for strict rather than semi-strict scrutiny.

[Q2155]

90. **B** First, since the continued existence of the office being painted was a major assumption on which the contract was based, the destruction of the office will cause both parties to be contractually discharged. Second, when contractual duties are discharged on account of impossibility, a party who has partly performed will generally be permitted to recover in quasi-contract for restitution, i.e., for the value of the benefit conferred on the other party. Therefore, the painter will be permitted to recover for the value of the painting that he had done as of the moment of the fire.

(A) is wrong because, as discussed in the analysis of Choice (B) above, a party who has partly performed by the time of the event causing the discharge is permitted to recover in quasi-contract for the value of his partial performance.

(C) is wrong because the lawyer's performance is discharged not because *it* is impossible, but because the performance which the lawyer was to receive in exchange for her own performance (a paint job) is impossible. When performance of one side of the agreed exchange is rendered impossible, the other side is discharged so as to prevent either side from being unjustly enriched.

(D) is wrong because: (1) both parties' contractual duties (not just the painter's) are discharged; and (2) the painter's damages would be measured by a restitution concept (value conferred on the lawyer just before the fire) rather than by a reliance concept.

[Q1121]

91. **A** Under FRE 608(b), a witness can be impeached with prior bad acts that bear upon truthfulness.

Failing to stop at a stop sign has no bearing on truthfulness. As a general matter, a witness also can be impeached with evidence that contradicts a part of his testimony that bears on an important issue in dispute. However, in this case, the prior bad acts do not contradict the witness's testimony that he stopped on this occasion. Essentially, the defendant is trying to show that the plaintiff is a careless driver. Carelessness is a character trait, and evidence of a person's character is not admissible in a civil case to prove how that person acted on the occasion in question. (FRE 404(a)).

(B) is wrong because, under FRE 608(b), a witness can be impeached with bad acts that do not result in convictions. The reason that the prior acts here are inadmissible is not because there were no convictions, but rather because the acts have no bearing on veracity or contradiction of prior testimony.

(C) is wrong because it's factually incorrect. It's true that under FRE 608(b), a witness can be impeached with prior bad acts that bear upon truthfulness by demonstrating falsity, dishonesty, or the like; so if the prior acts bore on truthfulness, they could be used for impeachment here. But in this case, the plaintiff's prior acts may demonstrate carelessness, but they do not demonstrate dishonesty.

(D) is wrong, because the conclusion does not follow logically from the premise. A person can be acting carefully on one occasion and not another, so the prior acts are not contradictory of the plaintiff's testimony that he was careful in this instance, as this choice asserts. If the plaintiff testified that he had never run a stop sign, then the prior acts *would* contradict his testimony, and would be admissible.

[Q7012]

92. **B** Normally, an owner's refusal to abate a naturally-occurring condition on his land will not be deemed to be a nuisance. But nearly all courts have long recognized an exception for trees that pose the risk of falling on the public highway, and some courts have extended this exception to trees that pose a risk of physical danger to those on adjacent non-highway property. A court would not necessarily find that the risk of danger from the fallen trees makes the condition a nuisance, but of the four choices this is the only one that could plausibly lead to a finding of nuisance.

(A) and (C) are wrong because, while these might be reasons for holding that a man-made feature poses a nuisance, they would not be grounds for overruling the usual rule that failure to abate a naturally-occurring condition is a nuisance.

(D) is wrong because the fact that a condition cannot be challenged by any other law or ordinance does not mean that the court will find it to constitute a nuisance — the man will have to show that the conditions here cause him a substantial interference with his use and enjoyment of his property, and the fact that the condition doesn't violate a law or ordinance doesn't say anything about whether the man can meet this standard.

[Q3175]

93. **C** The UCC controls. The seller is entitled to be put in the position it would have been in if the contract had been performed. The proper measure of damages here is set out in UCC §2-708(2), which provides that a seller is entitled to the profit the seller would have made ($2 per set), plus an allowance for costs reasonably incurred ($8 per set), minus payments received for resale of the goods ($2 per set) — here, the salvage. Accordingly, the seller should recover $2 + $8 − $2 = $8 per set.

(A) is wrong, because the seller is entitled to be put in the position it would have been in if the contract had been performed, and two dollars per set fails to accomplish that goal. This would have been a correct answer ONLY IF the seller had not yet begun manufacturing the ball bearings. The seller incurred those costs in preparing for performance, and is entitled to recover them in order to protect its expectation interest.

(B) is wrong, because the difference between the cost of manufacture and the salvage price fails to take account of the lost profit the seller ($2 per unit) is entitled to recover.

(D) is wrong, because the statutory section which controls, UCC § 2-708(2), tries to put the seller in the position it would have been in had the contract been performed, and contains no requirement that the goods be salvaged by sale at a public auction.

[Q7031]

94. **B** In judging the constitutionality of the display of a religious symbol such as a nativity scene, the most important single factor seems to be the context in which the religious symbol is displayed: If the religious symbol is presented by itself in what is clearly a space reserved by the government for its own property and its own messages, the Court is likely to conclude that a reasonable observer would believe that the government was endorsing the religious message. Conversely, the presence of other non-religious symbols nearby, or the existence of a sign indicating that the display was furnished by private parties, may well be enough to lead a reasonable observer to the conclusion that the government was *not* endorsing religion. [*Allegheny County v. ACLU*]

On this standard, the proposed display of the nativity scene here would be unconstitutional. The nativity scene would not be surrounded by non-religious symbols having to do with the holiday season (symbols that would make it seem that the nativity scene was just part of a secular celebration of the holiday season). The whole presentation here — and the fact that the governor and legislature supported it — would create in a reasonable observer the impression that the government was endorsing a religious message. And the fact that the display components would be contributed by private citizens would not be enough to prevent the reasonable observer from believing that the government was endorsing religion.

(A) is wrong because the ownership of the display would not be dispositive on the issue of whether government seemed to be endorsing religion. If the scene here seemed to be a celebration of Christmas as a primarily secular holiday, the fact that the government owned the display would not be fatal. But, for the reasons discussed in Choice (B) above, the context of the display here would suggest to a reasonable observer that the state was endorsing religion. Consequently, the display violates the Establishment Clause.

(C) is wrong because donation would be only one element considered in the total context of the display. If the display made it clear to the public that private citizens had donated the components, this would indeed be one factor (but just one) tending to demonstrate that the display was not a forbidden government endorsement of religion. But there's no indication here that the fact of private donations would be disclosed to the public. Furthermore, this fact, even if disclosed, probably wouldn't be enough to overcome the otherwise-powerful impression that the government is endorsing a religious message.

(D) is wrong because displaying the scene next to the products would not rebut the impression that the state was endorsing the nativity scene's religious message. When a religious symbol such as a nativity scene is displayed in a public place, the issue is whether a reasonable observer would believe that the government is endorsing a religious method. Context is all-important. If the nativity scene were displayed next to other objects that pertain to December as a primarily secular holiday (e.g., a Santa Claus figure), the impression of an endorsement of religion would be rebutted. But putting the scene next to the year-round display of in-state-manufactured products would not rebut the impression of an endorsement of religion, because an observer would realize that the two displays were separate, and that the nativity scene was its own stand-alone display on an explicitly religious topic.

[Q3165]

95. **C** The Court held in *Webster v. Reproductive Health Services* (1989) that a state could constitutionally forbid the use of all public facilities and publicly-employed staff in abortions, without thereby violating the substantive due process right to abortion. If the state forbade all facilities in the state

— public or private — from performing abortions, that would be an unconstitutional "undue burden" on abortion, but the availability of private-facility abortions here prevents an undue burden from occurring. And the fact that the state here is allowing the use of public facilities for those abortions necessary to save the life of the mother makes it even more clear that the regulation is constitutional. (Probably under *Webster* such an exception is not even required.)

(A) is wrong because the Court has held (in *Webster*, supra) that the availability of private-facility abortions means that a ban on the use of public facilities does not impermissibly interfere with the right of abortion.

(B) is wrong because the Court has held (in *Harris v. McRae* (1980)) that government's refusal to fund abortions for patients who cannot afford them does not constitute an interference with the constitutionally-protected right to abortion.

(D) is wrong because the Court no longer uses the privilege/right distinction in deciding cases involving the exercise of the important constitutional interests, and it is certainly not the case that the state may condition access to public facilities for an abortion "on any basis it chooses." (For instance, the state could not say that it will fund abortions at state-owned facilities for white women but not black women.)

[Q2162]

96. **A** Art. IV, Sec. 3, Cl. 2 gives Congress the power to "make all needful Rules and Regulations respecting the Territory or other Property belonging to the United States[.]" Since the National Forest is federally-owned property, this clause gives Congress the power to pass regulations governing it. Under the supremacy clause, those regulations would take precedence over any conflicting state regulations, such as the right to kill coyotes implied by the state bounty bill.

(B) is wrong because it suggests that there is an independent Congressional power to act to advance "the general welfare." This is not so — there's a power to "*tax and spend ...* for the general welfare," but that's not what's at issue here (because Congress is doing pure regulating, not taxing or spending).

(C) is wrong because if Congress has been given an explicit power in a certain area (here, the power to regulate on federal lands), Congress can indeed override whatever right the state might otherwise have to legislate in areas of traditional state governmental functions.

(D) is wrong because the Full Faith and Credit clause does not block Congress from punishing conduct that has been authorized by a state; the clause merely requires one state to enforce every other state's judgments.

[Q2079]

97. **C** One mental state that suffices for murder is an intent to commit serious bodily injury. Since it was the defendant's intention to severely injure the player, the intent element is satisfied. The only remaining issue is whether the defendant's act was a proximate cause of the player's death. If it was, then the defendant is guilty of murder.

An intervening cause will not be superseding (i.e., will not prevent the earlier cause from being a proximate cause) only if the intervening cause was not reasonably foreseeable. Although the player's allergic reaction to the drug was an intervening cause of harm to him, the drug was given to relieve pain which resulted from the beating, so the giving of the drug was certainly not unforeseeable. The fatal allergic reaction itself was unusual, but not so uncommon or bizarre as to be fairly called unforeseeable. Indeed, one of the standard risks from conduct that puts a person in need of medical attention is that medical negligence, hospital infections, allergies, and the like, will then ensue, so even if the particular intervening harmful medical event is unusual, the overall class of harmful medical events will be viewed as foreseeable and thus not superseding. And that is true even if the intervening medical event was the product of negligent medical treatment. So the allergy here will not be found to be a supervening event whether the use of the drug was negligent or not, and the defendant's attack will therefore be a proximate cause of the death.

(A) is wrong because, under the analysis in Choice (C) above, although the drug reaction was an intervening cause, it was not a superseding cause, and will therefore not prevent the defendant's attack from being deemed to be a proximate cause.

(B) is wrong because the player's death may have had several proximate causes. The fact that the doctor's conduct was one of them does not mean that the defendant's conduct was not also one of them. Since the doctor's conduct occurred after the defendant's, the doctor's conduct was an *intervening* cause of that death. But an intervening cause does not break the chain of proximate causation, unless that intervention was unforeseeable. As explained in Choice (C) above, the giving of the drug here, and the victim's fatal allergic reaction to it, would not be deemed unforeseeable. Therefore, the defendant will be criminally responsible for the death even if the death was also proximately caused by the doctor's negligence.

(D) is wrong as a statement of law. An intervening cause will be superseding only if that cause was not reasonably foreseeable. The fact that the intervening cause was the product of reckless or gross negligence will not by itself make that cause unforeseeable and thus superseding. Therefore, to the extent that this choice turns solely on whether the doctor's conduct was reckless or grossly negligent, it cannot be the best explanation of the fact that the defendant will be guilty.
[Q5099]

98. **B** The plaintiff owner of a parcel can't gain enforcement of either a covenant at law or an inequitable servitude against a defendant who is the "downstream" owner of a burdened parcel (i.e., one who took after the burden was imposed), unless: (1) there was an intent by the original parties to benefit the parcel now owned by the plaintiff; and (2) the defendant was on actual or constructive notice of the nature of the restriction at the time she took. In the case of the suit by the doctor on behalf of Lot 2, both of these requirements are satisfied: (1) the developer-to-doctor deed made it clear that both Lots 2 and 4 were being both burdened and benefited by mutual single-family-only restrictions (so the requisite intent to benefit Lot 2 is present); and (2) the pharmacist was on constructive (and probably actual) notice of the restriction on the lot she was buying at the time she bought because it was mentioned in the developer-to-doctor deed that was part of the pharmacist's title report (and, indeed, from this the pharmacist knew that that restriction was intended to benefit Lot 2). Therefore, the doctor will likely be entitled to his choice of an injunction and damages (i.e., to recover on the equitable servitude or, alternatively, for breach of covenant at law).

The owners of Lots 1, 3, and 5, by contrast, cannot satisfy either of these requirements: (1) nothing indicates that at the time the developer conveyed these three lots, he was intending (then or ever) to create any equitable restrictions on any of his five lots, so the present owners of the three lots cannot show that their parcels were ever intended to be benefited; and (2) the pharmacist, at the time she took, was not on notice that Lots 1, 3, and 5 were to be benefited by any restriction on the parcel she was buying. So these owners are unlikely to get any relief against the pharmacist.

(A) is wrong because there was no common development scheme at the time Lots 1, 3, and 5 were conveyed. It's true that had there been in place, at the time Lots 1, 3, and 5 were conveyed, a "plan of development" (say, a filed subdivision plat) showing an intent to keep the whole development single-family residential, the owners of Lots 1, 3, and 5 might succeed with an "implied reciprocal servitude" argument, that the developer implicitly promised them that he'd burden his remaining lots consistently with this plan and that the pharmacist should have known of this promise and be required to honor it. But the facts do not indicate that any such plan existed at the time the developer sold Lots 1, 3, and 5.

(C) is wrong because, as noted in the analysis of Choice (B), owners cannot recover damages (i.e., recover on a covenant at law) unless they can show that there was an intent to give their parcels the benefit of the restrictive promise, an intent which is absent as to Lots 1, 3, and 5. The fact that the developer later developed such a purpose to burden his lots doesn't help — there must have been an intent-to-burden at the time when the developer still owned the lots in question.

(D) is wrong because, the existence of a zoning scheme that allows the activity in question doesn't trump a stricter scheme of covenants. If the zoning scheme was stricter, it would prevail (landowners can't by mutual agreement cause strict zoning rules to be relaxed). But the converse is not true — indeed, the whole idea of restrictive covenants is that they can be used to forbid uses that are allowed by the zoning rules.

[Q3055]

99. **C** The doctrine of *res ipsa loquitor* ("the thing speaks for itself") permits the jury to infer negligence without the plaintiff's having produced any direct evidence of negligence. There are two main requirements: (1) the event must be of a kind which ordinarily does not occur in the absence of negligence; and (2) other causes, including the conduct of the plaintiff and third persons, must be sufficiently eliminated by the evidence. Rest. 2d, §328D. These requirements are satisfied here: (1) commercial airline flights normally do not crash into mountains in the absence of negligence; and (2) other causes have been essentially eliminated (for instance, the fact that the weather was good eliminates poor weather as the cause). Some courts add two additional elements for res ipsa: (3) that the instrument that caused the injury have been in the exclusive control of the defendant; and (4) that there be no direct evidence of how the defendant behaved. These two additional requirements, if the jurisdiction applies them, are also easily satisfied, since the airline was in control of the plane, and since there is no direct evidence of what went wrong. Therefore, res ipsa applies, and its effect is to permit the jury to infer: (1) that the defendant was negligent, and (2) that this negligence caused the accident.

(A) is wrong because, as described in (C) above, the doctrine of res ipsa permits the jury to infer that the crash was caused by the airline's negligence, even in the absence of direct evidence from the plaintiff about the cause.

(B) is wrong because, while res ipsa requires that the plaintiff show that the event was of a kind which "ordinarily" does not occur except through the fault of someone, the plaintiff is *not* required to show that the event couldn't possibly have been due to a cause not involving the defendant's fault (as the phrase "negating the possibility" implies). All plaintiff has to show is that, by a preponderance of the evidence (i.e., *more likely than not*), the airline's negligence was to blame, and the fulfillment of the "ordinarily does not occur without negligence" requirement for res ipsa satisfies this more-likely-than-not element of the plaintiff's prima facie case.

(D) is wrong because it misstates the rules for common carriers. Common carriers (including airlines) are required to exercise a very high degree of care toward their passengers and guests, which is to say they are liable for even slight negligence. But they do not have strict liability.

[Q3161]

100. **C** FRE 803(7) gives a hearsay exception for "evidence that a matter is *not included in the ... records ...* kept in accordance with [the business records exception], to *prove the nonoccurrence or nonexistence of the matter*[.]" This exception applies perfectly here: the editor has kept a business record of all retraction demands received by the newspaper, and is submitting here evidence that no retraction demand from the businessman is included in that business record. So this can be used to show that no such retraction demand was received by the paper.

(A) is simply wrong as a matter of law: where a record is kept that satisfies the business records exception, absence of a notation *can* be used as evidence that an event did not occur, as further described in (C) above.

(B) is wrong because the fact that evidence is self-serving is not, alone, sufficient to make it inadmissible.

(D) is wrong because, although almost anything may be used by a witness to refresh his recollection, the fact that a document was so used is not sufficient to permit its admission into evidence.
[Q5025]

ANSWERS
SELF-ASSESSMENT TEST P.M. EXAM

Answer Key

Use this Answer Key to quickly identify the correct answer to each question.

(101) B	(116) C	(131) C	(146) C	(161) A	(176) C	(191) C
(102) B	(117) A	(132) D	(147) B	(162) B	(177) C	(192) C
(103) A	(118) A	(133) D	(148) C	(163) D	(178) A	(193) C
(104) D	(119) A	(134) B	(149) A	(164) C	(179) D	(194) A
(105) A	(120) C	(135) D	(150) A	(165) B	(180) D	(195) C
(106) B	(121) D	(136) D	(151) D	(166) B	(181) C	(196) C
(107) A	(122) B	(137) D	(152) D	(167) A	(182) C	(197) B
(108) A	(123) D	(138) D	(153) A	(168) C	(183) A	(198) C
(109) B	(124) D	(139) C	(154) A	(169) B	(184) C	(199) B
(110) C	(125) A	(140) C	(155) A	(170) C	(185) B	(200) C
(111) D	(126) C	(141) D	(156) C	(171) B	(186) C	
(112) B	(127) D	(142) A	(157) D	(172) B	(187) A	
(113) A	(128) A	(143) C	(158) A	(173) D	(188) D	
(114) A	(129) C	(144) B	(159) B	(174) D	(189) D	
(115) D	(130) A	(145) C	(160) C	(175) A	(190) A	

101. **B** Normally, even where one party knows that the other is making a mistake about a basic assumption, the former's non-disclosure of the relevant fact will not constitute a misrepresentation that the relevant fact does not exist. But the non-disclosure *will* constitute a misrepresentation that the mistaken fact does not exist — and will be grounds for rescission — if it amounts to a "failure to act in good faith and in accordance with reasonable standards of fair dealing." Rest. 2d, §161(b). Where the non-discloser learns of the true fact through improper or questionable means, the court is likely to find a failure to act in good faith. Here, since the horse was the heir's property at the time the trainer secretly timed it in the exercise session, the case is analogous to the Restatement's example of a mining company trespassing on the seller's property to gain mineral-deposit information; a court would therefore likely conclude that the trainer's timing session pushed the entire transaction into the bad-faith category.

(A) is wrong because the trainer's undisclosed experience as a trainer would not alter the general principle that one party's failure to disclose that the other party is making a mistake about a basic assumption does not constitute the sort of misrepresentation that would allow the "innocent" party to rescind. The test is whether the non-discloser's failure to correct the other's mistake constitutes bad faith, and a court would be unlikely to conclude that the non-discloser's failure to disclose his own credentials pushes the entire situation over into the bad-faith column.

(C) is wrong because the party with superior knowledge is normally not required to correct the other party's mistake about even a basic assumption where that assumption is due to the latter's lack of diligence or knowledge — "if the other [party] is indolent, inexperienced or ignorant, or if his judgment is bad or he lacks access to adequate information, his adversary is not generally expected to compensate for these deficiencies. A buyer of property, for example, is not ordinarily expected to disclose circumstances that make the property more valuable than the seller supposes." Rest. 2d, §161, Comment d.

(D) is wrong because it cites a completely irrelevant fact. The trainer had no obligation to correct what he knew to be the heir's mistake as to a basic assumption, unless the failure to correct amounted to bad faith or a failure to follow reasonable standards of fair dealing. The fact that the mistaken party was angry does not push the more knowledgeable party's lack of disclosure into the bad-faith category, especially where (as here) there is nothing to indicate that the more-knowledgeable party even knew about the other's anger.

[Q2062]

102. **B** For a third party to be an intended beneficiary, it must first of all be the case that giving him the right to sue would be appropriate to effectuate the intentions of the parties. If he meets this test, he must further fit into one of the two following categories: (1) either the performance of the promise will satisfy an obligation of the promisee to pay money to the beneficiary; or (2) the circumstances indicate that the promisee intends to give the beneficiary the benefit of the promised performance. The dealer meets these requirements, and is thus an intended beneficiary of the uncle's promise. First, giving the dealer the right to sue would effectuate the intentions of the parties — the uncle intended to help the nephew get a minivan by his promise to pay, and letting the dealer sue on the promise is consistent with that intention. Next, the nephew (the promisee) has promised to pay money to the dealer (the beneficiary), so enforcing the promise satisfies alternate test (1) above (satisfaction of the promisee's obligation to pay money). Having met the requirements of an intended beneficiary, the dealer can enforce the uncle's promise to the nephew. The fact that the uncle's promise to the nephew did not explicitly name the dealer — and instead phrased the promise in terms of "anyone from whom you buy ..." — does not prevent the dealer from being an intended beneficiary, since there is no requirement of identification as long as the other requirements for being intended (stated above) are met.

(A) is wrong because the dealer was not a party to the uncle's promise to the nephew. The essence of the promissory estoppel idea is that the maker of a promise may be bound by that promise, even though it is not supported by consideration, if the *promisee* relies upon that promise to his detriment, and the promisor should have foreseen the reliance. The doctrine gives only the promisee the right to sue. Since the uncle's promise was made only to the nephew, not the dealer, this requirement isn't met.

(C) is wrong because the suretyship clause of the statue of frauds applies only where the promisor makes an oral promise *to the creditor.* So for the uncle to be a surety of the nephew, the uncle would have had to make a promise *to the dealer* (the creditor), which the uncle didn't do. The fact that the uncle promised the nephew (the debtor) that the uncle would make good on the debt is irrelevant for purposes of the suretyship provision.

(D) is wrong because there is no requirement either that the intended beneficiary be identified when the promise is made, or that he be aware that it was made at any particular moment. Therefore, the fact that the dealer was neither identified, nor aware of the promise when it was made, is irrelevant.

[Q3172]

103. **A** The manufacturer is the only one of the three potential defendants who can be liable in strict liability. A person who is engaged in the business of selling products, and who sells a defective product, is subject to liability for harm to persons or property caused by the defect. Rest. 3d (Prod. Liab.) §1. One type of defect is a "design defect." A design defect occurs "when the foreseeable risks of harm posed by the product could have been reduced or avoided by the adoption of a reasonable alternative design by the seller or other distributor, or a predecessor in the commercial chain of distribution, and the omission of the alternative design renders the product not reasonably safe." Rest. 3d (Prod. Liab.) §2(b). Here, the manufacturer will be strictly liable because it satisfies the required elements for strict liability: (1) it was in the business of selling products; (2) it sold the product that caused the harm here (the HVAC system); and (3) the HVAC system was "defectively designed," since a better HVAC system was a reasonably available alternative design that could have reduced or avoided the harm, making the omission of such alternative something that rendered the product not reasonably safe.

Neither the heating company nor the cooling company is liable under this test, since neither sold the defectively-designed product (the HVAC system). It's true that the heating company and the cooling company sold *components* that went into the defective HVAC system. But their components were not themselves defective at the time of sale, and these defendants did not do anything that contributed to the "downstream" design defect introduced by the manufacturer (e.g., they didn't give the manufacturer instructions that induced the manufacturer to design the ventilating system in a defective manner). So they cannot be said to have "sold" a "defectively-designed product."

Since (B), (C), and (D) all treat either the heating company or the cooling company as liable, these choices are wrong for the reasons described in the discussion of choice (A) above.

[Q4044]

104. **D** Larceny is defined at common law as: (1) the trespassory (2) taking and (3) carrying away of the (4) personal property (5) of another (6) with the intent to steal it. LaFave, §16.2, at 671. The defendant committed larceny: (1) She picked up the purse, a taking. (2) She moved it from its original position when she placed it under her coat and took a few steps toward the exit, a carrying away. (3) & (4) The purse is a tangible item owned by another, the clothing store. (5) The defendant took it without the clothing store's consent. (6) When she picked up the purse (exerted control over it), the facts state that she did so with the intent to take it without paying for it. The defendant's actions therefore satisfy all the requirements of larceny. The fact that the defendant did not exit from the store with the property is irrelevant — the crime was complete once she exerted dominion and carried the item a small distance, while intending to keep it. Nor does the fact that the defen-

dant took only couple of steps with the purse prevent the "carrying away" element from being satisfied — even the smallest movement of the item will suffice.

(A) is wrong because the defendant completed the crime once she exerted dominion over the purse and carried it a small distance, while intending to keep it. See the analysis of Choice (D) above.

(B) is wrong because the defendant completed the crime as soon as her actions matched her intent. The crime was complete once the defendant exerted dominion over the purse and carried it a small distance, while intending to keep it. Nothing she did thereafter — including "withdrawing" from the "criminal enterprise" — could undo the completed crime.

(C) is not wrong because the crime of larceny was complete once the defendant moved the item with intent to take it. Since this choice says that only attempted, not completed, larceny has occurred, it's wrong.

[Q3098]

105. **A** A negligent tortfeasor is not generally liable for the criminal acts of third parties made possible by his negligence, but there is an exception when the tortfeasor should have realized the likelihood of the crime at the time of his negligence. The issue of foreseeability is generally a question for the jury. In this case, there had been many thefts from the construction area during the course of construction. Accordingly, there was enough evidence to support a jury verdict for the plaintiff, but it was not so overwhelming as to require the judge to take the rare step of granting summary judgment for the plaintiff.

(B) is wrong because the issue of foreseeability is generally a question for the jury. In this case, there had been many thefts from the construction area during the course of construction. The jury should be asked to consider whether the failure to place warning lights could foreseeably create a situation in which a damaged vehicle would be left vulnerable to theft.

(C) is wrong because, while it is true that a negligent tortfeasor is not generally liable for the criminal acts of third parties made possible by his negligence, there is an exception when the tortfeasor should have realized the likelihood of the crime at the time of his negligence. In other words, third-party criminal acts are not "superseding" when they were reasonably foreseeable to one in the defendant's position. The issue of foreseeability is generally a question for the jury, and that's true here, where there had been many thefts from the construction area during the course of construction. Accordingly, there is enough evidence to support a jury finding that the theft was foreseeable, so the defendant's motion for summary judgment should be denied.

(D) is wrong because, while the fact that the goods would not have been stolen "but for" the construction company's negligence answers the question whether that negligence was a "cause in fact" of the thefts, it doesn't answer the question whether that negligence was the proximate cause of the thefts. The construction company's negligence was the proximate cause of the thefts if and only if the third-party criminal acts were reasonably foreseeable to one in the construction company's position. And such issues of foreseeability are generally a question for the jury, so that a grant of summary judgment for a plaintiff on that basis is rare. In this case, there remains a jury question as to whether the pattern of past thefts from the construction site made the theft of the goods from the delivery truck foreseeable.

[Q7032]

106. **B** Courts generally hold that one who possesses an adjoining landowner's land, under the mistaken belief that he has only possessed up to the boundary of his own land, meets the requirement of "hostile" possession and can become an owner by adverse possession. This is especially likely where the possessor has both planted and fenced in the land in question, since such actions are very likely to bring home to the record owner that the possessor is asserting an adverse claim. So the buyer is highly likely to be found to have gained title to the 10-foot strip of Lot 3 by adverse possession. On the other hand, the buyer has not met the requirement for "continuous" possession

of Lot 2. The requirement of "continuous" position does not mean that the possessor must be physically on the property 100% of the time. However, a court would almost certainly require more than the very occasional rabbit-hunting at issue here in order to conclude that the buyer had "continuously" occupied Lot 2.

(A), (C), and (D) are wrong because they are inconsistent with the above analysis.

[Q1063]

107. **A** The Eleventh Amendment generally forbids the federal courts from entertaining damage suits against states, and Congress cannot override this ban even when it is acting pursuant to some enumerated power (e.g., the Commerce Clause). But there is one exception: when Congress is using its special powers to enforce the post-Civil War amendments (the Thirteenth, Fourteenth and Fifteenth), it may authorize damage suits against the states that would otherwise be barred by the Eleventh Amendment. That is what's happening here.

(B) is wrong because it is overbroad. As a general rule Congress, even where it is acting pursuant to some power given to it by a specific provision in the Constitution, may not override the state immunity from federal-court damage suits conferred by the Eleventh Amendment; enforcement of the post-Civil War amendments represents the only exception to this rule.

(C) is wrong for essentially the same reason: the Eleventh Amendment *does* generally limit the power of Congress (not just the power of the federal judiciary) to modify the sovereign-immunity of the states, but the Supreme Court has held that in the special case in which Congress is enforcing the post-Civil War amendments this general limitation on Congress's power does not apply. *Fitzpatrick v. Bitzer* (1976).

(D) is wrong because it is a flat misstatement of law: the Supreme Court has held that the Eleventh Amendment protects a state from federal-court damage suits even where the suit is brought by a citizen of a different state. *Hans v. Louisiana* (1890).

[Q1027]

108. **A** When the brother conveyed his interest in the property to his wife, this conveyance acted as an immediate severance, transforming the joint tenancy into a tenancy in common between the wife and the sister. When the wife immediately reconveyed to the brother, the brother and sister were tenants in common. When the brother died, his interest as a tenant in common passed back to his wife, making her a tenant in common with the sister.

(B) is wrong because the joint tenancy was severed before the brother's will took effect (at the moment the brother conveyed to his wife).

(C) is wrong because once the joint tenancy was broken by the conveyance from the brother to his wife, it could only be reestablished by a new conveyance joined in by both tenants in common, i.e., the wife and the sister (or, later, the brother and sister).

(D) is wrong because a conveyance by either joint tenant severs the joint tenancy regardless of whether the conveying joint tenant had or breached any fiduciary obligation to the other.

[Q1047]

109. **B** The mortgage attached to the entire property, and payment of 1/2 the total amount therefore did not "free up" a 1/2 undivided interest. The investor as mortgagee has a lien on the *entire property*. That is, the investor received a security interest on the full property — and the concomitant right upon default to conduct a judicial sale of the full property to get her debt repaid — regardless of whether one party paid that party's full share. A.L.P. §16.172. In other words, the investor is entitled to say, "Who paid what is between the two of you — I've got the right to have the whole property sold at foreclosure if any part of my loan is in default and the default is not wholly cured." That's what happened here. (The sister's remedy is a suit in contribution against the brother for 1/2 the amount she paid to the investor.)

(A) is wrong, because the investor did not have title to the property. A mortgage is a security interest in a property securing a loan. The fact that the mortgage instrument contained a clause in which the brother and sister warranted that they owned the property free of encumbrances (which is what the general warranty clause did) is irrelevant to the issue of whether the sister is entitled to quiet title.

(C) is wrong, because the equitable doctrine of marshaling does not apply to these facts. Marshalling is the ranking of assets in a certain order toward the payment of debts. The concept arises in equity, and means that where there are two creditors, with the senior one having two funds to satisfy his debt, that senior creditor must resort first to the fund which is not subject to demand of the junior creditor. The concept is misapplied to this fact pattern, because the doctrine would be one a second mortgagee invoked to protect his interest from the first mortgagee's foreclosure. Under these facts there is only one mortgage on the property, and as a party who joined with the brother in making the mortgage on the property, the sister would not be able to have her interest released.

(D) is wrong, because the sister would lose even if the cotenancy was joint. Joint tenancy differs from tenancy in common only with respect to the right of survivorship, which exists as to the former but not the latter. There is no difference in the legal analysis here between the joint-tenancy and tenancy-in-common scenarios.

[Q3065]

110. C An invitee is a person who enters onto the premises in response to an express or implied invitation of the landowner. The landowner owes the invitee a general duty to use reasonable and ordinary care in keeping the property safe for the benefit of the invitee. That duty includes the duty to inspect and correct hidden dangers and defects. Under these facts, the mother accompanied the daughter, a minor patient. That makes the mother an invitee, since she entered the premises under the hospital's implied invitation. At issue then is whether the hospital used reasonable and ordinary care to keep the property safe. The mere fact that the mother injured herself on a protruding fixture does not establish that the hospital failed to use due care to protect one in the mother's position. (For instance, the fixture may have been necessary to the functioning of the emergency room, and there may have been nothing that could reasonably have been done to make it safer for one who happened to faint near it.) On the other hand, it's certainly possible that inspection of the fixture would have shown that its shape and/or size posed an unreasonable risk to passersby, one which could have been easily corrected by, say, use of padding. This choice is the only one, therefore, that turns on the relevant issue: whether the hospital's personnel took, or failed to take, reasonable steps to safeguard invitees like the mother from dangers posed by the fixture.

(A) is wrong because, while the mother was indeed an invitee, as such the hospital only owed her a general duty of reasonable and ordinary care, including the duty to inspect the premises and see to it that they were reasonably safe. So the only way the hospital would be liable for damages suffered by the mother was if it did not exercise ordinary care. To the extent that this choice suggests that the mother automatically wins because she was an invitee — that a landowner has in effect strict liability to invitees who are injured by a condition of the land — it's simply wrong as a matter of law.

(B) is wrong because whether the fixture on which the mother injured herself in her fall was obvious, commonly used, and an essential part of the hospital's equipment does not go to the level of care the hospital owed the mother, or to whether the hospital failed to exercise that level of care. For example, suppose that the fixture was *non-obvious* and rarely-used. As long as the device did not pose an unreasonable danger to those around it, the hospital would still not be liable, because the hospital would not have failed to use reasonable care in connection with the device. Conversely, even if the fixture *was* obvious, commonly-used, and essential, the hospital may have negligently failed to protect passersby from it (e.g., by putting padding around it, if this could be done without interfering with the device's function).

(D) is wrong because the hospital *did* owe the mother the duty of care owed to an invitee, which includes affirmative aspects. A landowner owes its invitee a general duty to use reasonable and ordinary care in keeping the property safe for the benefit of the invitee, a duty which includes the obligation to *inspect* the property so as to identify and correct hidden dangers. So, for instance, if inspection would have showed that the fixture's shape or location posed an unreasonable risk of injury to passersby, the hospital owed the mother the affirmative duty of finding and correcting the condition (e.g., by installing protective padding).

[Q3036]

111. **D** Hearsay is defined as an out-of-court statement offered to prove the truth of the matter asserted in that statement. Since the newspaper can only be offering the journalist's statement "When I wrote the article, I believed it" in order to prove that when the journalist wrote the article, he believed in it, the statement is indeed being offered to prove the truth of the matter asserted therein. So it's hearsay, and it's not admissible unless some exception applies. No exception applies; most notably, the exception for state of mind (discussed in Choice (B) below) does not apply.

(A) is wrong because if the out-of-court statement by the journalist were admitted as evidence of with whether the article was published without malice, the statement would be being admitted to prove the truth of the matter asserted therein, and would thus be hearsay not falling within any exception.

(B) is wrong because the choice's reference to the admissibility of the declarant's "declaration of [his] state of mind" could only be a reference to FRE 803(3)'s exception for "A statement of the declarant's *then existing state of mind* ... but not including a *statement of memory or belief to prove the fact remembered or believed* unless it relates to the ... the declarant's will." Here, the journalist's statement was not about his present belief as of the moment of the statement, but rather about what he remembered his mental state to have been at the moment in the past when he wrote the article. So the statement falls within 803(3)'s inapplicability to "a statement of memory ... to prove the fact remembered." (The "fact remembered" was the journalist's prior mental state.) As the idea is often put, 803(3) does not cover "backward looking statements."

(C) is wrong because there is no rule allowing a party to put in a self-serving statement made by that party (or in this case, made by an employee that party). Indeed, one of the main purposes of the hearsay rule is to prevent a party from putting in statements made out of court by that party, for fear that these may be self-serving attempts to "manufacture evidence."

[Q5024]

112. **B** The suit has been brought on a failure-to-warn theory. The facts stipulate that the dangers that the plaintiff says should have been warned of were not known or knowable at the time of the plaintiff's exposure. Therefore, the judge must at the outset answer a pure question of law: Does a defendant who is selling dangerous substances have a duty to warn of their dangerousness if that dangerousness is unknown at the time? Choice (B) encapsulates this issue, since if (and only if) the defendant is held to have a duty to warn of these not-yet-known dangers can a reasonable jury possibly find that the defendant is liable for failing to warn. It's not clear how the judge should rule, but it's clear that this is the central issue in the case. (By the way, Rest. 3d [Prod. Liab.], §2(c), seems to answer "no" to the question posed by Choice (B), since the Restatement imposes only a duty to warn of "foreseeable risks," which seems equivalent to the question's "risks [that] were reasonably discoverable" at the time.)

(A) is wrong because (1) the issue is irrelevant to plaintiff's failure-to-warn theory, and (2) in any event, this is a question of fact, to be left to the jury. Plaintiff has sued on a failure-to-warn theory. Therefore, even if no satisfactory, safe alternative exists even today, there could still be a duty to warn of these unavoidable dangers. (One in plaintiff's position would be entitled to conclude that in view of the dangers, he should take a different job.) Consequently, the existence of a satisfactory alternative is simply not relevant to the claim. In any event, even if this issue were relevant, the answer would be a pure question of fact, not law.

(C) is wrong because (1) the issue posed may not even be a relevant issue; and (2) the issue is in any event a question of fact. As to (1), the judge could quite plausibly decide (as a matter of law, and as described in Choice (B)), that the plaintiff should be held to have had a duty to warn of not-yet-discoverable risks. If the judge so held, then the issue here (whether D in fact knew of the risks) would be legally irrelevant. As to (2), in any event, what any defendant should reasonably have known at a particular moment is inevitably a factual issue, properly left to the jury.

(D) is wrong because (1) "inherent dangerousness" is probably not an issue; and (2) even if it were, this would be a factual issue to be left to the jury. The concept of "inherent dangerousness," to the extent that it's relevant in a product-liability suit, generally refers to the issue of "unavoidable danger." That is, if a product has some social utility, and is "unavoidably dangerous" (or as it is sometimes put, "inherently dangerous"), the defendant may be able to argue that the product is not "defective." (That's because the idea of a "defect" involves something that is "wrong" or "needlessly dangerous," and something that is unavoidably hazardous does not meet this standard.) Here, the case has been brought on a failure-to-warn theory. So even if asbestos is "inherently dangerous" (and thus not defective), this fact would not spare the defendant from having a duty to warn of its inherent dangers (assuming there is a duty to warn of not-yet-knowable dangers). So the inherent dangerousness of the product would be irrelevant. In any event, even if inherent dangerousness were a relevant issue, this would be a matter of fact, not law, and thus properly left to the jury.

[Q3023]

113. **A** The woman would have to assume the man's mortgage to be liable under it. When a person buys a mortgaged property without assuming the mortgage, the buyer has no liability on the mortgage. That's true even if the mortgage contains a due-on-sale clause — the clause will be enforced (and will entitle the mortgagee to accelerate the mortgage), but the clause won't cause the buyer to be deemed to have assumed the mortgage. Nor will the fact that the buyer actually makes several mortgage payments cause her to be deemed to have assumed the mortgage and thus be personally liable.

(B) is wrong because privity of estate is not an issue in mortgage cases. Privity of estate makes a difference in cases involving covenants at law — absence of privity of estate means that a successor to the covenantor won't be bound. But a mortgage is not a covenant running with the land, so privity of estate doesn't matter.

(C) is wrong because a due-on-sale clause wouldn't create liability on the part of the buyer. A due-on-sale clause allows a lender to demand full payment of the remainder of an existing loan if the mortgagor transfers any interest in the property securing the loan without the lender's consent. The violation of the due-on-sale clause would give the bank grounds for a case against the man, and grounds to accelerate the mortgage, but not grounds to obtain a personal judgment against the woman.

(D) is wrong for the same reason as (B): a mortgage is not a covenant running with the land, making privity of estate irrelevant.

[Q1033]

114. **A** Courts disagree about whether and when a person who wishes to use deadly force in self-defense must instead retreat if this could be done safely. But all courts agree that there is never a requirement to retreat if the defender does not intend to use deadly force. LaFave, §9.4(f) at 411. Since the defense here consisted of pepper spray, and since pepper spray is not a defense method that is likely to cause death or serious bodily injury, it did not constitute the use of deadly force. Therefore, the defendant had no duty to retreat instead of using that non-deadly force.

(B) is wrong because, while this answer correctly states that the defendant should not be convicted, it misstates the legal basis for this conclusion. While states disagree about whether or when a defendant may have to retreat before using deadly force, no jurisdiction requires a person who wishes to use non-deadly force to retreat, regardless of whether the structure is occupied. If this choice looked attractive to you, perhaps you were thinking of the fact that in states that require retreat before the use of deadly force, nearly all make an exception where the defender is in his own dwelling that is not also the dwelling of the person being defended against. But the fact that the force here was non-deadly means that this "dwelling" exception to the requirement of retreat could not matter.

(C) is wrong because even in those states requiring retreat in certain circumstances, retreat is not required if the defender is proposing to use only non-deadly force.

(D) is wrong because the defendant acted within his rights even though the husband did not threaten to use deadly force. A response of non-deadly force is justified where the defender reasonably believes the other is about to inflict unlawful bodily harm, and the threatened harm need not be deadly (i.e., need not consist of death or serious harm).

[Q7096]

115. **D** FRE 201(b) allows judicial notice of a fact that is "not subject to reasonable dispute" because it is either "(1) generally known within the territorial jurisdiction of the trial court" or "(2) capable of accurate and ready determination by resort to *sources whose accuracy cannot reasonably be questioned.*" The fact here would be very unlikely to fall within category (1), since even the federal judge seems not to know it. So the only hope is category (2). The clerk of the state court might be a reasonably accurate source, but not a "source whose accuracy cannot reasonably be questioned." For instance, the clerk might be relying on a faulty memory, or might have some hidden motive to intentionally misstate the facts. In any event, the custom in most courts (including ones following FRE 201) is not to take judicial notice of the determinations of courts other than the court which is doing the noticing.

(A) is wrong, because a certified copy would be permitted under FRE 902(4). FRE 902 lists a number of categories of documents that are self-authenticating. One of these is 902(4)'s category of "certified copies of public records," defined to include "a copy of an official record or report ... certified as correct by the custodian or other person authorized to make the certification." A certified copy of a record of conviction would clearly fall within this definition.

(B) is wrong, because testimony of someone who heard the sentence be issued would be a good means of authentication. FRE 901(b) gives a number of illustrations of acceptable methods of authentication, i.e., of (in FRE 901(a)'s language) "evidence sufficient to support a finding that the matter in question is what its proponent claims." Since the claim is that there has been a conviction, authentication consists of evidence sufficient to find that the conviction really occurred. The first illustration given in FRE 901(b) is (1), "Testimony of witness with knowledge" — the text of (1) recognizes authentication by means of "testimony that a matter is what it is claimed to be." So here, the plaintiff's testimony, from his own personal knowledge, that a sentence of conviction was pronounced, will qualify.

(C) is wrong because the defendant's statement would be admissible as an admission. The testimony here is a classic admission by a party-opponent. Under FRE 801(d)(2), an out-of-court statement is admissible (as an exclusion to the hearsay rule) if it is "offered against a party and is (1) the party's own statement..." Since the "oral admission" by the defendant that he had been convicted is a statement by the defendant being offered against him, the testimony by the witness is admissible.

[Q3167]

116. **C** Estoppel by deed applies to validate a deed, and in particular a warranty deed, that was executed and delivered by a grantor who had no title (or less-than-perfect title) to the land at that time, but

who represented that he had such title and who thereafter acquired such title. (The doctrine is sometimes called "after-acquired title.") In this case, estoppel by deed would apply in the woman's favor to estop the nephew from claiming ownership of the land upon the death of his uncle.

(A) is incorrect because the fact that the uncle was the owner of record on the date of transfer to the woman would be relevant in a dispute between the uncle and the woman, but is not relevant in a dispute between the nephew and the woman.

(B) is incorrect because while it is true that a title search would have revealed that the uncle was the owner of record on the date of transfer, the uncle's ownership is only relevant to a dispute between the woman and the uncle, not to a dispute between the nephew and the woman. In fact, the woman owns the land because of the operation of estoppel by deed, as described in Choice (C).

(D) is incorrect because although this option correctly states that the woman owns the land, it misstates the reason why this is so. The woman's recording of the deed provided notice to the world of her interest from the time of recording, but had no bearing on the validity of her claim vis-a-vis the nephew.

[Q7082]

117. **A** Hearsay is an out-of-court statement offered to prove the truth of the matter asserted in that statement. Since the statement by the dispatcher that a blue sedan was traveling at an excessive speed was made out of court, and since it was offered to prove that the defendant's blue sedan was traveling at an excessive speed, it is hearsay. No exception applies, as is analyzed below.

(B) is wrong because the "present sense impression" exception (given by FRE 803(1)), applies only to "A statement describing or explaining an event or condition *made while the declarant was perceiving the event or condition,* or immediately thereafter." The declarant would have to be the police dispatcher. But the dispatcher is extremely unlikely to have been perceiving the fact that "officers [are] in pursuit of a blue Ford sedan ... traveling ... at an excessive rate of speed" — rather, the dispatcher was almost certainly repeating information that the officers had themselves radioed to him, and he therefore did not have the requisite present sense impression.

(C) is wrong because the "past recollection recorded" exception (given by FRE 803(5)) allows a witness to read from a written record that satisfies various requirements. But here, the witness is not reading from the memorandum, she has instead used it to refresh her recollection, and that use does not qualify for the past recollection recorded exception.

(D) is wrong because the use here does not qualify for the present recollection refreshed doctrine. A witness may refresh her recollection while testifying by examining almost anything which will have that effect. She may then testify from her refreshed recollection, but *only if her testimony is otherwise admissible.* Since the statement to which the witness is attempting to testify is hearsay (the dispatcher's statement about the speed at which the officers were chasing the car), it is inadmissible, and is not made admissible by the fact that the witness properly refreshed her recollection by looking at a writing.

[Q5068]

118. **A** If parties to an existing contract agree to modify the contract for the sole benefit for one of them, the modification will usually be unenforceable in non-UCC cases, for lack of consideration. That's because of the pre-existing duty rule: When one party to an existing contract makes an additional promise, and the other party merely promises to do what she is already required to do, the former's promise is not supported by consideration. A primary function of the pre-existing duty rule is to refuse to reward "hold-up" behavior by a provider of services, who in the middle of the contract refuses to complete performance unless she gets a better price or other improved terms. That's exactly what happened here: The painter has unfairly extracted the $200 promise from the accountant when it's too late for the accountant to get a substitute. So the accountant's promise will be unenforceable unless some exception to the pre-existing duty rule applies. Two common excep-

tions are that: (1) there were unanticipated circumstances that made the painter's request for more money not unreasonable, or (2) the painter agreed to do some additional duty beyond what he was already required to do. But neither of these exceptions (or any other) applies here, so the pre-existing duty rule applies and the accountant's promise is unenforceable for lack of consideration.

(B) is wrong because the accountant's promise is not too uncertain. The parties were not agreeing to a charge of "whatever it takes" — they were instead agreeing to a charge of $200, with the accountant's "whatever it takes" remark being more in the nature of a side commentary (e.g., "I'm agreeing to the $200 because I would in fact agree to whatever it took to get you to finish the work.").

(C) is wrong because letting the accountant escape from her $200-extra-compensation promise would not lead to her unjust enrichment. The painter is only doing exactly what he always agreed to do for exactly the price the two parties agreed to, so depriving him of his unfairly-extracted extra $200 would not constitute unjust enrichment to the accountant.

(D) is wrong because a party's inability to complete performance due to that party's own delay or poor planning does not constitute the sort of extraordinary and unanticipated occurrence to which the impossibility doctrine applies. In general, only "external" events (e.g., an act of God, a strike, etc.) will qualify for the impossibility defense.

[Q1120]

119. **A** This choice is correct because: (1) it correctly implies that the only basis on which the glue manufacturer could be liable is on a strict product liability theory; and (2) it correctly asserts that if the glue manufacturer is strictly liable, then the paint company must be as well. Let's take these steps one at a time. As to (1), the glue manufacturer won't be found negligent, since it had no reason to believe that the product posed eye dangers, and since it warned of any danger (e.g., from lack of ventilation) of which it was aware. So if the glue manufacturer were liable, it would have to be on a product liability basis. As to (2), if the glue manufacturer were strictly liable, it would have to be because it sold a defectively dangerous product. If the product was defectively dangerous, then the paint company, as a "downstream" re-seller, would have exactly the same liability, since anyone who sells a defectively dangerous product is strictly liable for it. So there's no way the glue manufacturer could be liable without the paint company's also being liable.

(B) is wrong because it doesn't matter whether the secretary was an invitee of a tenant in the building or not. The recovery here would have to be on a strict product liability basis (see the analysis of Choice (A) for why), and any person who is injured by a defect in a defective product can recover against any seller of that product, whether the plaintiff was an invitee at the time of the injury or not. (Indeed, even if the secretary had been a trespasser, she could have recovered against the paint company in strict product liability.)

(C) is wrong because it ignores the possibility that the paint company is strictly liable as a non-negligent seller of a dangerously defective product.

(D) is wrong because it ignores the possibility that the paint company as a seller of a dangerously defective product would be strictly liable even though the product came in a sealed package. Sellers of dangerously defective products are strictly liable for the harm caused by the defect, and that is true even though the seller behaved with all possible care. So the fact that the product came in a sealed package — thus preventing the paint company from recognizing or altering the danger even if it wanted to — is irrelevant.

[Q4049]

120. **C** Since the government had previously agreed that the teacher could only be fired if she were shown not to have had "good behavior," she had a due process "property" interest in maintaining her job. The Supreme Court has held that once a person has a property interest in a job or benefit, only the

courts, not the government, may prescribe the procedures that are to be used to terminate that job or benefit. So the fact that the statute provides only for a post-discharge hearing does not mean that this is all the teacher is due. Instead, the Court has held that the job holder is entitled to a hearing before the termination (or at least before the termination of salary). *Cleveland Bd. of Ed. v. Loudermill* (1985). Since the statute here did not give the teacher such a pre-termination hearing, the statute was unconstitutional. And the statute did not get saved by the government's holding a hearing three months after the termination.

Choice (A) is wrong because it is not true that a claim that a state statute is unconstitutional is not ripe until all state-court remedies have been exhausted. When a litigant believes that a state statute violates the federal constitution, the litigant may sue immediately in federal court for a determination that this is so, as long as the requirements of justiciability are met. And although it's true that one of the requirements of justiciability is that the case be "ripe," ripeness merely means that the plaintiff has already suffered, or imminently faces, actual injury.

Choice (B) is wrong for at least two reasons: (1) not all state employees have the right not to be dismissed except for good cause (and this choice implies that all of them do); and (2) even if an employee such as the teacher here had a right not to be dismissed except for good cause, the burden of proof on the government would be just a preponderance-of-the-evidence standard, not the hard-to-satisfy "beyond a reasonable doubt" standard.

Choice (D) is wrong because the Supreme Court has held that, where a state employee has a right to hold her job during good behavior, the employee is entitled not only to a pre-dismissal statement of reasons but a pre-dismissal hearing (and the fact that the statute provides only for a post-dismissal hearing does not change the constitutional requirement of a pre-dismissal one). Cf. *Loudermill, supra.*

[Q1152]

121. **D** Where the defendant's statement is oral rather than written, any defamation action would have to be for slander rather than libel. The plaintiff is not entitled to recover for slander unless either: (1) the slander falls within one of four "slander per se" categories; or (2) plaintiff has shown "special damage" (which means economic or pecuniary harm). The four slander per se categories are accusations of: (1) a criminal offense; (2) a "loathsome" disease (i.e., a sexually transmitted disease); (3) a matter incompatible with the plaintiff's business, trade, profession or office; and (4) serious sexual misconduct. Rest. 2d, §570. Calling the plaintiff a "deadbeat" doesn't fall into any of these categories (at least if the plaintiff is a consumer rather than a businessperson, as is the case here). Therefore, since the statement is slander rather than libel, and since it's not slander per se, the customer can win only if he shows that he has suffered some "special damage," i.e., economic harm.

(A) is wrong because, although it mentions an element that will be necessary to the customer's recovery ("publication" to a third person), it omits any discussion of special harm, which is required for this slander-not-per-se action as discussed in Choice (D) above.

(B) is wrong because, although the fact that the conduct was extreme and outrageous (if indeed it was) would be relevant to an action by the customer for intentional infliction of emotional distress, it is not relevant to an action for defamation, which is what the question is asking you about.

(C) is wrong because the customer might be able to win even if the bill collector did not know that the customer didn't really owe any money to the store. Even under Supreme Court First Amendment-based restrictions, states are permitted to give a private (i.e., non-public-figure) plaintiff the right to win if the plaintiff can show that the defendant made a defamatory falsehood and behaved at least negligently with respect to the statement's truth. Therefore, assuming that the customer did not in fact owe the store anything (something that is not really clear from the facts), the customer can win even if the bill collector didn't know that the customer owed nothing, but negligently believed that the customer owed money. (The customer's problem is that he would have to show special damage, i.e., pecuniary harm, as detailed in the discussion of Choice (D) above.)

[Q4065]

122. **B** The Constitution requires unanimity where only a 6-person jury is used. *Burch v. Louisiana* (1979).

(A) is wrong because, while this answer correctly states that the conviction will be set aside, it misstates the legal basis for this conclusion. The Constitution does not require 12-person juries, and in fact allows 6-person juries. *Williams v. Florida* (1970).

(C) is wrong, because while this answer correctly states that the conviction will be set aside, it misstates the legal basis for this conclusion. The Constitution does not require 12-person juries, as discussed in Choice (A), but it does require unanimity where only a 6-person jury is used, as discussed in Choice (B).

(D) is wrong because the conviction will not be upheld, since the Constitution requires unanimity where only a 6-person jury is used, as discussed in Choice (B).

[Q7017]

123. **D** An anticipatory repudiation (what the choice calls simply a "repudiation") is a clear statement by a party, made before performance under a contract is due, that the party cannot or will not perform. An anticipatory repudiation is treated as if it were a present breach. For a statement by the promisor to constitute a repudiation, it must appear to the promisee that the promisor is either unwilling or very unlikely to perform. The buyer's statement here does not meet these requirements. The buyer has not made it clear that she probably won't perform — indeed, just the contrary, since she's indicated that she *will* perform, however grudgingly, if legally required to do so. Since the statement here is not an anticipatory repudiation, and since there is no other present breach (the time for performance won't arrive until December), there has been no breach, and the seller will lose if the case is decided before December.

(A) is wrong because, as described in the discussion of Choice (D) above, the buyer's statement did not meet the requirements for an anticipatory repudiation, because the buyer indicated that she would perform if required to do so.

(B) is wrong because the seller has not yet requested assurances. A party to a contract has the right to demand reasonable assurances when the other party to a contract gives the first party reasonable grounds for insecurity about whether the latter will perform; if the latter fails to provide these assurances, this failure will itself be considered a repudiation, and a breach. The buyer's October 1 statement may have created reasonable grounds for the seller's insecurity with respect to the buyer's performance, though even this is uncertain. However, before the seller could sue for breach of contract based on such insecurity, he was obligated to request assurances from the buyer. Here, the seller has not yet requested assurances, so the seller cannot successfully claim that the buyer's failure to provide further assurances, or the buyer's creation of insecurity in the seller, constitutes a breach.

(C) is wrong because it falsely implies that a seller can never bring suit for breach before the appointed date for performance. One of the major purposes of the anticipatory repudiation doctrine is that it allows the repudiatee to bring an immediate suit for breach, before the time for performance has arrived. So if the buyer had anticipatorily repudiated, the seller could bring an immediate suit, and Choice (C) would be an incorrect statement. But, as described in the analysis of Choice (D), the buyer has not anticipatorily repudiated.

[Q3142]

124. **D** Under common law, self-identifying statements are not sufficient to establish the source of a writing. FRE 902 creates some exceptions to this rule, but letterheads are not among them.

(A) is wrong because an expert may state an opinion concerning the authorship of a particular writing based upon a comparison of the writing in question with an exemplar of the defendant's writing. See FRE 901(b)(2), giving as an illustration of proper authentication "comparison by ... expert witnesses with specimens which have been authenticated."

(B) is wrong because the trier of fact may form a conclusion about the authorship of a particular writing based upon its own comparison of that writing with an exemplar of the defendant's handwriting.

(C) is wrong because any person may testify to what he had seen, if what he has seen is relevant to the facts in issue.

[Q4058]

125. **A** Even in a court that has a relatively tough standard for the enforceability of litigated damages clauses, the court will enforce the clause if *both* of the following are true: (1) the forecast was a reasonable estimate of likely damages at the time the contract was entered into; and (2) the party seeking to enforce the clause has suffered actual damages that are hard to calculate accurately. Here, these two conditions are satisfied: (1) at the time the contract was made, the captain faced a real risk that the customer would fail to show up at the last minute, and that she would be unable to get another charter for that same day; therefore, a deposit of 40% of total contract price was a reasonable forecast of likely damages, especially since most of the captain's costs for a one-day charter are fixed (cost of boat) so that if she doesn't do the trip she recoups relatively little expense; (2) while the captain has collected $400 from the replacement as well as $200 from the customer, giving her a total for the day of $600 (i.e., $100 more than she would have gotten from the customer alone if the contract had been fulfilled), she had to stay out two hours beyond the customary return time, so some of her $100 "surplus" may have been due to this extra-long day rather than being a windfall; consequently, the captain's actual damages are indeed hard to calculate accurately after-the-fact.

(B) is wrong because it is a misstatement of law. In non-sales cases, there is no single formula that determines the outer bounds of permissible liquidated damages, as this choice suggests that there is. The examiners may have been trying to trick you into thinking of the formula applied in UCC cases, under which if the buyer of goods makes a deposit and then breaches (e.g., by canceling), and the contract does not contain a liquidated damages clause, the buyer gets back any part of his deposit in excess of "20% of the value of the total [contract price] or $500, whichever is smaller" if the seller does not establish actual damages. §2-718(2)(b). Since this is a contract for the sale of services rather than goods, this provision does not apply (and the 10% amount in the choice doesn't match up with the UCC percentage anyway).

(C) is wrong because, while it arguably describes a treatment that puts the captain in the same position she would have been in had the contract been performed (she has collected $600 for the day from the combination of the customer and the replacement, versus $500 if the customer contract had been performed, so she arguably needs to give back $100), this choice ignores the liquidated damages clause. So long as the liquidated damages clause meets the rules for enforceability of such clauses, the fact that the clause gives the person trying to use it some slight benefit over the actual damage amount that a court might compute is irrelevant.

(D) is wrong because the liquidated damages clause here would not operate as a penalty. As long as such a clause at least meets the two-part test described in Choice (A), it by definition does not constitute a penalty. In other words, the "penalty" label is simply a shorthand method of stating that the clause doesn't pass the two-part test, which the clause here does pass.

[Q2086]

126. **C** Either co-tenant has the right, at any time, to demand partition. During the course of partition, the court will order an accounting, to determine whether either party owes the other money for rents collected, taxes paid, etc. It is not clear what substantive rules will govern that analysis — for

instance, jurisdictions differ on whether a co-tenant who occupies the premises himself must account for the imputed value of rent received beyond his pro rata share. But the one thing that we can be sure of is that the court will require an accounting, and that's what this choice specifies.

(A) is wrong because the man never occupied the property in a "hostile" manner.

(B) is wrong because the court would grant partition, for the reason described in the discussion of (C).

(D) is wrong because a court would conduct an accounting to determine if either party has an obligation to pay money to the other.

[Q3025]

127. **D** The terms of the bequest made it clear that only a child who survived the testator's wife would take. Each child had a contingent remainder as of the testator's death. When the lawyer died before his mother (the widow) died, the lawyer's contingent remainder was nullified without ever becoming vested, leaving nothing to pass to the lawyer's friend by devise. At the widow's death, the contingent remainders in the accountant and the doctor vested (and, simultaneously, became possessory).

(A) is wrong for the same reason (D) is right: the remainders were intended by the testator to be contingent unless and until the remaindermen survived the widow, at which time they would vest. So when the lawyer died, his contingent remainder was destroyed by his failing to have survived the widow, and he had no interest to pass to the friend.

(B) is wrong because under the common law approach to the Rule against Perpetuities, the time for evaluating a will is when the testator *dies*, *not* when the will was *executed*. At the time the testator died, his widow (and, indeed, his children as well) were necessarily already in existence, and could therefore serve as measuring lives. So there was no risk that the remainder to the testator's children would vest beyond "measuring lives plus 21 years," making the gift to those children valid contingent remainders.

(C) is wrong as a matter of law: some remainders can indeed descend by intestacy. *Example*: O bequeaths "to A for life, then to B." Assume B is living at O's death, but dies intestate before A, and with C as his heir at law. At B's death, the vested remainder in B passes by intestacy to C, and C will have a fee simple once B dies.

[Q2187]

128. **A** A search will be valid if consent to it is given by a person who the police reasonably but mistakenly believe has joint authority over the premises. *Ill. v. Rodriguez* (1990). Here, if the cheerleader actually had been the defendant's roommate, she would have had authority to consent to a search of the common areas of their shared room. Since she told the police that she was, and since she had a key to the room, it was reasonable for them to believe her. When the police went inside and saw the marijuana on a coffee table, it was reasonable for them to believe that this was a portion of the room shared by the defendant and her roommate (reasonably assumed by them to be the cheerleader). The cheerleader's apparent authority therefore justified the search, and makes the search legal even though it was not supported by a warrant. And this is true even though the police were (reasonably) mistaken in believing that the cheerleader actually had authority.

(B) is wrong because, even if the police did have probable cause to believe that they would find marijuana in the room (and they probably did), they would still need a search warrant, unless some exception to the warrant requirement applied. Since this answer does not give any hint of the need for a warrant or an exception to the warrant requirement, it cannot be the best answer, even though it correctly predicts the result.

(C) is wrong because, while it is true both that the police did not have a warrant and that the cheerleader did not have authority, neither of these facts matters. That's because, as further described in the analysis of Choice (A) above, the cheerleader had apparent authority, so the police's mistake was a reasonable one and the case is treated as if the cheerleader had had actual authority.

(D) is wrong because: (1) the police probably *did* have probable cause, based upon the cheerleader's suspicions and her explanation of how she came to have those suspicions, to believe that they would find marijuana in the room; and (2) in any event, whether the police had probable cause or not, the cheerleader's apparent authority to consent to a search of what the police thought was the area shared by the cheerleader and the defendant overcame both the need for a warrant and the need for probable cause.

[Q5073]

129. **C** FRE 1006 says that "the contents of voluminous writings, recordings or photographs which cannot conveniently be examined in court may be presented in the form of a chart, summary, or calculation." The individual timesheets here meet the "voluminous writings" standard, since they would be almost daily over a five-year timeframe, a stack that would be hard for the judge or jury to examine in court. FRE 1006 also says that "the originals, or duplicates, shall be made available for examination or copying, or both, by other parties at reasonable time and place." So the fact that the underlying timesheets were made available to the client prior to trial, as specified in this choice, is a necessary condition for the summaries' admission under FRE 1006. By the way, the summaries: (1) become evidence (i.e., they're not just non-evidentiary testimonial aids); and (2) substitute for the underlying originals, which means that those originals must be independently admissible. Here, the underlying timesheets are hearsay, but they fall within FRE 803(6)'s business records exception.

(A) is wrong because the summary-of-voluminous-writings provision of FRE 1006 applies as described in Choice (C) above, and that provision does not require that the underlying writings being summarized be offered into evidence (although they may be).

(B) is wrong because, under FRE 1006, the summaries can come in as substantive evidence, as described in choice (C) above.

(D) is wrong because the summaries can come in under FRE 1006 even if the underlying timesheets have not been lost. If you picked this choice, you may be thinking of FRE 1004(1), under which the B.E.R. can be satisfied by something other than the original writing or a duplicate thereof (e.g., a summary) if "all originals are lost or have been destroyed, unless the proponent lost or destroyed them in bad faith[.]" But FRE 1006 provides an independent means of getting summaries into evidence (one that does not depend on loss of originals), and that means 1006 is available here as discussed in Choice (C) above.

[Q6002]

130. **A** Only the testimony about peaceableness is a "pertinent trait" of the accused. FRE 404(a), after stating the general rule against character evidence to prove action in conformity therewith, gives an exception for "evidence of a pertinent trait of character offered by an accused[.]" Since peaceability and truthfulness are each "traits of character," the evidence will be admissible if and only if it concerns a "pertinent" trait. What traits are "pertinent" depends on the nature of the crime charged and any defenses raised. Here, what's charged is a crime that involves violence, but not untruthfulness. Therefore, the accused's reputation for peaceableness involves a "pertinent" trait (one who is peaceable is less likely to have committed a crime involving violence). However, the accused's reputation for truthfulness would probably be held not to be pertinent (since one who is truthful is not less likely to have committed a murder than one who is untruthful). (Note, however, that if the defendant took the stand and the prosecution attacked his credibility, then the "reputation for truthfulness" testimony would become admissible because the defendant's truthfulness or untruthfulness would be in issue and thus a "pertinent" trait.)

To the extent that Choices (B), (C), and (D) each fail to admit the peaceableness testimony or

admit the truthfulness testimony, it's wrong for the reasons described in the analysis of Choice (A).
[Q3164]

131. **C** Because the only person whose rights have been arguably affected by the new statute is the friend, who is not a claimant, there is no live case or controversy between the litigants, so standing rules prevent the court from hearing it.

(A) is wrong because the lack of standing prevents the court from deciding the case on its merits even though the plaintiff is claiming that the Constitution has been violated (which would of course raise a federal question if there were a case or controversy before the court).

(B) is wrong because, if there were not any standing problem, the question of the constitutionality of the statute would not be a nonjusticiable political question (a category limited to a few special situations, none of which applies here).

(D) is wrong, because the Eleventh Amendment bars only suits seeking money damages against states, and the suit here is seeking a declaratory judgment rather than money damages.
[Q1133]

132. **D** The most common test for insanity is the M'Naghten Rule, which requires that defendant have a diseased mind which caused a defect of reason, such that when Defendant acted he *either* didn't know his act was wrong *or* he didn't understand the nature and quality of his actions (e.g., mistaking someone's head for a baseball and hitting it with a bat). The M'Naghten Rule is also the toughest test for the defendant to meet, so if the defendant can meet it here, he can satisfy virtually any test the jurisdiction is at all likely to use. Here, the defendant satisfies the M'Naghten Rule, because he did not know his act was wrong — he thought he was being mercilessly attacked, and he therefore believed that his act was self-defense and thus not either legally or morally wrong.

(A) is wrong because an intoxication defense would not exonerate the defendant under a murder charge. Murder requires an unlawful killing with malice aforethought. Malice can take the form of intent to kill or inflict great bodily injury, felony murder, or "depraved heart" (acting in spite of an unjustifiably high risk to human life). Voluntary intoxication, which is involved here, is only a defense to prove a lack of capacity for so-called "specific intent" crimes. Murder, because of the variety of mental states that will suffice for it, is classified as a "general intent" crime, meaning precisely that voluntary intoxication will not furnish a defense as long as the defendant meets any of the possible mental states for the crime. Since the defendant's intoxication did not prevent him from having the desire to kill, the intoxication will not furnish him with a valid defense.

(B) is wrong because it mischaracterizes the facts. It's true that murder requires an unlawful killing with malice aforethought. But "malice aforethought" refers to a variety of mental states any of which can suffice: intent to kill, intent to do great bodily harm, felony murder, or acting with reckless indifference to the value of human life ("depraved heart"). Since the defendant intended to strangle the woman, he intended either to kill her or at least to do her great bodily injury, so he meets the malice aforethought requirement.

(C) is wrong because self-defense would not be a valid defense to murder on these facts. Self-defense has both an objective and a subjective element: the defendant must *in fact* believe the danger exists (the subjective part), and the defendant must be *reasonable* in this belief (the objective part). Here, the defendant misapprehended the danger – the old woman was only slapping him, and thus deadly force was not required. Since the defendant's perception of danger was not reasonable, self-defense will not be available as a defense.
[Q4040]

133. **D** The landowner's use of the easement put the bank on notice of her interest, preventing the bank from being a purchaser "without notice" who is entitled to the protection of the recording act. Under a recording statute like the one here, a subsequent BFP prevails over a prior grantee who

failed to record by the time of the subsequent grant. But the statute gives subsequent purchaser protection only if she had *no actual or constructive notice* at the time of the conveyance. One type of constructive notice is "inquiry notice": notice of any matter as to which the grantee is (or should be) in possession of facts which would lead the grantee to make an investigation. One source of inquiry notice is that where the property is in possession of one other than the record owner, the prospective grantee is under a duty to inquire about the facts that put that person into possession (since the reason may be that the possessor has an unrecorded interest). Here, the bank should have noticed that even though the strip was shown as belonging to the neighbor's parcel, it was "possessed" by the landowner in the form of the driveway. Had the bank made inquiry of the landowner, she would presumably have told the bank about her easement. Consequently, the bank is deemed to have been on notice of the landowner's easement, preventing the bank from being the "subsequent purchaser for value and without notice" required for protection under the recording statute. Since the landowner's interest precedes the bank's, the bank could win only with the protection of the recording act, so it loses.

Choice (A) is wrong, because the landowner's recording of the deed prior to the foreclosure action would not protect the landowner's rights. If the bank had been a BFP without notice of the landowner's interest at the time the bank made the mortgage, the landowner's interest would be subordinate to the bank's recorded mortgage, and the fact that the landowner later (after the mortgage) recorded would not change this. In other words, under this statute, the time for testing whether the first conveyance (here, the easement) was "recorded according to law" would be at the time that the "subsequent purchaser" took its interest, not the time when that subsequent purchaser tried, say, to gain title by foreclosure. (You can see how this would have to work this way if lenders are to be able to lend in reliance on the records — once the loan is made, the lender needs to be able to be confident that no later-filed interest can take priority over its own interest.)

Choice (B) is wrong, because the mere fact that the easement provided access to a public street from Blackacre would not prevent the recording act from causing the landowner to lose. The examiners were probably trying to trick you into thinking that because the easement provides access from Blackacre to a public street, the easement would be one of "necessity," and remain valid even though unrecorded. But even in courts recognizing easements by necessity, the easement here would not qualify, because the facts tell us that Blackacre also has direct access to a different public street. The easement here was an express easement, and if it is not recorded, the grantee risks losing it to a subsequent grantee from the original grantor.

Choice (C) is wrong because it misstates how the assignment of appurtenant easements works, and also ignores the significance of the recording act. The easement here is, indeed, "appurtenant" rather than "in gross." (That is, it pertains to a particular benefited parcel, Blackacre.) It's true that an easement appurtenant generally passes with the property — so if the landowner sold Blackacre, the easement would pass with Blackacre, rather than being extinguished. But here, these mechanics are irrelevant; for one thing, the landowner isn't transferring her interest in Blackacre. The recording act operates completely separately from the assignment of appurtenant easements — the easement is an interest in the neighbor's parcel, and needed to be recorded if it was not to be subordinated to a BFP of the neighbor's parcel. (In other words, it was only the bank's inquiry notice that prevented the bank from getting protection of the recording statute vis-a-vis the landowner's easement).

[Q3010]

134. **B** The man met all the requirements of the recording statute: he took for value, he took without notice of the prior conveyance, and he recorded before the prior conveyance was recorded. Once the man met those requirements, his interest cut off all rights of the prior grantee (the woman) who didn't record first. The man therefore had the ability to pass a valid title to his nephew, even though the nephew did not take for value, and even though the nephew was on record notice of the woman's

claim at the time he took (since by then the woman had recorded).

(A) is wrong because it is not the woman's status as a donee that causes her to lose, it is the fact that she did not record before a subsequent BFP (the man) recorded. Remember that under recording acts, it is never significant whether the *first* grantee took for value; it only matters whether the *subsequent* grantee, who is trying to take advantage of the recording act, took for value.

(C) is wrong because the fact that the woman recorded before the nephew cannot save her; once a subsequent grantee (the man) took for value and without notice and then recorded first, a person downstream from that subsequent grantee (the nephew) wins against the original late-filing grantee regardless of whether the downstreamer took for value, took without notice, or recorded first.

(D) is wrong because the fact that the nephew did not give value doesn't matter; as with choice (C), once the subsequent grantee (the man) got the protection of the recording act, it doesn't matter whether a person downstream from him gave value, recorded first, or took without notice.

[Q2163]

135. **D** A landowner has no legal right to have sunlight continue to reach her building. Therefore, it is not a nuisance or other violation for one owner to block another owner's access to sunlight, even if the consequence of the blockage is to reduce the latter building's rental or market value.

Since the defendant has done nothing wrong, (A), (B), and (C) are all incorrect.

[Q1157]

136. **D** The plaintiff's testimony would be hearsay within hearsay, and the "outer level" is not within any exception. The FRE defines hearsay as "a statement, other than one made by the declarant while testifying at the trial or hearing, offered in evidence to prove the truth of the matter asserted." FRE 801(c). Anytime the evidence in question consists of an out-of-court statement by *A* repeating another out-of-court statement by *B*, you have to analyze *both A*'s statement and *B*'s statement — if *either* statement is hearsay not falling within any exception, the combined statement cannot come in.

Here, the "inner" level (the defendant's statement to the plaintiff's husband) is an admission being used against a party-opponent, so it falls within the admissions exception to the hearsay rule. But the "outer" level (the husband's statement to the plaintiff, "Here's what the defendant told me...") is hearsay not within any exception. First, notice that the statement ("The defendant told me he'd blow my head off one day") is being offered to prove the matter asserted: it's being offered to prove that the defendant indeed made the threat — if the defendant hadn't made the threat, the evidence would be of no probative value in the case. (The statement is also being offered for the additional not-really-hearsay inference that if the defendant made a threat to kill the husband by shooting, that's evidence tending to show that the fatal shooting of the husband by someone unknown was done by the defendant. But this "secondary" purpose doesn't detract from the fact that the primary purpose — to prove that the defendant made the threat — is a hearsay purpose.) Now, let's look at whether the husband's statement falls within any exception. It doesn't. For instance, it doesn't fall within the state-of-mind exception, because the husband wasn't saying, "I'm scared of the defendant because he threatened to kill me..." — it's offered for the pure purpose of showing that the defendant made the threat, and that purpose doesn't qualify for state-of-mind, excited-utterance, or any other exception.

(A) is wrong because the state-of-mind exception doesn't solve the problem that the husband's statement to the plaintiff is, separately, hearsay. It's true that the defendant's statement alone might well be admissible as evidence of the defendant's state of mind vis-a-vis the husband, under FRE 803(3) (covering declarant's "then existing state of mind, emotion, sensation, or physical condition"). But the problem (as further discussed in Choice (D) above) is that what's offered is what the husband said out of court that the defendant told him out of court. So if the husband's statement (the "outer" statement) is hearsay not within an exception, the fact that the defendant's statement (the "inner" statement) falls within a hearsay exception doesn't help. Here, the statement by the husband is hearsay not within any exception, as shown by the analysis in Choice (D). Therefore, the combined statements of the husband and the defendant can't come in.

(B) is wrong because the admissibility of statements made by, and offered against, a party-opponent doesn't solve the combined hearsay-on-hearsay problem present here. It's true that the defendant's statement, if made directly to the testifying witness (the plaintiff) could be repeated by her on the stand, since then it would be a statement made by a party opponent admitted against that opponent, a non-hearsay use under FRE 801(d)(2)(A). But the problem (as further discussed in Choice (D) above) is that what's offered is what the husband said out of court that the defendant told him out of court. So if the husband's statement (the "outer" statement) is hearsay not within an exception, the fact that the defendant's statement (the "inner" statement) is a non-hearsay admission doesn't help.

(C) is wrong because it mischaracterizes the evidence, and it also doesn't address the hearsay within hearsay issue. First, the answer choice characterizes the evidence incorrectly, as proof of a prior bad act, when it is being offered as a statement. Secondly, it does not address the pivotal issue: the hearsay problem presented by the husband's statement (the "outer" statement).

[Q3045]

137. **D** FRE 615 says that "At the request of a party the court <u>shall</u> order witnesses excluded so that they cannot hear the testimony of other witnesses..." Although the eyewitness has already testified, the fact that he is expected to be re-called for further cross means that he's still to be treated as a witness who has not yet testified. By using the word "shall," the rule does not give the trial judge the discretion to allow the witness to remain. (The purpose of the sequestration rule is to prevent the witness from tailoring his testimony to that of other witnesses. This purpose would be thwarted by letting the eyewitness here be in the courtroom before his re-cross.)

(A) is wrong because the court has the discretion to permit inquiry into additional matters. FRE 611(b) says that as a general rule cross "should be limited to the subject matter of the direct examination and matters affecting the credibility of the witness." But that section goes on to say, "The court may, in the exercise of discretion, permit inquiry into additional matters as if on direct examination." The court's discretion would be especially proper in this case, since the defendant is effectively the direct examiner (because the plaintiff called the defendant as an adverse, or "hostile," witness).

(B) is wrong because leading questions are not proper on these facts. Here, if the defendant's lawyer is conducting "cross examination" of the defendant, it must be because the plaintiff called the defendant as an adverse witness (which is, indeed, what Choice (A) specifies happened). In that scenario, this "cross" is to be treated by the court as if it were a direct exam, since the questioner is sympathetic to the witness. In that instance, the cross should not be allowed to make use of leading questions, any more than a standard direct exam may use leading questions. See FRE 611(c), stating the general rule that leading questions "should not be used on the direct examination of a witness except as may be necessary to develop the witness' testimony."

(C) is wrong because matters of credibility are within the scope of cross-examination. FRE 611(b), in defining the permissible scope of cross-examination, says that the cross may include, in addition to "the subject matter of the direct examination," "matters affecting the credibility of the witness." So the fact that credibility was not placed in issue in the direct does not bar it from being covered on cross.

[Q3153]

138. **D** FRE 104(a) says that "Preliminary questions concerning ... the admissibility of evidence shall be

determined by the court.... In making its determination it is *not bound by the rules of evidence except those with respect to privileges.*" The pedestrian's statement to the nurse is admissible if, and only if, the statement qualified for the dying-declaration exception. That exception requires that the declarant knew or believed that he was about to die. The affidavit is relevant to that issue. It's true that the affidavit is hearsay (it's an out-of-court statement offered to prove the truth of the matter asserted, i.e., that the pedestrian really knew or believed he was dying). And this hearsay does not fall within any exception. But under 104(a), the judge may consider this inadmissible hearsay in making her preliminary ruling on the admissibility of the pedestrian's statement to the nurse.

(A) is wrong because even though the affidavit is hearsay not within any exception, it may still be considered on the preliminary matter of the admissibility of the statement to the nurse. As described in Choice (D) above, the fact that the affidavit is hearsay not within any exception does not prevent the court from using it to resolve a preliminary question about the admissibility of other evidence.

(B) is wrong because: (1) dying declarations are admissible in civil cases; and (2) the admissibility of the affidavit is irrelevant to whether it can be considered on the preliminary question here. First, FRE 804(b)(2) gives a hearsay exception for, "In a prosecution for homicide *or in a civil action or proceeding*, a statement made by a declarant while believing that the declarant's death was imminent, concerning the cause or circumstances of what the declarant believed to be impending death." So the proposition asserted in Choice (B) — that dying declarations can't be used except in homicide prosecutions —is simply incorrect as a matter of law. Furthermore, even if this statement of law were true, it would be irrelevant — as described in the discussion of Choice (D) above, the judge may consider inadmissible material in ruling on an evidentiary question.

(C) is wrong because: (1) the affidavit is the "outer level" of a two-level hearsay statement, and that outer level doesn't qualify for the then-existing-state-of-mind exception; and (2) the affidavit's admissibility doesn't matter here anyway. First, notice that we have hearsay-within-hearsay. The "outer" level is the doctor's affidavit (a statement made out of court, repeating some other statement). The "inner" level is the pedestrian's statement to the doctor. Each must satisfy a hearsay exception. It's true that the inner statement arguably qualifies for the then-existing-state-of-mind exception (though even this is far from clear, since under FRE 803(3) "A statement of ... belief to prove the fact ... believed" does not qualify for the exception.) But the *outer* statement is not a statement about *the declarant's* then-existing state of mind — for this purpose, the declarant is the doctor, and he's not summarizing his own then-existing state of mind (except insofar as he's making a statement of what he currently remembers the pedestrian to have said, which is inadmissible since FRE 803(3) denies the state-of-mind exception for "a statement of memory ... to prove the fact remembered"). Since one of the two levels is inadmissible hearsay, the entire statement-within-a-statement is inadmissible. Nonetheless, as described in Choice (D) above, the statement need not be admissible to be considered by the judge in making a preliminary admissibility ruling.
[Q3147]

139. **C** The operations of the federal government are indeed immune from state regulation, no matter how reasonable the state regulation, and even though the regulation is a generally-applicable one that treats the federal government no differently than anyone else. Since the office building is owned by and operated by the federal government, this regulatory immunity applies.

(A) is wrong, because even though the regulation of pollution may be a legitimate state police power concern, that regulation must give way to federal regulatory immunity.

(B) is wrong because, even if regulation of pollution is a joint concern of the federal and state governments, and even though both governments can regulate private parties (assuming that the state regulation is not inconsistent with the federal regulation), it does not follow that the state can regulate the federal government — under the principles of regulatory immunity, the state cannot do so.

(D) is wrong because there is no "de minimis" exception to the principle that states may regulate pursuant to their inherent police power. (The sole problem here is the federal immunity from regulation, which applies whether the asserted violation of the state's regulation is de minimis or not.)

[Q1195]

140. **C** This answer is correct because the beatings would tend to prove that the killing was not accidental. Under FRE 404(b), "Evidence of other crimes, wrongs, or acts is not admissible to prove the character of a person in order to show action in conformity therewith." So if the prosecution were offering the prior beatings on the theory that "These beatings showed that the defendant had a violent character, making it more likely that he acted violently on this occasion," the evidence would be barred by the above-quoted portion of 404(b). However, FRE 404(b) goes on to say that such other-crimes-or-wrongs evidence "may, however, be admissible for other purposes, such as proof of motive, opportunity, intent, preparation, plan, knowledge, identity, or *absence of mistake or accident*..." Here, that's exactly what's happening: the defendant has claimed that the shooting was accidental, and the prosecution is offering the prior beatings to show "absence of mistake or accident." So the evidence is admissible.

(A) is wrong because the acts of violence here are not being offered as character evidence. It's true that if the evidence were offered as pure character evidence, to show that the defendant acted in conformity with his character (character for violence, say) on the present occasion, the evidence would be barred by FRE 404(b). But as described in the analysis of Choice (C), the evidence here is being offered to show "absence of mistake or accident," not to show "character," so it's admissible.

(B) is wrong, because the beatings show lack of accident regardless of who started the fights. The fact that the witness doesn't know first-hand who started the fights is irrelevant, if the mere existence of the fights would tend to show that the shooting on the present occasion was no mistake. For instance, even if the father started the two prior fights, the fact that the defendant responded by beating his father would make it at least somewhat less likely than it would otherwise be that the shooting now was an accident. So the evidence is relevant, and it's admissible (as described in Choice (C)) as tending to prove absence of accident.

(D) is wrong because evidence of a character for violence is not admissible under these circumstances. Under FRE 404(b), "Evidence of other crimes, wrongs, or acts is not admissible to prove the character of a person in order to show action in conformity therewith." So if the evidence of the prior beatings were really being offered to show that "the defendant has a character for violence, and is thus likely to have acted violently on the present occasion," the quoted sentence would apply to make the evidence inadmissible (not admissible, as this choice posits). However, "character for violence" is not what the prior-acts evidence is being offered for. Instead (as shown in the analysis of Choice (C)), it's being offered to show absence of accident, and that purpose is admissible under 404(b).

[Q3064]

141. **D** Government may take generally-applicable actions that advance important public interests, without giving an exemption to those whose religious beliefs are thereby burdened. The facts tell us that the rules against overnight camping and campfires are "consistently enforced" because of "very great dangers," so the "generally applicable" and "advancement of important public interests" standards are met here. The fact that the Superintendent doesn't like cults doesn't matter, because there is no indication that his decision to deny the permit here was motivated by anything other than a desire to enforce these generally-applicable rules.

(A) is wrong, for the same reason that (D) is right: government may impose a generally-applicable rule to promote an important interest, even if government knows that its enforcement of that rule will interfere with religious conduct.

(B) is wrong because the Park Service's action did not "purposely and invidiously discriminate" against the group — what was being enforced was a generally-applicable rule that was not enacted for anti-religious purposes.

(C) is wrong because it misstates the law governing the Establishment Clause as well as the facts — if non-religious groups were permitted to take the same general type of action in question (here, overnight camping and campfires), which they are not, then it would not be a violation of the Establishment Clause for the government to allow a religious group to do the same thing (and, indeed, it would probably be a violation of the Free Exercise Clause for the government *not* to allow the religious group to do the same thing that the non-religious are permitted to do.)

[Q2112]

142. **A** The landowner's wife had a determinable life estate, evidenced by the words "for life" and "until remarriage" in the landowner's will. The daughter had a vested remainder (following the determinable life estate) and an executory interest (following the remarriage contingency). Both of the daughter's interests could be assigned to the friend. On the remarriage of the landowner's wife, the wife's life estate ended and it automatically went to the holder of the future interest, who at that time was the daughter's friend.

(B) is incorrect, because the landowner's wife had a determinable life estate, evidenced by the words "for life" and "until remarriage" — a fee simple estate has no such words of special limitation.

(C) is incorrect, because the landowner's wife had a determinable life estate. Had she not remarried, her life estate would have been transferable; however, the words of limitation regarding remarriage terminated her life estate immediately upon her remarriage, and her estate automatically went to the holder of the future interest.

(D) is incorrect, because the wife's new husband got nothing, for the reason discussed in Choice (C).

[Q7023]

143. **C** Generally, an assignee "stands in the shoes of his assignor." That is, the assignee generally takes subject to all defenses, set-offs, and counterclaims that the obligor could have asserted against the assignor. Here, therefore, the banker as assignee of the contractor's rights stands in the contractor's shoes, and is vulnerable to any counterclaim or defense to which the contractor would have been vulnerable if it was the contractor that was suing the homeowner. If the contractor had not made the assignment and had sued the homeowner for the $10,000 contract price (or any part of it), the homeowner could have raised the counterclaim or defense for damages for breach due to the contractor's abandonment, and used that counterclaim/defense as a set-off, i.e., to reduce any amount which the homeowner would otherwise owe. Consequently, the homeowner can make this same counterclaim or defense when sued by the banker as the contractor's assignee. (The homeowner could not achieve an affirmative recovery against the banker, but the homeowner isn't trying to do that here, just reduce the amount he owes the banker.)

(A) is wrong because it does not matter either that the contractor-homeowner contract was already in existence at the time of the notice of assignment or that the contractor was not yet in breach at that time. In a suit by the assignee against the obligor, the obligor can raise any defenses or counterclaims that it could have raised against the assignor, regardless of when those defenses or counterclaims came into existence. (If you selected this choice, you may be thinking that about the rules on *modification*, under which the giving of notice of assignment by assignee to obligor will deprive the obligor and assignor of the subsequent right to modify the contract if the assignor has fully performed.)

(B) is wrong because it states a completely fictitious rule of law. It is true that the homeowner's claim is unsecured and that the banker's is secured; this fact might prevent the homeowner from getting and collecting an *affirmative recovery* against the contractor (since the banker's secured claim would take priority over the homeowner's later-acquired judgment for the affirmative recovery). But what the homeowner cares about here is using its claim as a set-off (something that can reduce the banker's recovery against the homeowner), and the homeowner's claim is fully operative as a set-off even though the set-off claim is in a sense "unsecured."

(D) is wrong because, while it states the correct result, it gives the wrong reason. Whether or not the homeowner's claim against the contractor arose prior to the contractor's default on the loan from the banker, the homeowner gets to raise against the banker any defense he could use against the contractor (for reasons described in the discussion of choice (C) above).
[Q2032]

144. **B** Ordinarily, the parol evidence rule bars proof of an oral clause offered to supplement or contradict a completely integrated writing (which the writing here probably was). But an oral agreement that the writing will simply *not be legally enforceable at all* unless some condition precedent is satisfied is *not* barred by the parol evidence rule. This exception applies here: the owner's spouse's approval of the design was a condition precedent to the enforceability of the agreement, so that oral condition, and its non-satisfaction, may be proved.

(A) is wrong because it gives an incorrect reason for the correct result. It is not the fact that a third party's approval was required that makes evidence of the oral agreement admissible in the face of the parol evidence rule; it's the fact that the oral agreement established a condition precedent to the writing's enforceability that exempts proof of the oral agreement from the rule.

(C) is wrong for two reasons: (1) it misstates the "partial integration" branch of the parol evidence rule (under which an oral agreement that supplements rather than contradicts a partial integration *is* admissible); and (2) the parol evidence rule simply doesn't apply to an orally-agreed-upon condition to the writing's enforceability, as analyzed in Choice (B) above.

(D) is wrong because, while it correctly summarizes the branch of the parol evidence rule that bars oral understandings that contradict any sort of integration (partial or complete), it fails to reflect the fact that the parol evidence rules simply doesn't apply to an orally-agreed-upon condition to the writing's enforceability, as analyzed in Choice (B) above.
[Q1044]

145. **C** First, education is not a fundamental right for equal protection purposes. *San Antonio Sch. Dist. v. Rodriguez* (1973). Second, wealth classifications are not a suspect category. This choice therefore correctly asserts that (1) no fundamental right or suspect classification is involved in this case; and (2) where this is true, the plaintiff must bear the very difficult burden of proving that there is no rational relationship between the classification being used and any legitimate state interest. (By the way, it is very unlikely that the plaintiffs would win under this test; a school-funding scheme relying principally on local property taxes was upheld against rational-basis equal protection attack in *San Antonio v. Rodriguez, supra.*)

(A) is wrong because classifications based on wealth are not "inherently suspect" for equal protection purposes, so such classifications do not have to satisfy the strict scrutiny standard that this choice articulates.

(B) is wrong because the Court has held that education (or at least the right to have a public education that goes beyond minimally-adequate standards) is not a fundamental right for equal protection purposes; therefore, the strict scrutiny standard articulated by this choice would not apply.

(D) is wrong because it articulates an intermediate level of scrutiny, and that level is only used in cases involving semi-suspect classifications (e.g., ones based on gender).

[Q1073]

146. **C** Consent — plaintiff's willingness — is a complete defense to most intentional tort actions. Consent is implied if the reasonable person would infer from the plaintiff's conduct and the surrounding circumstances that the plaintiff is willing for the defendant's act to occur. The fact that the defendant and the plaintiff had been enjoying each other's jokes for years could result in the inference that the plaintiff was willing to have a joke like this one played upon him. Although it is not certain that a court would come to this conclusion, the argument in (C) is the only one listed which could support the defendant's defense.

(A) is wrong because as long as the plaintiff has an apprehension of an imminent harmful or offensive contact, it does not matter that what the plaintiff fears is a contact from a third person or a force of nature rather than from the defendant. See Rest. 2d, §25, and Illustr. 1 thereto (D liable for assault for making a noise that tricks P into thinking he is about to be bitten by a rattlesnake).

(B) is wrong because if the defendant's act is intended to put the plaintiff in apprehension of an immediate bodily contact and succeeds in so doing, it does not matter that that act would not have put a person of ordinary sensitivity or courage in such apprehension. Rest. 2d, §27.

(D) is wrong because, although it is true that knowledge that a particular result is substantially certain to occur is deemed the equivalent of intent to bring about the result, the fact that the defendant was not substantially certain that the plaintiff would be injured will not help the defendant. That's because what must be intended for assault is merely either the creation of a harmful or offensive bodily contact (not an injury), or the creation of an apprehension of such contact. Here, a bite from a real spider would be harmful or offensive, so the defendant intended to bring about in the plaintiff an apprehension of a harmful or offensive contact (the bite) despite the fact that the defendant knew that no such bite would occur. Since the defendant intended to put the plaintiff in apprehension of being bitten, the fact that the defendant neither intended to injure the plaintiff nor knew with substantial certainty that the plaintiff would be injured is irrelevant.

[Q5112]

147. **B** The victim's statement about the defendant was hearsay, but was properly admitted under FRE 804(b)(2)'s "dying declaration" exception, because it was made by a person now unavailable to testify, believing he was about to die, concerning personal knowledge of the cause of death, and the statement is offered at either a criminal homicide trial or a civil wrongful death suit. Since that statement came in, his prior inconsistent statement (about Jack) can be used to impeach his credibility, since hearsay declarants *can* be impeached. Note that this impeaching evidence would not be admissible *substantively*, since it does not fulfill the requirements of 801(d)(1)(A)'s prior-inconsistent-statement hearsay exclusion — the prior inconsistent statement is only admissible substantively if the statement was made under oath, at a prior proceeding, subject to perjury, with the declarant now being the testifying witness; here, the victim's statement about Jack was not made under oath or at a proceeding.

(A) is wrong because the witness' testimony does not fit an exception to the hearsay rule; it's inadmissible hearsay. In particular, the statement does not fit the most obvious exception, the "dying declaration" exception to the hearsay rule, because the victim did not have an impending sense of death when he made the statement. FRE 804(b)(2). The rationale behind the exception is that no one wants to die with a lie on his lips; where a person thinks he's going to *live*, this is not applicable. (Also, the statement will not be admissible *substantively* as a prior inconsistent statement, for the reasons discussed in Choice (B) above).

(C) is wrong because the FRE do not condition the admissibility of a statement on whether it addresses an "ultimate issue." See FRE 704(a).

(D) is wrong, because the testimony *is* relevant to a substantive issue in the case. A piece of evidence is logically relevant if it tends to prove or disprove a material fact. FRE 401. If the victim's prior statement about Jack is true, it will tend to prove that the victim was lying about the defendant's stabbing him, and thus make it less likely that the defendant is guilty of murder. As a result, it's *extremely* relevant!

[Q4022]

148. **C** This is a classic illustration of a state regulation in the economic or social-welfare area, where no fundamental right is involved. (Insurers don't have a fundamental right to adopt any particular pricing mechanism.) Since the "one price for all" scheme is rationally related to achieving one or more legitimate state objectives (e.g., promoting a sense of fairness and non-discrimination among insurance customers living in a particular county, or avoiding race-based redlining), the scheme does not violate the insurer's due process rights.

(A) is wrong for the same reason (C) is right — the company may have a due process right not to be irrationally deprived of its desired pricing mechanism, but the requirement of uniform pricing here is not irrational.

(B) is wrong, because the statute does not unduly burden interstate commerce (it only applies to policies written in-state, and it does not discriminate against out-of-state insurers).

(D) is wrong because federal courts do not have a duty to abstain from passing on the case until the state courts have had an opportunity to pass on the constitutionality of this state statute. When a litigant believes that a state statute violates the federal constitution, the litigant may sue immediately in federal court for a determination that this is so, as long as the requirements of justiciability (e.g., ripeness, actual injury to the plaintiff, etc.) are met. In other words, there is no sense in which state courts get "first shot" to determine the federal constitutionality of a state statute.

[Q2008]

149. **A** An inter vivos gift (i.e., one made during the giver's lifetime) may be made of real estate. The gift is deemed made when "delivery" occurs, accompanied by the requisite donative intent. Here, the homeowner had the requisite donative intent as shown by his words. Delivery occurred when the homeowner physically handed the deed to the nephew's friend as the agent of the nephew; this was delivery because it is clear from the homeowner's words that he intended the gift to take place immediately rather than at some future time. Acceptance is presumed if the gift is beneficial. Once delivery occurred, the homeowner could not recall the gift.

(B) is incorrect, because although the recording of a deed may create a presumption of delivery, here the delivery occurred prior to the recordation of the deed (at the moment the homeowner physically handed the deed to the nephew's friend as the agent of the nephew, with the intent to pass the title).

(C) is incorrect, because a gift causa mortis may only be made of personal property. In addition, the gift was not made in view of pending death from a stated peril (the facts only note that the homeowner was ill).

(D) is incorrect, because a testamentary document takes effect at the death of the testator and must have been executed with the requisite testamentary intent. Here, the homeowner wanted the nephew to have title immediately and thus delivered the deed to the nephew's friend; the homeowner did not want to postpone delivery until his death.

[Q7070]

150. **A** Common-law burglary is defined as the breaking and entering of the dwelling house of another in the nighttime with the intent to commit a felony. LaFave, Criminal Law, §8.13, at p. 883. The woman satisfies this definition because she unlawfully entered the neighbor's house at night with intent to commit a felony therein (larceny). The "breaking" element is satisfied because the woman opened a window — there is no requirement that the breaking occur by means of force, or that the premises have been secured, such as by a lock. *Id.* at 884. The "entering" element is more

questionable on these facts, but the woman's actions satisfy this element as well. See LaFave, Criminal Law, §8.13(b), at p. 886 (to constitute burglary it is "sufficient if any part of the actor's person intruded, even momentarily, into the structure. Thus it has been held that the intrusion of a part of a hand in opening a window, or the momentary intrusion of part of a foot in kicking out a window, constituted the requisite entry.").

(B) is wrong because the woman's action proceeded beyond the point of attempted burglary to the completed crime of burglary, as discussed in the analysis of choice (A) above.

(C) is wrong because, while the woman may have been guilty of attempted larceny, that crime arguably would merge into, and in any event was less serious than, the burglary crime.

(D) is wrong because the woman is guilty of burglary, since she unlawfully entered the neighbor's house at night with intent to commit a felony (larceny), as more fully discussed in the analysis of Choice (A) above.

[Q7027]

151. **D** Under FRE 406, evidence of an established business practice is admissible as circumstantial proof that it was followed on a particular day. So the proof here of the daily mailing practice is admissible to prove that the notice was mailed on the particular day in question.

(A) is wrong because when past conduct has a regularity amounting to a "routine practice of an organization," it is deemed relevant to the issue of whether the practice was followed on a particular day, and under FRE 406 is admissible on that issue.

(B) is wrong for the same reason (D) is right: evidence of an established business practice is admissible as circumstantial proof that it was followed on a particular day, without the need to prove directly that the practice was following on the day in question.

(C) is wrong because FRE 406 says that the regular practice is admissible to prove that the practice was following on the particular occasion in question, "whether corroborated or not and regardless of the presence of eyewitnesses." So, any office employee who knows about the practice of his own knowledge may testify to it.

[Q5087]

152. **D** The federal concession statute, by requiring a nominal rental on account of the great public benefit from concessions, shows a federal intent to keep the total occupancy costs for concessionaires low. The state occupancy tax has the effect (and purpose) of making occupancy costs higher for the affected taxpayers than it would otherwise be. This fact is coupled with the fact that the state is singling out taxpayers on non-state-taxed property, including federally-owned property, so the interference with federal interests is especially acute. Therefore, a court might well hold that the state law so undermines the federal purposes as to be invalid under the Supremacy Clause. The court would not *necessarily* reach this conclusion, but this is the most powerful of the four arguments.

(A) is wrong because the occupancy tax does not discriminate against interstate commerce (since the effect on tourists from inside Purple is the same as on out-of-state tourists), and it is unlikely that subjecting the plaintiff to the same overall level of overall taxation as businesses located in state-taxable facilities would be found to be an "undue burden."

(B) is wrong because the Fourteenth Amendment's P&I Clause protects only certain very limited rights of "national citizenship" (mostly the right to travel from state to state), and the Clause has never been interpreted to protect a "fundamental right to do business on federal property." (It's true that the P&I Clause of Art. *IV* protects the fundamental right to pursue one's business or profession, but the examiners have tried to trick you here by using the Fourteenth Amendment's P&I Clause, not the Art. IV Clause.)

(C) is wrong because the Fourteenth Amendment Equal Protection Clause protects only against a given state's unfair classification of multiple persons, not against one state's treating a person less favorably than other states treat similarly-situated persons. (Also, any classification being done by Purple here does not involve a suspect or semi-suspect class or a fundamental right, so the classification merely has to be rationally related to the achievement of a legitimate state objective, and the occupancy tax here meets this easy-to-satisfy standard.)

[Q2150]

153. **A** The plaintiff does not meet the requirement of "injury in fact." He clearly has not been injured yet; the real question is whether he faces sufficiently imminent injury from the residency requirement. A court would likely hold that because the plaintiff has not yet even made the decision to run, and could not be injured unless he decided to run, any threatened injury to him is too uncertain and speculative to meet the requirement that prospective injury be reasonably concrete and imminent. The fact that the chairman has joined the suit does not change this, since the chairman (and the chairman's party) would not be injured unless some actual candidate was blocked by the residency requirement, and there is no such candidate now.

(B) is wrong because: (1) the absence of a case or controversy would prevent the court even from getting to the issue of whether there was a substantial federal constitutional question in the case; and (2) the fact that something is a local election does not prevent it from presenting a substantial federal constitutional question (for instance, an unduly long residency requirement probably *would* constitute a violation of an actual candidate's equal protection rights).

(C) is wrong because, while the residency restriction might well constitute an equal protection violation of the rights of an actual candidate, the plaintiff's lack of actual-candidate status prevents him from raising a case or controversy.

(D) is wrong because there is no basis (certainly not a federal constitutional basis) for the court to conclude that "substantially complying," rather than fully complying, with the residency requirement here would be sufficient.

[Q2153]

154. **A** The events satisfy all the requirements of FRE 803(5)'s exception for recorded recollection (sometimes called "past recollection recorded"). These requirements are: (1) the memorandum must relate to something of which the witness once had first-hand knowledge; (2) the record must have been made by, or adopted by, the witness when the matter was fresh in the witness' memory; (3) there must currently be some impairment of the witness' memory of the events; and (4) there must be evidence that the record correctly reflects the witness' original knowledge. The tape satisfies all these elements: (1) the tape relates to something of which the witness once had first-hand knowledge, since the witness personally saw the events, including the license number; (2) the tape was made when the matter was fresh in the witness's memory, and although he didn't make it he adopted it by listening to the playback and verifying that his wife had relayed the license number correctly; (3) there is presently an impairment of the witness's memory, since he has said that he has no present memory of the license plate number; and (4) the witness's listening to it and concluding that it was accurately satisfies the requirement that the tape correctly reflects his original knowledge.

(B) is wrong because the witness is not a public official who had a duty to make the report. There is indeed an exception to the hearsay rule for public records and reports. This exception is codified in FRE 803(8), which allows the admission of "records, reports [or] statements ... of public offices or agencies" "setting forth ... (B) matters *observed pursuant to duty imposed by law* as to which matters there was a *duty to report*, excluding, however, in criminal cases matters observed by police officers and other law enforcement personnel[.]" But the public records exception does not apply in this case because the witness (the one who made the "observation") was not a public official, nor was the report he made to the police of the break-in part of an official duty. (And even if the witness *was* a police officer, the last clause quoted above starting with "excluding" would prevent the report from coming in against the defendant in the defendant's criminal trial.)

(C) is wrong because the tape recording of the call to the police falls within the past recollection recorded exception. (See the discussion of Choice (A) for why this is so.)

(D) is wrong because the witness's wife did not have to have first-hand knowledge of the license number in order for the recorded recollection exception to apply. It's true that the witness's wife was the one who "made" the recording (in the sense that she was the one who spoke the license number on to the tape). But the requirements of FRE 803(5)'s past recollection recorded exception do not require that witness be the one who physically made the record. All that 803(5) requires in this respect is that the record be one that is "made *or adopted* by the witness when the matter was fresh in the witness' memory," and that the witness have had first-hand knowledge. Here, when the witness immediately listened to the playback and pronounced the relayed number correct, the witness adopted the record; since he had the first-hand knowledge about the license number, the first-hand knowledge requirement is also satisfied.

[Q3040]

155. **A** The defendant can be found guilty of all three crimes. Let's take the crimes one at a time.

First, let's look at burglary. Common-law burglary is: (1) the breaking, (2) and entering, (3) of the dwelling, (4) of another, (5) at nighttime, (6) with the intent to commit a felony within. The defendant's actions satisfy all the requirements for burglary. Requirements (1) and (6) are the only ones that are even worth discussing here. As to (1) (breaking), courts recognize "constructive breaking" — if D uses fraud or threat of force to induce the occupants to let him in, that counts as breaking. That's what happened here. As to (6) (intent to commit a felony within), where D commits a felony once inside the premises, courts will in the absence of other evidence presume that D had the intent to commit that felony at the time of entry. So here, the defendant would readily be found to have intended, at the time he entered, to commit the felony of robbery once he was inside. Thus the requisite intent-to-commit-a-felony-within is satisfied.

Next, let's examine robbery. Robbery is: (1) a taking, (2) of the personal property of another, (3) from the other's person or presence, (4) by force or intimidation, (5) with the intent to permanently deprive. Here, the only interesting question is whether taking the property from the safe (rather than directly from the person) of the victim meets requirement (3). But the taking will suffice if it's from the "person or presence" of the owner, and the safe would be found to have been within the husband and wife's presence at the time the defendant took the necklace.

Finally, let's look at murder. There are of course multiple types — ways of committing — murder. Here, the relevant type of murder is felony murder. Felony murder is a killing, even an accidental one, committed during the commission of certain dangerous felonies. The defendant's actions satisfy the requirements of felony murder. The defendant was committing robbery, and robbery is one of the "dangerous" felonies recognized at common law as a predicate crime for felony murder. The interesting question is whether the fact that the defendant was arrested before the husband had his heart attack prevents the husband's death from being "during the commission of" the robbery. Notice that the husband's death was very closely causally related to the robbery — the husband had his heart attack because he was trying to free himself from his bonds and gag, and he was bound and gagged because, and solely because, the defendant wanted to commit, and escape from, the robbery. Where there is a close causal relationship between the underlying felony (or the attempt to escape from it) and the death, the requirement of a death "during the commission of" the felony is generally deemed satisfied, even if the death doesn't come until after the felony-and-escape period is in some sense over.

(B), (C), and (D) are not the best response, because each fails to cover at least one of the three crimes that in fact was committed, as described in Choice (A).

[Q3101]

156. **C** Plaintiff bears the burden of proving by a preponderance of the evidence that defendant actually caused his injury, just as he must bear the burden of proving the other parts of his prima facie case. Under these facts, the customer cannot produce any real evidence that the restaurant caused him to become sick. At best the customer can introduce facts that raise a mere suspicion that the restaurant was the cause — he can show that he had an upset stomach later in the evening and that various health code violations had been found at the restaurant. What he cannot show is that the meal was the but-for cause of his becoming ill. In response to the customer's facts, the restaurant can show that the customer had three meals after eating in their restaurant, any of which could have caused his infection. The restaurant could also argue that the bacterium causing the customer's illness could have come from the customer's own hands. While this "no causation" defense might not work, it is the restaurant's best chance of those defenses listed.

(A) is wrong because the fact that no one else became ill creates only an inference that the restaurant was not the cause. The fact that no one else got sick certainly doesn't prove that the restaurant wasn't the cause — perhaps one employee failed to wash his hands, prepared the one dish eaten by the customer, then washed them. In any event, the restaurant is better off making the much more general argument (listed in Choice (C)) that the customer is required to make an affirmative showing that the restaurant's negligence caused the illness, and that he has failed to carry this burden by a preponderance of the evidence.

(B) is wrong because the restaurant is responsible for the acts of its employees while in the course of their duties, even if they disregard instructions. Under the doctrine of respondeat superior, an employer is vicariously liable for the negligent acts of its employees, done within the scope of the employment. The fact that the employee has disobeyed rules formulated by the employer is not a defense. Thus as long as there was evidence that an employee failed to wash her hands and then prepared a dish eaten by the customer, the fact that this happened in violation of the restaurant's instructions would not prevent respondeat superior from applying against it.

(D) is wrong because assumption of risk would not apply here. The assumption of the risk doctrine bars a plaintiff from recovery if he voluntarily consented to take the chance that the harm in question would occur. Here, the customer may have assumed the risk of an upset stomach caused by spicy food, but he did not assume the risk of becoming ill because of a bacterium in contaminated food, and his claim is that the latter is what occurred.
[Q3090]

157. **D** Strict liability crimes generally have the following attributes: (1) they are regulatory in nature; (2) they do not involve serious penalties (i.e., they are usually limited to a fine, not imprisonment or even probation); (3) they involve serious harm to the public; and (4) it was easy for the defendant to find out the true facts before he acted. Cf. LaFave, §4.5, p. 188. In fact, statutes regulating food, drugs and misbranded articles, as well as hunting license requirements and the like, are all common forms of valid strict liability statutes. So this choice, involving the sale of adulterated milk, satisfies these tests fairly well: (1) the crime is essentially regulatory; (2) it's a misdemeanor rather than a felony; (3) it involves serious harm to the public; and (4) the defendant ought to be able readily to determine whether milk he's selling was adulterated (though admittedly this is the weakest of the four factors as to this choice).

(A) is wrong because it's highly unlikely shoplifting would be regarded a strict liability crime, even if the statute did not specify which *mens rea* it would require. Here, the main thing that would make this statute a less-than-perfect candidate for strict liability is that it is not regulatory in nature (like firearms registration rules, hunting license requirements, and the like). Also, shoplifting is a type of larceny, and thus a court would likely infer a *mens rea* requirement – that is, the intent to steal. So the fact that, in this case, the most severe penalty is a $200 fine, would not be dispositive, in view of the moral opprobrium, relation to larceny, and non-regulatory nature of the offense.

(B) is wrong because it's unlikely possessing heroin, defined as a felony, would be a strict liability crime, even if the statute did not mention a *mens rea*. The more serious the potential punishment, the less likely a crime is to be a strict liability one. So the fact that it's a felony here is enough to make it not the best choice.

(C) is wrong because a statute making failure to register a gun a felony is unlikely to be a strict liability crime. What makes this option tempting is that firearms registration statutes are classic strict liability offenses, because they have a regulatory flavor. However, the wrinkle here is that the crime is defined as a *felony* – thus, in view of the stiff potential penalty (more than one year's imprisonment, under common law), the court is likely to infer that the legislature intended to require some sort of *mens rea*, at least negligence.

[Q4036]

158. **A** Under the doctrine of "negligence per se," where a legislature has enacted a statute that is intended to prescribe the standard of conduct of a reasonable person in a particular situation, an excused violation of that standard that leads to the harm will constitute a prima facie showing of negligence if certain requirements are met (e.g., that the statute was intended to guard against the type of harm, and to protect the class of persons, at issue in the present case). So if the statutory violation were the only evidence regarding negligence that had been presented on either side, the plaintiff would win. But notice that the above formulation refers to an *"unexcused"* violation of the statute. Here, the decedent's estate, by demonstrating that the decedent had an unforeseeable heart attack while otherwise driving reasonably, has established that the statutory violation was excused. See, e.g., Rest. 2d, §288A(2)(a) (giving an excuse for a statutory violation where "the violation is reasonable because of the actor's incapacity"). Since this evidence of excuse is undisputed, and since there is no other evidence of negligence, the decedent's estate wins.

(B) is wrong because, while this answer correctly states that the decedent's estate will prevail, it misstates the legal basis for this conclusion. The plaintiff's evidence that the decedent violated the statute by crossing over into her lane of traffic *does* establish a prima facie case of negligence. (That is, if it were the only evidence of negligence in the case, plaintiff would be entitled to go to the jury.) Nevertheless, the decedent's estate successfully rebutted the plaintiff's evidence by providing an uncontested explanation of how the accident happened that is inconsistent with a finding of negligence (that the decedent's unforeseeable heart attack made her unable to comply with the statute, or indeed with any standard of care). Keep in mind that when a statement says that the plaintiff has or has not "established a prima facie case for liability," the statement is referring merely to the facts presented by the plaintiff in the plaintiff's case, not referring to the overall set of proven facts after both sides have rested. So it can happen — as it did here — that the plaintiff establishes a prima facie case in her own case, but that the defendant then produces counterproof to rebut that prima facie case, entitling the defendant to a verdict (perhaps even a directed verdict that takes the case away from the jury).

(C) is wrong, because while it may or may not be true that accidents of this type do not ordinarily happen in the absence of negligence, that is beside the point. This choice is suggesting the applicability of *res ipsa loquitur*, one requirement for which is that the accident be of a type that ordinarily does not happen in the absence of negligence. There are two problems with the use of *res ipsa* here: (1) it is far from clear that median-crossing accidents "do not ordinarily happen in the absence of negligence" (there are a lot of heart attack, seizure, and other involuntary median-crossing scenarios, perhaps amounting to a majority); and (2) even where the "does not usually happen without negligence" requirement is met, the doctrine will not be applied where there is direct and unrebutted evidence that something other than the defendant's negligence was the cause (and here, that evidence exists in the form of the heart attack evidence).

(D) is wrong because the plaintiff's evidence that the decedent violated the statute and crossed over into her lane of traffic establishes only a prima facie case of negligence. The decedent's estate successfully rebutted the plaintiff's evidence — and thus made the negligence per se doctrine inapplicable — by providing an undisputed explanation of how the accident happened that is inconsistent with a finding of negligence.

[Q7059]

159. **B** A license is permission to use the land of another. It is ordinarily revocable, and is not subject to the Statute of Frauds. In this case, because the neighbor had the landowner's permission to use the road and did not expend any money, property, or labor pursuant to the agreement (i.e., the neighbor did substantially rely on the continued availability of the license), the neighbor had a license that was revocable — and effectively revoked — by the grantee.

(A) is incorrect because, while this option correctly states that the grantee will prevail, it misstates the reason why this is so. A license (unlike an easement) is not subject to the Statute of Frauds; it may be oral, written, or implied.

(C) is incorrect because for estoppel to apply to make a license (which is ordinarily revocable) irrevocable, the neighbor must have expended money, property, or labor pursuant to the agreement. In this case, the landowner alone maintained the road. The neighbor's use of the land by permission, without expense, was therefore a revocable license that was effectively revoked by the grantee.

(D) is incorrect. An open and notorious use of the road suggests a claim for an easement by prescription. However, the use was with permission, which prevents a prescriptive claim. (Also, the use was for just three years, making it extremely unlikely that the statutory period for adverse possession-type claims could have run.) Instead, the neighbor's use of the land was a license that was effectively revoked by the grantee.

[Q7098]

160. **C** This is a race notice statute, since it says that it protects only "subsequent purchasers for value without notice, *who shall first record.*" Therefore, the investor could only obtain the protection of the recording statute if he recorded before the prior interest (the bank's mortgage) was recorded. Since the bank recorded on Jan. 18 and the investor on Jan. 23, the investor did not satisfy the record-first requirement. Therefore, the recording act does not apply, and the bank wins under the common-law principle that the first-in-time conveyance takes priority over the second conveyance.

(A) is wrong because, while the investor's paying valuable consideration and taking without notice prior to the bank's recording were *necessary* elements for him to be covered by the recording act, they were not *sufficient* elements — he was also required to record first.

(B) is wrong because there is no principle of estoppel by which a party who delays in recording loses the right to rely on the recording act; the only risk taken by the delaying party is that during the delay, a subsequent purchaser may meet the requirements for protection under the recording act.

(D) is wrong because it gives an incorrect explanation for the correct result: after the bank received its mortgage, it would still lose to a subsequent purchaser for value without notice who beat it to the recording office.

[Q1054]

161. **A** In order for a deposit / liquidated damages clause in a land sale contract to be enforceable, even in an easy-to-satisfy court the amount fixed must be reasonable relative to *either* the *anticipated* loss (viewed as of the time the contract was signed) or to the *actual* loss (as determined by the passage of time). The clause here does not meet this standard. It was not a reasonable forecast viewed as of the time the contract was made, because a loss of $50,000 in value during the contract-closing gap is highly unlikely given that the market value at the outset was $100,000 (i.e., a 50% loss of value during a relatively short 2- or 3-month period). Nor was the amount set in the clause reasonable compared with the actual damages, since we're told that the value of the property had actually

increased between the signing and the time for closing. So the clause was not reasonable relative to either the anticipated or actual loss, making it an unenforceable penalty.

(B) is wrong as a matter of law — the death of the purchaser under a land-sale contract does not terminate the contract. Instead, both sides remain liable, with the purchaser's estate legally obligated to pay the purchase price assuming that all conditions to closing are satisfied.

(C) is wrong, because the court would not enforce an unenforceable term of a contract.

(D) is wrong because it reaches the wrong outcome, and because equitable conversion has nothing to do with this fact pattern. Equitable conversion, if a court decides to apply it, causes the risk of loss to pass from seller to buyer at the signing of a land-sale contract. Here, it was not equitable conversion that prevented the purchaser's death from terminating the contract. And in any event, the purchaser is entitled to a return of the deposit less any actual damages (which will be zero or negligible in light of the run-up in value).

[Q3119]

162. **B** When a state (or subdivision of a state, like a city and its municipally-owned operations) regulates a right that is "fundamental to national unity," and does so in a way that disadvantages out-of-staters, that regulation will essentially be subject to strict scrutiny under the Art. IV Privileges and Immunities clause. (Among other things, the state must show that the discrimination against non-residents bears a "substantial relationship" to the problem the state is attempting to solve.) Practice of one's business or profession is a right "fundamental to national unity" for P&I purposes.

The case here is on all fours with *New Hampshire v. Piper* (1985), where the Court held that New Hampshire's attempt to restrict the right to practice law to state residents violated the Art. IV P&I clause. Applying *Piper*, since there's no showing that out-of-state doctors are the peculiar source of any special problem that the hospital is trying to solve, the restriction violates the P&I Clause.

(By the way, there's no exception under the P&I Clause for activities in which the city or state is a "market participant," as there is under the dormant Commerce Clause. *United Bldg. and Constr. Trades Counc. v. Camden* (1984). So the fact that the city owns the hospital that's making the rule doesn't help it, as it would against a Commerce Clause attack.)

(A) is wrong because the legislature of state Red was not trying to punish the doctor. A bill of attainder is a legislative act that attempts to inflict punishment without a judicial trial upon individuals who are designated by name or in terms of past conduct. The constitutional prohibition against a bill of attainder would not be helpful to the doctor because the hospital here merely took the purely regulatory action of changing the residency requirement for practicing medicine at the hospital — no public entity named the doctor as a criminal, or attempted to punish or stigmatize him, which is what a bill of attainder would have done.

(C) is wrong because the doctor would have to show that the licensing requirement was not rationally related to a legitimate government interest, a showing the doctor probably couldn't make. The Due Process Clause of the Fourteenth Amendment provides that no state shall make or enforce any law which shall deprive any person of life, liberty, or property, without due process of law. When a fundamental right is not involved, substantive due process requires only that a law be "rationally related" to the achievement of a "legitimate government interest." So to win on due process, the doctor would have to prove that Red's new residency requirement was not rationally related to some legitimate government purpose. This standard is very lenient and easy-to-satisfy. Here, for instance, the hospital could plausibly claim that it wants to have on staff only doctors who live very nearby, and that it's entitled to use state of residence as a proxy for nearby-ness. Although the fit between means and end isn't very tight under this rationale, it's almost certainly tight enough to meet the extremely lenient rational-relation standard.

(D) is wrong because state Red was not legislating against past acts. The Ex Post Facto clauses,

Article I, §9 and §10, prohibit both the federal government and the state, respectively, from passing legislation that retroactively alters the criminal law as to offenses or punishments, in a substantially prejudicial manner. A retroactive change in civil regulations, such as licensing requirements, cannot violate the prohibition, since the prohibition applies only to "penal," i.e., punitive, measures. Here, the facts make it clear that the hospital was not making a rule penalizing past acts, but was instead making residency a requirement to practice medicine in state Red going forward.

[Q3190]

163. **D** The statement in (D) is incorrect. When the distributor wrote the letter and induced the customer to present the letter to the manufacturer, the distributor was making an offer for a unilateral contract — that is, it's clear that the distributor was expecting the manufacturer to accept (if he accepted at all) by extending the credit, rather than promising the distributor that he would extend the credit. When the manufacturer extended the credit, this was an acceptance of the distributor's offer by performance, so the distributor's guarantee of repayment came into effect. However, because of the requirement that an offeree who accepts an offer for unilateral contract must give prompt notice of acceptance to the offeror, if the manufacturer had not given the distributor prompt notice of the sale (which the facts say he did), the distributor's guarantee duty would have been discharged. Notice that it was up to you to spot the fact that this was an offer for unilateral contract — the facts don't highlight this, and if you hadn't noticed it yourself, you would probably not have seen why notice by the manufacturer was important.

(A) is wrong because the statement is correct: the distributor's promise would not have been enforceable had it not been embodied in a signed writing. That's because the distributor's offer was a promise to "answer for the debt of another." As such, it fell within the suretyship provision of the Statute of Frauds, and was therefore required to be in a writing signed by the party to be charged (the distributor).

(B) is wrong because the statement is correct: as the discussion of Choice (D) describes, the distributor's offer was an offer for a unilateral contract (i.e., one to be accepted by performance rather than return promise), and the manufacturer accepted that offer by doing the requested act, i.e., extending credit to the retailer.

(C) is wrong because the statement is correct. It's true that the distributor received no consideration from the customer. However, the distributor received consideration *from the manufacturer* — the distributor bargained to have the manufacturer give credit to the customer, and got the performance he bargained for. (The fact that the performance ran to the customer rather than to the distributor [the promisor] does not prevent it from being consideration to support the distributor's promise.) The customer was a third-party beneficiary of the distributor's promise, and in a third-party beneficiary arrangement the fact that the third-party beneficiary does not give consideration to the promisor does not make any difference.

[Q2174]

164. **C** The test for unconscionability is whether in light of the general commercial background and the commercial needs of the particular parties, the contract is so one-sided as to be unconscionable. Here, there are two facts that support an unconscionability claim: (1) a purchase price that was 70% below market; and (2) the landholder's lack of knowledge about timber values. It is not certain that the landowner will prevail with the unconscionability claim as the basis for rescission, but of the four choices it is the only one that could plausibly work for him.

(A) is wrong because the logger has not behaved in bad faith. A buyer who proposes a very below-market price has not thereby behaved in bad faith. In any event, "bad faith" in some abstract sense is not grounds for canceling a transaction to which the other party has agreed, in the absence of misrepresentation or unconscionability.

(B) is wrong because the landholder did not make a misrepresentation, which is necessary for equitable estoppel. Equitable estoppel is a doctrine applied by courts of equity to allow one party to rescind when the other misrepresents a fact on which the first party justifiably and detrimentally relies. Here, the landholder would have to show that the logger misrepresented something, and it's not likely that the landholder could make that showing.

(D) is wrong because the landholder can't show coercion. The defense of duress will rarely be successful where one party merely takes economic advantage of the other's pressing need to enter the contract. For the concept of duress to work for the landholder, he would have to argue that the logger coerced him into entering the contract. There are no facts here to show coercion — all the logger did was take advantage of the landholder's scant knowledge about timber values and his pressing need for immediate money, and that's not the same thing as coercion.
[Q3082]

165. **B** This choice correctly states the three-part *Lemon v. Kurtzman* (1970) test for government action that is alleged to benefit some religious interest. On the facts here, the statute passes all three parts: there is no evidence that the city's decision to operate the cemetery under these rules was intended to benefit religious groups; the primary effect of the cemetery operation is not to benefit those who put religious monuments on their plot; and the city's work in maintaining the religious monuments is so incidental to the overall operation of the cemetery — and so comparable to the work needed to maintain non-religious monuments — that there is no excessive entanglement between government and religion.

(A) is wrong because the amount of government funds spent is not dispositive; if the city was intending to benefit only religion (e.g., by providing a $20 reimbursement to the first 100 people who bought a piece of religious jewelry), the fact that only a "small amount" of city funds was spent would not save the expenditure from being a violation of the Establishment Clause.

(C) is wrong because it misstates the test for Establishment Clause violations; a city may maintain a "religious object" if the maintenance is part of a religiously-neutral program that is not intended to, and does not have the primary effect of, benefiting religion.

(D) is wrong because, if the government acts neutrally as to religion (as it has done here), there is no Establishment Clause violation whether the government has pursued a compelling interest or not.
[Q1138]

166. **B** The landowner has used deadly force, so the standards for using it are tougher than for using non-deadly force. A person is privileged to use deadly force (defined as force intended or likely to cause death or serious bodily harm) against another when the person believes that: (1) the other is about to inflict upon him an intentional contact or other bodily harm; and (2) the person is thereby being put in peril of death, serious bodily harm, or sexual assault, which can safely be prevented only by the immediate use of such deadly force. Rest. 2d, §65(1). Furthermore, even where deadly force would otherwise be permissible in self-defense, no amount of force (deadly or otherwise) may be permitted in excess of that force which the person reasonably believes to be necessary for his protection. Rest. 2d, §70. Since the hunter's shotgun was being pointed at the landowner, Choice (B) correctly applies these two rules, since the landowner would be privileged to use self-defense if and only if he reasonably believed that the hunter would fire, and that no lesser amount of force would safely prevent that firing. Notice also that there is no real issue of the possibility of retreat here, because the shotgun is pointed at the landowner, and a shotgun has a significant range; therefore, the landowner would reasonably believe that he could not retreat in safety — he might be shot in the back. (The range of the gun matters, because even in those courts imposing a duty to retreat outside of one's own dwelling, retreat is only required if it can be done so with apparent safety, and that is not the case here.)

(A) is wrong because it overstates the landowner's right to protect his property against trespass. A landowner *does* have the right to use force to prevent or terminate another's intrusion upon the owner's land, if (1) the owner reasonably believes that the intrusion cannot be prevented by lesser force; and (2) the owner has first asked the other to leave and he has refused, or the owner reasonably believes that such a request will be useless or dangerous. Rest. 2d, §77. So based on this formulation, Choice (A) could be right. However, where the intruder does not threaten death or serious bodily harm to the owner or another who is on the premises, the owner *may not use deadly force*, i.e., force intended or likely to cause death or serious bodily harm. Rest. 2d, §79. This choice, insofar as it asserts that the landowner was entitled to fire his pistol merely to cause the hunter to leave the premises if this couldn't be done with lesser force, is therefore wrong — a landowner is required to summon the authorities rather than use deadly force to repel an intruder who does not pose a danger of death or serious bodily harm to the occupants.

(C) is wrong because the fact that the landowner made the first use of force is irrelevant in this case. At the beginning of the encounter, the landowner asked the intruder to leave and the intruder refused; that was enough to entitle the landowner to use non-deadly force to repel the intruder if no lesser degree of force recently seemed as though it would suffice (see Choice (A) above for why this is true). The landowner's use of a gentle push met this requirement. (Even if the push went beyond what was privileged, it is still the case that after the hunter escalated the encounter by using deadly force, the landowner would have been privileged to use deadly force in self-defense if no lesser force seemed as though it would suffice.)

(D) is wrong because the fact that the landowner waited to make the first use of even non-deadly force against the hunter until after the hunter was already completely on the property is irrelevant; an owner is entitled to try to persuade the intruder to leave voluntarily, and does not thereby forfeit his right to use an appropriate level of non-deadly force if the persuasion fails.
[Q5052]

167. **A** If the parties orally agree on a deal, but mistakenly prepare and execute a document which incorrectly reflects that oral agreement, either party may obtain a court order for reformation (i.e., a rewriting of the document). That's what would happen in this choice, since both parties agreed on what acreage was to be covered by the agreement, and a clerical mistake caused the document to diverge from the oral agreement.

Choices (B), (C), and (D) are all wrong for the same reason: the parties did not in fact have a meeting of the minds about a key issue, so reformation to match their "actual" (subjective) agreement is not possible. In this situation, discharge for mutual mistake, rather than reformation, is the appropriate remedy.
[Q1128]

168. **C** Ballot restrictions that are so severe that minor-party and independent candidates have no realistic opportunity to get on the ballot are given strict scrutiny, under both the equal protection clause and the First Amendment's freedom of association clause. [*Williams v. Rhodes* (1968)] The statute here is such a restriction, because it makes it completely impossible (not just somewhat harder) for someone who fails to get a major-party nomination to then run as an independent or minor-party candidate in the general election, no matter how much public support that person can demonstrate. Consequently, the choice here, by articulating strict scrutiny as the standard, is correct.

(A) is incorrect because, although it correctly articulates the strict-scrutiny standard, it incorrectly says that the plaintiff who is challenging the government bears the burden of persuasion; in those scenarios triggering strict scrutiny, the burden of persuasion is on the government.

(B) is wrong because it incorrectly uses the easy-to-satisfy mere-rationality standard, when what is at issue is a serious impairment of the fundamental right to be a candidate (and the right of voters to choose the best candidate).

(D) is wrong because, for the reasons stated above, the court would apply the strict scrutiny stan-

169. **B** Normally, a contract for the sale of goods having a value of more than $500 is not enforceable unless memorialized in a writing signed by the party against whom enforcement is sought, here, the retailer. However, there is an important exception for confirmations sent between merchants. According to UCC §2-201(2), "Between merchants if within a reasonable time a writing in confirmation of the contract and sufficient against the sender is received and the party receiving it has reason to know its contents, it satisfies the requirements of [the Statute of Frauds] against such party unless written notice of objection to its contents is given within 10 days after it is received." So here, even though the retailer didn't sign anything, the confirmation makes the contract good against her under 2-201(2), because: (1) the retailer and the manufacturer are both merchants; (2) the manufacturer signed the confirmation, so that the confirmation would have been binding against the manufacturer; (3) the retailer had "reason to know [the confirmation's] contents" (because she read it); and (4) the retailer did not indicate her objection to the memorandum's contents within 10 days after receiving it.

(A) is wrong because the fact that the goods were "identified to the contract" is irrelevant to the enforceability of the contract — even if the retailer had canceled before the goods were shipped (or even before the goods were identified within the manufacturer's plant as being the ones that would be shipped to the retailer), the manufacturer would still have been entitled to sue for breach if more than 10 days had passed since the retailer received the confirmation. (The MBE examiners are probably trying to fool you into thinking of §2-709, under which the fact that the goods have been identified to the contract will entitle the seller to sue for the full contract price if the seller cannot resell them at a reasonable price — but this provision doesn't turn an otherwise-unenforceable contract into an enforceable one, it merely governs the measure of damages for an already-enforceable contract.)

(C) is wrong because the retailer is liable despite never having signed a writing, due to her receipt of a confirmation and her lack of objection to it, as described in the discussion of Choice (B) above.

(D) is wrong because the fact that the retailer never paid for or accepted any of the goods is irrelevant — the retailer is bound by virtue of the fact that she received a signed confirmation and failed to object to it, and this is true regardless of whether she paid for or accepted any of the goods.

[Q2185]

170. **C** On these facts, we cannot rule out either a conviction for murder or one for manslaughter. If the defendant fired the third shot while still in the heat of passion from the prior attack by the neighbor, the defendant will qualify for manslaughter of the "imperfect self-defense" variety. If the defendant was *not* still in the heat of passion at the time of the fatal shot, then the defendant will meet all the requirements for murder, since he will have intentionally killed another with no mitigating circumstances or defenses. Because of this absence of information about heat of passion, we do not know which of these two crimes will be applicable, but we know that neither can be excluded.

(A) is wrong because of the word "only." States disagree whether a defendant who succeeded can be convicted of attempt (with the modern view being that he can; see LaFave, §10.5, p. 449); so if the defendant fired in cold blood rather than in heat of passion, the fact that the defendant committed murder might or might not preclude a conviction of attempted murder. But because the defendant is guilty of at least the completed crime of manslaughter, if not murder, for the reasons described in choice (C) above, it cannot be the case that attempted murder is the "only" crime for which there can be a conviction.

(B) is wrong because we cannot be certain that manslaughter is the only crime for which there could be a conviction. As further described in the discussion of choice (C) above, there will have to be a conviction of either manslaughter or murder, depending on whether the defendant was still in the heat of passion at the time he fired the last shot. So it's not accurate to say, as a matter of law, that there could be a conviction "only" for manslaughter.

(D) is wrong because we can be certain that at the least, there will be a conviction for manslaughter. Taking the facts most favorable to the defendant, at the time he fired the final and fatal shot he was no longer in fear of being attacked by the neighbor. Therefore, a prerequisite for the defense of self-defense — fear of attack — was not met at the critical moment. If the defendant was still in the heat of passion at the time of the third shot, he will qualify for "imperfect self-defense," entitling him to be convicted only of voluntary manslaughter, not murder. If he was not still in the heat of passion, this will be murder. But the one thing we know is that it will not be "no degree of homicide."

[Q7069]

171. **B** The defendant's mistaken belief that the briefcase was his own prevented him from having the required mental state for robbery. Robbery is the: (1) taking, (2) of personal property of another, (3) from the other's person or presence, (4) by force or intimidation, (5) with the intent to permanently deprive him of it. The intent required for robbery is the intent to use force to take "the property of another." Therefore, if D mistakenly (even unreasonably) believes that the property in question is his own, the required "intent to take the property of another" is lacking. The fact that that mistake was brought about by voluntary intoxication — and the fact that the mistake may have been "unreasonable" — makes no difference.

(A) is wrong because: (1) the absence of threats would not prevent this from being robbery; and (2) the intoxication would not necessarily prevent this from being robbery. Robbery is the taking of personal property of another from the latter's person or presence, "by force or intimidation." A taking can involve force without involving threats. Here, the defendant struggled with the owner, and knocked him to the floor, so the requisite force was present even though the defendant made no threats. Also, the fact that the defendant was drunk would not necessarily prevent him from being guilty — it was only the defendant's mistaken belief that the briefcase was his that caused him to avoid guilt. (It's true that the intoxication may have been what caused the defendant to have the mistaken belief — but no matter why the mistaken belief occurred, the defendant would have avoided guilt.)

(C) is wrong because voluntary intoxication can still prevent the required specific intent from existing. Robbery requires an intent to take "the property of another." If D fails to have the requisite intent, whatever the reason, the crime has not been committed. Here, the defendant thought the briefcase was his, so he lacked the requisite intent to take "property of another." The fact that the intoxication was "voluntary" would not make a difference, if for any reason (including intoxication) he lacked the requisite intent.

(D) is wrong because mistake *can* be a defense to specific intent crimes. If a mistake of fact prevents the defendant from having the requisite intent for a "specific intent" crime, that mistake is indeed a defense. Here, robbery requires an intent to take "the property of another." If a mistake causes D to believe (whether reasonably or not) that the property is his own rather than another's, that mistake causes D not to meet the intent element for the crime.

[Q3007]

172. **B** The facts here are very similar to those of *Rankin v. McPherson* (1987), where the Court held that: (1) the clerk's statement supporting a recent assassination attempt (of Pres. Reagan) was indeed on a matter of "public concern"; and (2) the fact that the clerk had no policy-making role and that his statement had little negative impact on his job effectiveness made it unreasonable to dismiss him for that statement.

(A) is wrong because even a "permanent" public employee (i.e., one with a property right in his post) may have his job taken without just compensation, as long as procedures constituting due process are followed. In other words, what the due process clause guarantees on these facts is that the clerk's job won't be taken arbitrarily or capriciously, not that the job won't be taken "without just compensation" (a standard that would more properly be applied to the taking of tangible real or personal property rather than a job).

(C) is wrong because the Court has held (in *Rankin, supra*) that although the government has an interest in having loyal and supportive employees, this interest does not outweigh the employee's interest in commenting on matters of public concern, where the comment does not undermine the employee's effectiveness in light of the non-policy-making and limited scope of the employee's job (which, like the job here, was clerical).

(D) is wrong because: (1) the Court does not use the right/privilege distinction in First Amendment public-employment cases; and (2) even if the Court did believe that public employment was a "privilege" rather than a "right," the Court would almost certainly view the case as justiciable.
[Q2184]

173. **D** Even where the writing is a complete integration, as it is here, the court will look to course-of-performance evidence to determine what the parties meant as to a point on which the writing is ambiguous. This is true in both sales and non-sales cases. Thus in sales governed by UCC Article 2, §2-208(1) says that "Where the contract for sale involves repeated occasions for performance by either party with knowledge of the nature of the performance and opportunity for objection to it by the other, any course of performance *accepted or acquiesced in without objection* shall be *relevant to determine the meaning* of the agreement." Here, the evidence proffered by the retailer — that the manufacturer permitted him to return undamaged radios for credit earlier during the course of the present contract — fits §2-208(1) exactly, since the retailer is claiming that the manufacturer's knowing acquiescence in the retailer's repeated requests for a credit for non-defective returned goods was a course of performance, admissible to show that the parties intended the writing to mean that such returns are allowed.

(A) is wrong because, as further explained in Choice (D) above, even though the writing here is a complete integration, the proffered evidence is course-of-performance evidence, which is admissible notwithstanding the parol evidence rule to show the meaning of the agreement.

(B) is wrong because it states an irrelevant point. It's true that the express terms control if those terms are inconsistent with the course of performance; thus UCC §2-208(2) says that "The express terms of an agreement and any ... course of performance, as well as any course of dealing and usage of trade, shall be construed wherever reasonable as consistent with each other; but when such construction is unreasonable, *express terms shall control course of performance* and course of performance shall control both course of dealing and usage of trade[.]" But here, there *is* no express term dealing with the retailer's right to return non-defective goods for credit (the writing is silent on this point), so the priority of express terms over the course of performance simply doesn't apply.

(C) is wrong because it relies on an irrelevant fact. The retailer is not trying to show an "agreement" to modify the original agreement — if he were, then there might be a Statute of Frauds issue. Instead, he's trying to show what the original written agreement *meant* (by the use of course-of-performance evidence), and his ability to do that has nothing to do with the Statute of Frauds.
[Q1108]

174. **D** When a state or local government uses its taxing powers (just as when it regulates), the state violates the dormant Commerce Clause if the tax: (1) intentionally discriminates against (i.e., treats less favorably) out-of-state competition to the benefit of local economic interests; or (2) unduly burdens interstate commerce. By reducing the amount of taxes paid by assemblers of computers in

an amount equal to the portion of computer components manufactured in Green, Central City is discriminating against out-of-state component-makers to benefit local component-makers (the in-state makers get an effective price advantage). This discrimination causes the tax measure to violate test (1) above.

(A) is not the best response, because the ordinance has the effect of making parts manufactured outside of Green more expensive. It is true that the tax directly falls only on companies resident in Central City. But the *effect* of the tax is to make components manufactured in Green less expensive than those manufactured outside of Green, making this intentional discrimination against out-of-staters, even though the out-of-staters aren't being directly taxed.

(B) is not the best response, because the dormant Commerce Clause *does* place some limits on a state's right to foster resident corporations. Although a state may sometimes foster local businesses by encouraging its residents to "buy local," some methods of encouragement violate the dormant Commerce Clause. Where a state uses its tax system to confer a direct financial benefit to those who buy locally-manufactured goods, at the expense of out-of-state makers, the state crosses the line into forbidden "economic protectionism," and violates the dormant Commerce Clause. That's what the tax here does.

(C) is not the best response, because taxes based on gross receipts are not a per se violation of dormant Commerce Clause principles. Some tax schemes violate the dormant Commerce Clause because they either discriminate against, or unduly burden, interstate commerce. But the mere fact that a tax is "measured in whole or in part by [the taxpayer's] gross receipts" does not automatically mean that either forbidden discrimination or an undue burden on commerce is present. It's true that if a state enacted a tax on a multi-state taxpayer's gross receipts, and made no distinction between receipts from in-state activities and those from out-of-state activities, that tax might well be found to be an undue burden on commerce, and thus a violation of the dormant Commerce Clause. But Choice (C) goes way beyond this principle, and doesn't tie in to the problem with the tax here (which is that it intentionally discriminates against out-of-state component makers).
[Q3114]

175. **A** Where the witness is an accused (a criminal defendant), FRE 609(a)(1) says that the court "shall" allow impeachment by proof of a less-than-10-year-old felony conviction, "if the court determines that the probative value of admitting this evidence outweighs its prejudicial effect to the accused." Choice (A) exactly matches this standard. It's important to note that the conviction here was for burglary, a crime whose elements do not include "an act of dishonesty or false statement"; if the conviction *were* for such a dishonesty/false-statement crime (whether felony or misdemeanor), FRE 609(a)(2) says that it "shall" be admitted, without any provision for the trial judge to determine that its probative value outweighs its prejudicial effect to the accused.

(B) is wrong because it ignores the fact that (as described in the analysis of Choice (A) above), where the witness being impeached is a criminal defendant and the crime is not a crime of dishonesty/false-statement, the conviction is admissible only if the trial judge determines that its probative value outweighs its prejudicial effect to the accused. So on the facts here, admission is not "a matter of right" as this choice asserts.

(C) is wrong because the fact that the crime here (burglary) is not a crime of dishonesty or false statement doesn't prevent its use. Under FRE 609(a), any felony (crime punishable by at least one year in prison), or any felony or misdemeanor involving dishonesty or false statement, can be used to impeach a witness. Where the crime does not involve dishonesty, it's admissible only "if the court determines that the probative value of admitting this evidence outweighs its prejudicial effect to the accused." If it *does* involve dishonesty, admission is mandatory (with no balancing). So the fact that the crime here didn't involve dishonesty or false statement doesn't automatically block its admissibility, as this choice asserts.

(D) is wrong, because the conviction *can* be proven through intrinsic impeachment (i.e., on cross examination of the witness being impeached). FRE 609(a) allows impeachment on these facts (as analyzed in the treatment of choice (A) above), and that rule does not impose any requirement that the impeachment occur by means of the court record of the conviction. So impeachment by asking the witness, "Isn't it true that you were convicted ..." is proper.

[Q4044]

176. C A state may grant broader rights under its own constitution than are granted by the federal Constitution. See *Michigan v. Long* (1983). Here, the state has a clear precedent that the recording violated the employee's state constitutional rights, and that the recording should be excluded as a remedy. The state court should apply this precedent to grant the employee's motion. In other words, where evidence is obtained in violation of a state constitutional provision and would be inadmissible under the state's policy of excluding evidence obtained in violation of the state constitution, the fact that there has been no federal constitutional violation should not prevent the state court from applying the state exclusionary policy.

(A) is wrong because a state may grant broader rights under its own constitution than are granted by the federal constitution. As further discussed in Choice (C) above, when the state gives broader rights than would be granted by the federal Constitution, a court of that state should apply any state-law exclusionary principle.

(B) is wrong because it is irrelevant what the police thought about the propriety of their actions under the federal Constitution, if the state has granted broader rights under its own constitution. Furthermore, this choice mischaracterizes the federal Constitution on this point: the police's actions *were* allowed by the federal Constitution, so the fact that the police had a "good faith" belief in the correctness of their action under the federal Constitution does not add anything to the analysis.

(D) is wrong because the secret recording of a conversation with a defendant by a government informant, like the recording in this case, does not violate the Fourth Amendment. See *United States v. White* (1971). (Instead, the evidence should be kept out because the state court can and should uphold the policy reflected in the state constitution's ban on the collection of such evidence, as buttressed by the state's exclusionary rule.)

[Q7086]

177. C Because Charles was dead at the time of the purported conveyance to the vendee and Charles as tenants in common, the deed's attempt to pass an interest to him was not effective (i.e., the deed was "void" as to him). Therefore, no interest passed through to his estate or via his estate to his nephew. The "Charles" portion of the tenancy in common therefore remained in the vendor. The deed was effective as to the vendee's interest, however, since she was correctly named and the deed was delivered to and accepted by her; therefore, she has the tenancy in common interest that the vendor intended to convey to her.

Choices (A), (B), and (D) are wrong because they are inconsistent with the above analysis.

[Q2114]

178. A FRE 803(18), the learned treatise exception, provides that if the court finds a publication to be a reliable authority, then "statements" in it may be read into evidence, but that the publication may not be received as an exhibit (which is what would have to happen if the jury were to "examine the book" as the question asks). Thus, the jury is not allowed to bring learned treatises into the jury room — there is a concern that if juries were allowed unrestricted access to the whole publication, they might rely on parts of the publication that are not germane to the case. Moreover, the intent of the rule is that juries need to be guided through the pertinent parts of the publication by the testifying experts.

(B) is wrong because FRE 803(18), the learned treatise exception, allows statements from a treatise to be read into evidence where the treatise is "called to the attention of an expert witness" and is found to be reliable by the court. The rule does not require that an expert rely on the treatise. In this case, the publication was called to the attention of the defendant's expert.

(C) is wrong because it's not enough that one expert testifies that the treatise is reliable. FRE 803(18) allows statements from a treatise to be read into evidence when the treatise is "*established as a reliable authority* by the testimony or admission of the witness or by other expert testimony or by judicial notice." In this case, one expert testified that the publication was reliable, but the other expert contests that assertion. The decision on reliability is for the court; it is not correct to say that the court should find the publication reliable simply because one expert has found it to be so. In addition, the rule allows "statements" from a learned treatise to be read into evidence, but does not allow the publication to be received as an exhibit (which would be required if the jury were to "examine the book" as the question asks).

(D) is wrong because, although the statement is true so far as it goes, it does not mean that the jury gets to consider any evidence that the parties wish to present. FRE 803(18), the learned treatise exception, requires the judge to determine that the publication is reliable before it can be considered by the jury. In addition, the rule allows "statements" from a learned treatise to be read into evidence, but does not allow the publication to be received as an exhibit (and since the question is asking whether the court should allow the jury to "examine the book," this should only happen if the book was received as an exhibit).

[Q7005]

179. **D** An owner of a wild animal or an abnormally dangerous animal is strictly liable for harm caused by that animal's dangerous nature. Part of what makes wild animals dangerous is that third persons who encounter the animal may well experience acute fear, whether that fear is well-founded or not as to the particular animal. Rest. 2d, §507, Comm. g and Illustr. 1. Here, even though the snake was defanged, the worker had no reason to know this. Therefore, his injury was caused by a foreseeable aspect of the animal's wild and dangerous nature, namely, its tendency to cause fear of being bitten.

(A) is wrong because owners of dangerous animals are strictly liable even when the harm would not have occurred but for the operation of a force of nature.

(B) is wrong because an owner of a wild animal or an abnormally dangerous animal is strictly liable for harm caused by that animal's dangerous nature. The contributory negligence of the worker would not be a defense to strict liability, and in any case there is nothing in the facts to indicate that the worker would have reason to foresee the risk of a poisonous snake.

(C) is wrong because, while this answer correctly states that the worker will prevail, it misstates the legal basis for this conclusion. There is probably not enough evidence here to support a finding of negligence. In any event, whether the owner did or did not take precautions that would be "adequate" (i.e., that would constitute reasonable care), this won't matter — the whole point of strict liability for keeping wild animals is that if the wild animal causes harm in a way that is related to its wildness, the plaintiff does not have to show negligence by the owner. Nor does it matter that the snake was defanged; the worker had no reason to know this, and his injury falls within the risk run by the homeowner because it was caused by the worker's foreseeable reaction to seeing an escaped snake.

[Q7075]

180. **D** The retailer's order was an offer. The wholesaler's shipment of goods in response to the offer was an acceptance, even though what the wholesaler shipped was non-conforming goods. That's so because UCC §2-206(1)(b) says that "an order or other offer to buy goods for prompt or current shipment shall be construed as inviting *acceptance* ... by the prompt or current *shipment* of con-

forming or *non-conforming goods*[.]" A buyer who receives non-conforming goods has the right to reject those goods, sending them back to the seller or holding them for the seller's pickup. That's because §2-601 says that, subject to some limitations not applicable here, "If the goods or the tender of delivery fail in any respect to conform to the contract, the buyer may (a) reject the whole; or (b) accept the whole; or (c) accept any commercial unit or units and reject the rest." So the retailer could reject all or some of the bushels.

(A) is wrong because the wholesaler's shipment was not a counteroffer, since that nothing in the facts surrounding the shipment indicated that the wholesaler was rejecting the retailer's offer (its order). Instead, the wholesaler's shipment was an acceptance (as well as a breach).

(B) is wrong because: (1) the wholesaler's shipment was not a counteroffer (for the reason described in the analysis of choice (A)); and (2) under UCC §2-602(2), if the retailer wants to reject rather than accept the peaches, it is merely required "after rejection to hold [the goods] with reasonable care at the seller's disposition for a time sufficient to permit the seller to remove them." So despite the peaches' perishability, all the retailer has to do is to promptly notify the wholesaler, "We don't want the peaches because they don't conform; we'll hold them for you to pick up."

(C) is wrong because, although a contract was indeed formed when the wholesaler shipped the peaches, their non-conformity to the retailer's order entitled the retailer to reject the goods rather than accept them.

[Q1141]

181. **C** One is liable for a crime, as an accomplice, if he procures, counsels, or commands the commission of that crime. Naturally, this would require that he intend that the crime be committed. Here, Sam's liability would rest on his statement "Kill him." Intent could be established by presumption, since a person of sufficient intelligence to understand the nature of his actions is presumed to intend the natural and probable consequences of his actions. Here, Sam encouraged Bill to kill Vic, so it could be said that Sam intended that Bill kill Vic. Furthermore, his statement would be considered counseling or commanding the commission of the crime of murder. As a result, Sam will be liable as an accomplice for murder.

(A) is wrong because it arrives at the wrong result, and it applies the wrong rule to these facts. The "clear and present danger" test is the test used to determine the validity, for First Amendment purposes, of a law designed to forbid advocacy of unlawful conduct. It provides that advocacy can only be forbidden if its aim is to produce or incite imminent illegal action, and it is likely to produce or incite such action. Whether Sam's speech is protected by the First Amendment is not the issue here; instead, the issue is whether Sam can be held liable for murder for encouraging Bill to kill Vic. Since A does not apply the correct rule, and, beyond that, arrives at the wrong result, it's wrong.

(B) is wrong because it's too broad. Given the requisite intent, "mere presence and oral encouragement" *are* sufficient to make Sam guilty as an accomplice. An accomplice is one who procures, counsels, or commands the commission of a crime. Choice (B) asserts that "mere presence and oral encouragement" are insufficient to make one liable as an accomplice; however, under the definition of accomplice, encouragement would constitute "counseling" or "commanding," and so, if accompanied by an intent that the person being encouraged commit the underlying crime, *would* create accomplice liability.

(D) is wrong because although it arrives at the correct result, the reasoning it gives would not be sufficient to hold Sam liable for murder. It's not Sam's presence and his intent which make him liable, as D suggests – rather, it's his act of *encouraging* the killing that makes him liable. Mere presence wouldn't make him liable, since, in general, one is not obligated to act affirmatively for the benefit of others; furthermore, his intent is not sufficient to create liability, since intent is merely a state of mind and, with nothing more, it's not criminal (until it produces action to bring about the desired results). It's Sam's active encouragement – "Kill him" – which makes him liable.

[Q4013]

182. **C** Since an employer is vicariously liable for the negligence of an employee committed within the scope of employment, statements tending to establish that the accident resulted from the deliveryman's negligence are relevant in the plaintiff's action against the restaurant. The evidence should, thus, be admitted unless excluded under the hearsay rule. Hearsay is an out of court statement offered to prove the truth of the matter asserted. These facts raise what is sometimes called a multiple-level hearsay problem (i.e., an out-of-court statement that contains another out-of-court statement). This is so because the deliveryman's testimony at the reckless driving trial was not made during the negligence trial and so is an "out of court" statement, and because the evidence of his statement is contained in a transcript which was also not made as part of the negligence trial and so is an "out of court" statement. In order for multiple-level hearsay to be admissible, each level must be separately admissible. (See FRE 805, saying that "hearsay included within hearsay is not excluded ... if *each part* of the combined statements conforms with an exception to the hearsay rule[.]")

The first level of hearsay is the testimony by the deliveryman at the reckless driving trial. But FRE 801(d)(2)(D)'s vicarious admission provision gives a hearsay exclusion for an agent's (including an employee's) statement concerning a matter within the scope of his employment, made while the agency (employment) relationship existed. (Note that under this provision — and in contrast to the common law — an agent's statement concerning a matter within the agency relationship qualifies, even if the principal, i.e., the employer, did not authorize the making of the statement.) The deliveryman's statement therefore qualifies as a vicarious admission, making it not hearsay.

The second level of hearsay is the transcript. Since it was made by a public official (the court reporter), regarding "matters observed pursuant to duty imposed by law as to which matters there was a duty to report" (that the deliveryman made the admission), the transcript qualifies as a public record or report under FRE 803(8)(B).

(A) is wrong because, under FRE 804(b)(1), prior testimony is admissible as an exception to the hearsay rule *only if the party against whom it is offered had an incentive and an opportunity to cross-examine* when the testimony was first given. Since the restaurant was not a party to the proceeding at which the deliveryman's testimony was given, the testimony does not qualify for admission under this exception.

(B) is wrong because the "past recollection recorded" exception (FRE 803(5)) applies only where (1) it concerns a matter about which a witness (the person on the stand) "once had knowledge but now has insufficient recollection"; and (2) the record was "made or adopted by the witness when the matter was fresh in the witness' memory[.]" Since the deliveryman never "made or adopted" the transcript, the only witness whose sponsorship of the record could possibly qualify was the court reporter who made the transcript. But the court reporter is not a "witness" here, and is not stating that his memory is now insufficient. (In any event, even if the past recollection recorded exception applied, it would only allow the transcript to be "read into evidence," not received as an exhibit as the restaurant is requesting.)

(D) is wrong because, while the facts do present a serious hearsay issue, the combination of the vicarious admission exclusion and the public records exception make the transcript admissible, as described in (C) above.

[Q5040]

183. **A** The professor can state a prima facie case of defamation, but he cannot prevail because the dean has a valid defense based on his reasonable belief that the professor invited him to speak. See Rest. 2d, §583 ("The consent of another to the publication of defamatory matter concerning him is a complete defense to his action for defamation.") By authorizing his agents to investigate his case,

the professor apparently consented to limited publication in response to their inquiries. By the way, ill will on the part of the dean, even if it existed, would be irrelevant to this defense.

(B) is wrong because, while this answer correctly states that the professor will lose, it misstates the legal basis for this conclusion. Some jurisdictions may require evidence of pecuniary loss for oral statements that are not slander per se, but this is a written statement. Under the common law applicable to libel (written defamations), damages to the professor's reputation would be presumed, allowing him to recover even if he sustained no provable pecuniary loss.

(C) is wrong because the tort of defamation does not turn on whether an investigation, reasonable or not, has been conducted. It is true that defamation is not a strict liability tort, and requires at least negligence by the defendant (and indeed requires knowledge of falsity or reckless disregard of the truth if the plaintiff is a public figure). So the dean's failure to investigate might constitute negligence, thereby supplying the requisite mental state. But even with the mental-state requirement satisfied, the professor would lose on the grounds of consent, as further detailed in the discussion of Choice (A).

(D) is wrong because the fact that the statement was in writing does not affect the outcome here. Even if the statement were oral, the professor could recover for slander if the dean were shown to have behaved negligently (e.g., by not investigating the rumor) and if no defense applied. But a defense does apply, namely the defense of consent, as further detailed in Choice (A).

[Q7050]

184. **C** FRE 702 imposes five requirements that expert testimony must meet in order to be admissible: (1) it must be the case that *scientific, technical, or other specialized knowledge* will *assist* the trier of fact to *understand the evidence or to determine a fact in issue*; (2) the witness must be qualified as an expert by *knowledge, skill, experience, training, or education*; (3) the testimony must be *based upon sufficient facts or data*; (4) the testimony must be the *product of reliable principles and methods*; and (5) the witness must have *applied these principles and methods reliably to the facts of the case*. The proposed testimony by the investigator meets these requirements: (1) The investigator's testimony about the speed of the train will help the trier of fact to understand the evidence in the case. (2) The facts state that the police accident investigator is experienced and has received training. (3) The investigator's testimony is based on his examination of the physical evidence, and he has stipulated that these types of physical data are the ones examined in such matters. (4) There is no indication that the investigator's methodology is not the product of reliable principles and methods. (5) The investigator made his conclusion about the train's speed after applying his training and experience to the physical evidence of the case. Having satisfied all five requirements, the accident investigator's testimony is proper and admissible.

(A) is wrong because there is simply no principle that says that "there cannot be both lay and expert opinion on the same issue." (For instance, it is perfectly proper for one side to put on lay eyewitness opinion testimony about the approximate speed of the train, and for the other to put on expert scientific opinion on the same subject.)

(B) is wrong because there is no principle that scientific or other expert testimony must reach its conclusion with any particular degree of "scientific certainty." All that is required is that the conclusion be sufficiently "reliable." For the reasons discussed in Choice (C), this reliability standard is satisfied here. To the extent that this choice is referring to the fact that the investigator is testifying merely that the speed falls within a range, instead of giving a single number, the existence of a range does not pose a problem. (Indeed, use of a range is probably more, not less, reliable, since it's less likely to give a false impression of precision.)

(D) is wrong because the only requirements for expert testimony are those discussed in the analysis of Choice (C) above. There is no requirement that the other side have first introduced some sort of opinion evidence on the issue.

[Q3117]

185. **B** The Thirteenth Amendment permits Congress to forbid the "badges and incidents" of slavery. This power has been interpreted by the Court to include the power to forbid even private acts of racial discrimination against black people, on the theory that such discrimination is the relic of slavery.

(A) is wrong because Congress does not have any "authority to enact laws for the general welfare" (only the power to "tax and spend" for the general welfare.).

(C) is wrong because this might be an explanation of why the statute couldn't be supported by Congress' commerce power, but the Thirteenth Amendment power allows Congress to forbid even purely local racial discrimination (i.e., discrimination that does not involve interstate commerce).

(D) is wrong because if Congress' action falls within a specific grant of power (here, the Thirteenth Amendment grant), the Tenth Amendment acts as a limitation only in the highly specialized case of Congress' attempt to take over state lawmaking mechanisms.

[Q2101]

186. **C** As a general rule, a landowner owes no duty to a trespasser to make her land safe. There are several exceptions, but none of those exceptions applies here. The exception that comes closest to applying is that an owner may have a duty of reasonable care to a trespassing child, if the owner has maintained an "attractive nuisance." But for reasons described in the analysis of Choice (B) below, this exception does not apply here.

(A) is wrong because the duty of a landowner to trespassers to keep the property free of dangerous artificial conditions exists only where the owner has reason to know that trespassers are in dangerous proximity to the condition and that they are unlikely to appreciate the risk. Even then, the duty is only to exercise reasonable care to warn trespassers of the danger, which was done here.

(B) is wrong because, while it is true that an owner may be liable to a trespasser if the owner has maintained an "attractive nuisance," the condition here was not an attractive nuisance. For a condition on land to be considered an attractive nuisance, there must be evidence that the possessor had reason to know that children were likely to trespass, as well as evidence that the plaintiff did not appreciate the risk involved. No such evidence is mentioned in the facts; for instance, there is no suggestion that children often stray from the day care center, and there is no reason to believe the child was not aware of the danger (since we're told he was a "bright nine-year-old" and that the danger was well-marked).

(D) is wrong because, while, this answer correctly states that the corporation will prevail, it misstates the legal basis for this conclusion. Even if the day care center had a duty to keep children from the ice, the corporation could also be liable if it was negligent. That is, if A is negligent as to a risk, the fact that B was also negligent as to the same risk is unlikely to save A from liability.

[Q7093]

187. **A** FRE 408 excludes, when offered to prove liability for a disputed claim, evidence of "conduct or statements made in compromise negotiations regarding the claim[.]" Here, there is a disputed claim, and the manager's statement was made in an effort to settle that dispute. As such the entire statement is protected under Rule 408.

(B) is wrong because the fact that the statement denied that the slipperiness was the cause of the problem does not prevent the overall statement from falling within FRE 408's ban on "conduct or statements made in compromise negotiations regarding [a disputed] claim." Even though the manager's statement contained a large portion of self-serving "it's not our fault," the entire statement is inadmissible because uttered during the course of compromise negotiations.

(C) is wrong because, although the statement is true as far as it goes, it does not go far enough. The fact that the statement was an admission by an agent about a matter within the scope of his authority only means that the statement is not excluded as hearsay. There is another ground for exclusion, so the statement is inadmissible even though it satisfies the hearsay rule. FRE 408 excludes evidence of conduct or statements made in compromise negotiations, as further discussed in choice (A) above.

(D) is wrong because FRE 408 protects not only offers of compromise, but also "conduct or statements made in the course of compromise negotiations regarding [a disputed] claim." The rationale is to allow the parties and counsel to speak freely during settlement negotiations, without having to worry that their statements will be used against them at trial. Here, there is a dispute, and the manager's statement was made in an attempt to settle that dispute. Therefore, the entire statement — including those portions consisting of statements of fact — would be excluded under FRE 408.

[Q7058]

188. **D** This answer is correct because the seller's acceptance was effective on dispatch. First, the buyer's signed order was an offer. Next, under UCC §2-206(1), "Unless otherwise unambiguously indicated by the language or circumstances . . . (b) an order or other offer to buy goods for prompt or current shipment shall be construed as inviting acceptance either by a prompt promise to ship or by the prompt or current shipment of conforming or non-conforming goods[.]" So this order authorized the seller to accept by either promising to ship or shipping; his letter was an acceptance by promise. Since there was a contract at the moment the seller mailed the acceptance on Jan. 7, the buyer's purported Jan. 8 revocation was ineffective.

(A) is wrong because the offer could be accepted by a promise to ship, not just by shipment, as explained in the discussion of Choice (D) above.

(B) is wrong because the seller's letter, although it supplied a price not previously mentioned by the buyer, was effective as an acceptance. UCC §2-207(1) says that "A definite and seasonable expression of acceptance . . . which is sent within a reasonable time operates as an acceptance even though it states terms additional to or different from those offered or agreed upon, unless acceptance is expressly made conditional on assent to the additional or different terms." So the fact that the seller's letter contained a price term that wasn't mentioned in the buyer's order — i.e., contained an "additional" term — didn't prevent the seller's letter from operating as an acceptance. (The seller's letter didn't say something like "But my acceptance is expressly conditional on your telling me you agree to the $10 price," so the situation referred to in the "expressly made conditional" clause at the end of the above-quoted portion of 2-207(1) doesn't apply.)

(C) is wrong because nothing made the buyer's offer irrevocable for any length of time. Offers ordinarily are not irrevocable. It's true that §2-205 authorizes "firm offers" (i.e., irrevocable ones) even without consideration for the irrevocability. But under §2-205, an offer is not "firm" unless it "by its terms gives assurance that it will be held open[.]" Nothing in the buyer's order "by its terms" gave that assurance. Therefore, the buyer had the usual common-law right to revoke before acceptance. (His problem was that his revocation didn't happen until after the acceptance, for the reason described in Choice (D).)

[Q3194]

189. **D** It is a core principle of Anglo-American criminal law that a person (let's call her the "defendant") does not have a duty to warn others of a peril or to assist them to avoid a peril. There are some exceptions to this rule — situations in which there is an affirmative duty to act (e.g., where the defendant brought about the peril) — but none of those exceptions applies here. Therefore, the wife did not have a legal duty, enforceable by the criminal laws, to warn the others about the bomb. See M.P.C., §2.01, Comm. 3; LaFave, §5.2, at 213-17.

Since (A), (B), and (C) would all make the woman guilty of some crime, these choices are wrong for the reason discussed in the analysis of choice (D) above.

[Q7026]

190. **A** The situations in which a plaintiff can recover for purely emotional distress caused by negligence are limited, and this is not one of them. Recovery for negligent misrepresentation is usually limited to pecuniary loss unless there was a risk of physical harm. In this case, the applicant found a comparable position promptly, so he suffered no pecuniary harm from the personnel director's misrepresentation, and therefore cannot recover for the non-pecuniary harm of emotional distress.

(B) is wrong because, while this answer correctly states that the applicant will not prevail, it misstates the legal basis for this conclusion. It is not the case that the director's statement is purely speculative. Some of the information conveyed to the job applicant was factual; it was clearly intended to assure the applicant that the company was in fact at the time economically strong, and to induce reliance. Therefore, the information was sufficiently concrete that it could serve as the basis for a negligent misrepresentation action.

(C) is wrong because, while reliance is essential for recovery in negligent misrepresentation, it is not sufficient. (For instance, the reliance must be reasonable.) The biggest problem is that this choice does not reflect the fact that while there are situations in which a plaintiff can recover for purely emotional distress caused by negligence, this is not one of them. Recovery for negligent misrepresentation is usually limited to pecuniary loss unless the misrepresentation also involved a risk of physical harm. In this case, the applicant found a comparable position promptly, so he suffered no pecuniary harm from the personnel director's misrepresentation.

(D) is wrong because recovery for negligent misrepresentation does not extend to all foreseeable damages. The applicant cannot prevail because recovery for negligent misrepresentation is usually limited to pecuniary loss, unless the misrepresentation produced a risk of physical harm. Here, there was never any risk of physical harm to the applicant. Since the applicant found a comparable position promptly, he suffered no pecuniary harm from the personnel director's misrepresentation, and therefore is not permitted to recover for his non-pecuniary harm (from emotional distress).

[Q7040]

191. **C** One who enters the realty of another to retrieve a chattel which got there through no fault of her own has a qualified privilege to do so, but must compensate the landholder for any actual damage which results.

(A) is wrong because, while the trucker had a qualified privilege to go on to the landowner's land to retrieve the gravel, it was required to pay for any damages caused by the retrieval operation. Therefore, limiting the landowner's recovery to nominal damages would not be adequate compensation.

(B) is wrong because liability for the initial spill would have to be premised on either trespass, negligence, or the conducting of an abnormally dangerous activity. There is no trespass liability here, because trespass requires that the defendant had intended to make contact with the property that belongs to the plaintiff. Here, since the contact (the spilling of gravel onto the plaintiff's property) occurred by accident rather than by the intent of the trucker, this requirement of intent is not satisfied. Nor does negligence liability apply, because we are told that the blowout was not due to any fault on the part of the trucker. Liability based on abnormally dangerous activity does not apply because the transporting of gravel is not an abnormally dangerous activity. Therefore, the trucker has no liability for the initial spill.

(D) is wrong because the trucker, although he correctly exercised a qualified privilege to recapture his chattels, must pay for the damage caused by the recapture operation, as further described in Choice (C) above.

[Q5075]

192. **C** For the day care center to be liable, its liability would have to be premised upon either intent, negligence, or strict liability. There is no indication of an intent by the day care center to harm the child, nor is there anything that would impose strict liability. So liability would have to be based

upon negligence. But a defendant cannot be liable for negligence unless the defendant failed to use a level of care that would be reasonable in the circumstances. The facts stipulate that the center's personnel used reasonable care to prevent a child from sneaking out, so there was no negligence by the center.

(A) is wrong, because day care centers are not strictly or absolutely liable for all injuries that occur to children under their care. The center's negligence must be established. Under the facts as described, there is no evidence of lack of reasonable care, and the day care center will prevail.

(B) is wrong because the mere fact that the center is located near a pond is not in itself evidence of negligence. It might mean that reasonable care requires extra-vigilant supervision, but the facts specify that the center staff was in fact exercising "reasonable care." Accordingly, the day care center will prevail.

(D) is wrong because the child's status as a trespasser would only be relevant in litigation against an owner or possessor of the land where the accident occurred. Since the suit is against the center, not the corporation that owned the land containing the pond, the child's status as trespasser is irrelevant.

[Q7094]

193. C The standard measure of contract damages is the expectation measure, which attempts to put the plaintiff in the position he would have been in had the contract been performed. Here, performance meant that the contractor would have a foundation, at a total cost to it of $200,000. The contractor paid the subcontractor $100,000, then paid another $120,000 to the replacement subcontractor, for a total of $220,000. So the contractor is $20,000 worse off than had the subcontractor performed. The contractor will need to recover this $20,000 in order to be in the position that performance would have left it.

(A) is wrong because the subcontractor's restitutionary recovery must be computed after subtracting breach damages owed by the subcontractor. A materially-breaching plaintiff may recover in quasi-contract for the value to the defendant of the rendered performance. But this recovery must be computed on a "net" basis, by subtracting from the unpaid-for value rendered to the defendant any damages caused by the breach. So in this case, if the contractor had been able to finish the work for, say, $10,000 (so that it would have spent a total of $130,000), the subcontractor would have been entitled to recover in quasi-contract the $50,000 difference between the $150,000 value that it rendered to the contractor and the $100,000 the contractor had made in progress payments (since the subcontractor's breach would not have caused any damages to the contractor). But on the actual facts here, even if the subcontractor recovered nothing in quasi-contract, the contractor would still have been damaged by $20,000 (as analyzed in Choice (C)). So the subcontractor obviously can't recover anything in quasi-contract, since each dollar given to it would just make the contractor's net damages worse. Instead, the subcontractor owes the contractor the $20,000 needed to make the contractor whole. Furthermore, in many jurisdictions a plaintiff who "wilfully" breaches isn't even eligible for a quasi-contract recovery, so in such a jurisdiction we wouldn't even get to the point of calculating whether the subcontractor was entitled to anything.

(B) is wrong because this computation would not leave the contractor whole. The contractor has $20,000 in damages (see Choice (C)) only on the assumption that the contractor doesn't have to pay the subcontractor anything in the litigation on a quasi-contract theory. If the subcontractor recovered $50,000, the contractor's net damages would mount to $70,000 from the original $20,000.

(D) is wrong because this computation, too, would not leave the contractor whole. The overriding principle is that the contractor, as a non-breaching counterclaimer, gets expectation damages to put it in the net position it would have been in had the contract been performed. If the subcontractor didn't have to pay anything (and didn't receive anything), the contractor would be $20,000 worse off than if the contract had been performed.

[Q3145]

194. **A** As the result of *Massiah v. U.S.* (1964), once a suspect has been charged and has counsel, it is a violation of his Sixth Amendment right to counsel for a secret agent to "deliberately elicit" incriminating statements from him in the absence of counsel, and to pass these on to the prosecution. The post-*Massiah* case of *U.S. v. Henry* (1980) establishes that even if the secret agent does not engage in actual questioning, if the agent is motivated to obtain confidences and succeeds in doing so, the agent will be deemed to have "elicited" the statement, and the *Massiah* rule will still be deemed violated. Therefore, since Ulrich was a police officer and was placed in a cell for the purpose of obtaining incriminating remarks outside the presence of the defendant's counsel, use of those remarks would violate the defendant's Sixth Amendment right to counsel as interpreted by *Massiah*.

(B) is wrong because "entrapment" refers only to conduct by a police officer which induces the defendant to commit a crime which he was not otherwise inclined to commit, not conduct that induces the defendant to confess.

(C) is wrong because even a warrant does not justify a police interrogation in violation of the *Massiah* rule described in the discussion of Choice (A) above.

(D) is wrong because even the eliciting of a voluntary statement violates the *Massiah* rule if done as a result of police operation conducted without the presence or consent of the defendant's attorney.

[Q5021]

195. **C** It was a condition precedent to the enforceability of the contract that the buyer give written notice to the seller by Jan. 2 that the buyer had found a buyer. However, when the buyer explained the difficulty with a written notice to the seller on Dec. 16, the seller's "That's okay" response clearly indicated to the buyer that the seller would not insist on the written notice. This oral response constituted a waiver of the condition, i.e., a knowing intent to abandon the benefit of the condition.

(A) is wrong because the requirement of a writing by Jan. 2 was an express condition to the enforceability of the contract. Complete, not just substantial, compliance with an express condition is normally required. Since the oral notice did not completely comply with the requirement of a written notice, the fact that it may have constituted substantial performance will not help the buyer.

(B) is wrong because: (1) the condition here was a condition precedent (the condition had to be satisfied before the contract would ever become enforceable), not a condition subsequent (i.e., something that if not satisfied would "unenforce" the previously-enforceable contract); and (2) even in the unlikely event that the condition was found to be a condition subsequent, its nonoccurrence could only help the seller, not the buyer.

(D) is wrong because the concept of a novation has nothing to do with these facts. A novation occurs when the two original parties to a contract — an obligor and an obligee — agree that a stranger can be substituted for the original obligor. So, for instance, if the seller and the buyer agreed that the third person would substitute for the buyer as the party who was under contract to buy the engine from the seller, a novation would have occurred. But on the actual facts here, no substitution of either of the original parties to the contract has occurred, so there is no novation.

[Q2052]

196. **C** The central problem with these facts is that they don't indicate an active misrepresentation by the engineer, and there's no duty on the engineer to disclose the true value of the stock. Such a duty only arises where, for instance, there is a specific query about the matter, a special (e.g., fiduciary) relationship exists, or there are other circumstances meriting disclosure (e.g., a half-truth, subsequent information which makes prior statement misleading, or knowledge of undisclosed facts basic to a transaction). None of these apply to these facts; thus, for there to be liability, an option

would have to add facts *creating* liability. That's what C does, by adding a misrepresentation – that the stock is not worth more than $6. This qualifies because the fact pattern now satisfies all the requirements of liability for intentional misrepresentation: (1) defendant's misrepresentation of a material past or present fact; (2) defendant's knowledge of falsity or reckless disregard for falsity; (3) defendant's intent to induce plaintiff's reliance; (4) plaintiff's actual, justifiable reliance; and (5) damages. Here, the misrepresentation about value obviously satisfies (1), and without that misrepresentation about value, requirement (1) would not be satisfied.

(A) is wrong because the general rule is that liability for misrepresentation requires some form of active concealment or active misleading, not just mere failure to disclose a material fact. There are a number of exceptions (e.g., the telling of a half-truth, or the existence of a fiduciary relationship between the parties). But no exception applies on these facts, so the engineer's silence about the material fact doesn't constitute an actionable misrepresentation.

(B) is wrong for the same reason (A) is wrong: liability for misrepresentation requires some form of active concealment or active misleading, not just mere failure to disclose a material fact. There are a number of exceptions, but none applies here.

(D) is wrong because the availability of the financial statement would not be relevant to the seller's claim. Even if the financial statement was not available to the seller, the engineer would not be liable for here mere failure to disclose a material fact that she knew, for the reasons described in the discussion of Choice (C) above.

[Q4045]

197. **B** Congress can only delegate powers it possesses, so you first have to determine whether Congress itself has power to regulate federal lands. The answer is "yes," because Art. I, Sec. 8, Clause 17 gives Congress power to regulate federal lands. Next, you have to determine whether Congress validly delegated this power that it possesses. Here, too, the answer is "yes." Congress may delegate rule-making authority to federal agencies through statutes that set concrete objectives for the agency, and that list adequate criteria for carrying out those objectives. The Supreme Court has been very deferential in applying these "concrete objectives" and "adequate criteria" requirements. The objective being pursued here (control of campfires on federal lands) is quite concrete, and the criteria specified by Congress for achieving that objective (use of a penalty schedule for rule violators) seem quite adequate. Therefore, the statute's provision of authority to the Forest Service would likely be held to satisfy the requirements.

(A) is incorrect, because the executive branch does not have inherent rule-making authority over public lands. The only source of federal power to regulate public lands is the grant in Art. I, Sec. 8, Cl. 17, to *Congress* to regulate such lands, as discussed above. So the executive's rule-making authority over public lands comes from delegation by Congress, not from any inherent authority.

(C) is wrong because the compelling nature of the government's regulatory interest is neither necessary nor sufficient to justify the Forest Service's regulation. The constitutional requirement is merely that the regulation be pursuant to a valid act of Congress, and that it not violate any specific constitutional prohibition. Since the act is a valid exercise of Congress' power to regulate federal lands, and since the delegation was validly done (as described in (B) above), that's the end of the matter, and the strength of the federal interest never becomes relevant.

(D) wrong because, although law enforcement is an executive function, the constitutional exercise of that function requires that the executive act pursuant to congressional authorization provided by law.

[Q7036]

198. **C** The daughter is the primary obligor on the debt to the friend. The father, by promising to make the payment if the daughter doesn't, has promised to "answer for the debt of another," making him a

surety. Since the father's promise is oral, it is rendered unenforceable by the suretyship provision of the Statute of Frauds, unless some exception makes it inapplicable. The most important exception to the suretyship provision is the main purpose rule. But here, the fact that the father's promise was not made for the "primary purpose" (i.e., "main purpose") of benefiting the father's own economic interests means that the main purpose rule does not apply, making the suretyship provision applicable. (Notice that nowhere in this choice do the examiners mention either the Statute of Frauds, the concept of suretyship, or the significance of the fact that the promise was oral — it's up to you to notice that the reference to the absence of "primary purpose" means that the suretyship provision will apply.)

(A) is wrong because the father *did* receive consideration for his conditional promise — the friend's making of the loan to the daughter. Consideration need not be given to the promisor, but can instead be given to a third party, as long as the promisor bargained for it.

(B) is wrong because it refers to the not-performable-within-one year provision of the Statute of Frauds, and that provision does not apply to the father's promise here. The reason is that there is a special exception under which "the one-year provision does not apply to a contract which is *performed on one side at the time it is made, such as a loan of money*, nor to any contract which has been fully performed on one side, whether the performance is completed within a year or not." Rest. 2d, §130, Comment d. Since the friend has fully performed on his side by making the loan, the full performance removed the entire contract from the one-year provision.

(D) is wrong because the law will supply a reasonable interest rate under the circumstances, so that the contract (and the father's promise) will not be void for indefiniteness. As long as the term omitted by the parties' agreement is not so basic as to prevent them from having had a meeting of the minds, the court will supply the missing term by implication. Here, since the friend cares mainly about getting his principal back, he can stipulate that the interest rate was 0%, and the court will certainly be willing to apply that rate to save the contract from indefiniteness.

[Q1089]

199. **B** This was an accommodation shipment under UCC §2-206(1)(b) — in the words of that section, the supplier "seasonably notifie[d] the buyer that the shipment [was] offered only as an accommodation to the buyer." Therefore, the supplier's shipment did not constitute an acceptance. Instead, it was a counteroffer to sell three gross of red widgets. At that point, the retailer could choose between accepting the red and paying for them, or rejecting the red, in which case there would be no contract (because there never was an accepted offer).

(A) is wrong because when a seller makes an accommodation shipment, the buyer has the right to reject the shipment but does not have the right to recover for breach. That's because the shipment is not an acceptance but instead a counteroffer, and the buyer's rejection of the goods constitutes a rejection of the counteroffer, with the result that there is no breach by the seller for which the buyer could recover.

(C) is wrong for two reasons: (1) if the retailer accepts the shipment, he cannot deduct any damages because of the nonconformity (since this type of accommodation shipment constitutes a counteroffer rather than acceptance, making the buyer's decision to keep the goods an acceptance of the goods as shipped, meaning that the nonconformity to the original order is irrelevant); and (2) if the retailer rejects the shipment, he has simply rejected the supplier's counteroffer, and there is no breach for which the retailer can deduct.

(D) is wrong for two reasons: (1) if the retailer accepts the shipment, he cannot deduct any damages because of the nonconformity (for the reasons described in the analysis of Choice (C) above); and (2) if the retailer rejects the shipment, he may do so without covering by obtaining conforming widgets from someone else. (He may, for instance, decide that he doesn't need widgets of any color after all.)

[Q2111]

200. **C** Although killing with the intent to cause great bodily harm is ordinarily classified as murder, it may be reduced to voluntary manslaughter if the defendant was acting in the heat of passion. This is only so, however, if the provocation which produced the passion would have caused a person of ordinary temperament to become enraged. (The reasonable person would not become so enraged as to kill; but the test is whether the provocation is such that a reasonable person might have become enraged so as to lose complete control.) So if the judge believes that no reasonable jury could conclude that an ordinary person in the wife's situation would have become enraged by the dancing, the judge must deny the instruction.

(A) is wrong because it is a misstatement of law: there is no "theory of deliberate provocation," and a person who kills will not be entitled to a voluntary manslaughter instruction merely because the victim deliberately provoked the defendant.

(B) is wrong because the objective standard described in the discussion of Choice (C) above (i.e., the likely reaction of a person of ordinary temperament) makes the wife's emotional peculiarities irrelevant.

(D) is wrong because it reflects a misstatement of law. An intentional killing may be reduced from murder to voluntary manslaughter if the defendant was acting under the mistaken belief that the killing was justified (e.g., D mistakenly thought he was being attacked with deadly force). This is known as the theory of mistaken justification. But (D) is wrong because the wife did not act in the mistaken belief that she was justified. Also, this choice suggests that the theory of mistaken justification would apply to prevent a manslaughter instruction, whereas if the theory applied it would require such an instruction.

[Q5048]

RAW-TO-SCALED SCORE CONVERSION CHART

Your raw score is the total number of questions you answered correctly. The MBE examiners convert each raw score to a "scaled score," to adjust for the fact that some instances of the MBE are harder than others. The examiners attempt to make it be the case that a given scaled score (say 133) represents the same level of competence whether obtained in July 2006 or February 2009. Your scaled score is never lower than your raw score. Here is a rough conversion chart to let you figure out approximately what scaled score you would have achieved on the 200-question Self-Assessment Test for any range of raw scores on that test. Note that on our Self-Assessment Test, you have 200 "chances" at raw points, whereas on the actual MBE you have only 190 chances (since 10 questions — and you can't tell which ones — won't be counted towards your raw score on the real exam).

If you can obtain a scaled score of *144 or better*, you are probably in good shape to pass your state's overall exam, since a scaled 144 is the "you're just barely on track to pass" threshold in California, generally considered the toughest bar exam in the nation. (Virtually all states add your MBE and non-MBE scores together in some fashion, so there's no true "minimum passing MBE score" — you can make up for a weak MBE showing with a strong state-law showing, or vice versa.)

Raw Score	Scaled Score
105-110	121-125
111-117	126-131
118-123	132-136
124-129	137-141
130-135	142-146
136-142	147-152
143-148	153-157
149-154	158-162
155-160	162-167
161-166	168-172
167-173	173-177

ANSWER SHEETS

The following pages of "bubble-style" answer sheets have been provided for your use. As on the actual MBE, each sheet covers a session (A.M. or P.M.), consisting of 100 questions. For each session, fill in the corresponding oval for each answer. As you answer each question, make a note on a separate piece of paper of the answers which were only good guesses, and not firmly based on your knowledge of the law, so that you can check the answers to those questions more carefully.

NATIONAL CONFERENCE OF BAR EXAMINERS
Multistate Bar Examination

A.M. EXAM

TEST FORM: 78526

NATIONAL CONFERENCE OF BAR EXAMINERS
Multistate Bar Examination

P.M. EXAM

TEST FORM: 78526

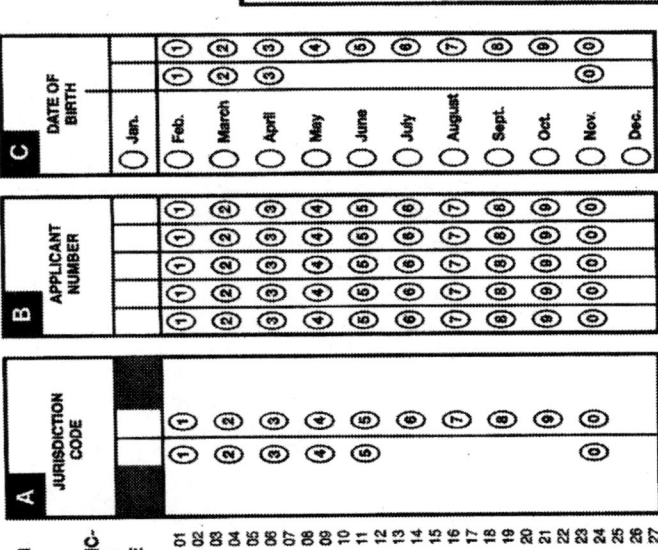